Pennsylvania's Criminal Justice System

CAROLINA ACADEMIC PRESS
State-Specific Criminal Justice Series

North Carolina's Criminal Justice System
Second Edition
Paul E. Knepper and Mark Jones

Georgia's Criminal Justice System
Deborah Mitchell Robinson

Florida's Criminal Justice System
William G. Doerner

California's Criminal Justice System
Christine L. Gardiner and Stacy L. Mallicoat, eds.

Missouri's Criminal Justice System
Frances P. Reddington, ed.

Illinois's Criminal Justice System
Jill Joline Myers and Todd Lough, eds.

Pennsylvania's Criminal Justice System
Mary P. Brewster and Harry R. Dammer, eds.

Pennsylvania's Criminal Justice System

Edited by

Mary P. Brewster

PROFESSOR AND CHAIR OF CRIMINAL JUSTICE,
WEST CHESTER UNIVERSITY OF PENNSYLVANIA

Harry R. Dammer

PROFESSOR AND CHAIR OF SOCIOLOGY/
CRIMINAL JUSTICE/CRIMINOLOGY,
THE UNIVERSITY OF SCRANTON

CAROLINA ACADEMIC PRESS
Durham, North Carolina

Library of Congress Cataloging-in-Publication Data

Pennsylvania's criminal justice system / edited by Mary P. Brewster and Harry R. Dammer.
    pages cm. -- (State-specific criminal justice series)
  Includes bibliographical references and index.
  ISBN 978-1-61163-460-0 (alk. paper)
  1. Criminal justice, Administration of--Pennsylvania. 2. Criminology--Pennsylvania. 3. Criminal procedure--Pennsylvania. I. Brewster, Mary P. II. Dammer, Harry R., 1957-

  HV9955.P4P456 2014
  364.9748--dc23

                            2014002479

CAROLINA ACADEMIC PRESS
700 Kent Street
Durham, North Carolina 27701
Telephone (919) 489-7486
Fax (919) 493-5668
www.cap-press.com

Printed in the United States of America

Contents

List of Figures and Tables

Series Note

Carolina Academic Press' state-specific criminal justice series fills a gap in the field of criminal justice education. One drawback with many current introduction to criminal justice texts is that they pertain to the essentially non-existent "American" criminal justice system and ignore the local landscape. Each state has its unique legislature, executive branch, law enforcement system, court and appellate review system, state supreme court, correctional system, and juvenile justice apparatus. Since many criminal justice students embark upon careers in their home states, they are better served by being exposed to their own states' criminal justice systems. Texts in this series are designed to be used as primary texts or as supplements to more general introductory criminal justice texts.

Acknowledgments

We would like to thank Beth Hall and the entire staff at Carolina Academic Press for providing us with the opportunity to publish this manuscript. Sincere gratitude goes to all of our contributors for sharing their knowledge and expertise, not only in their own chapters, but also collaboratively through providing thoughtful and critical feedback to other chapters' authors. Additional peer reviewers to whom we are deeply indebted include Randolph T. McVey, Brian F. O'Neill, Maureen G. Raquet, and Nathan M. Schenker. We also greatly appreciate the hard work of graduate student Adrianna Hughes in her assistance with the instructor's manual. Finally, our most heartfelt thanks go to our families for their understanding, patience, and support throughout the writing and editing of this text.

—MPB and HRD

Author Bios

Robert Boyer is a Professor of Criminal Justice at Luzerne County Community College in Nanticoke, Pennsylvania. He earned his Master's Degree in Public Administration from Marywood University and a Bachelor's Degree in Criminal Justice from King's College. He is a former police sergeant with the Kingston, Pennsylvania Police Department and is a state-certified Municipal Police Instructor. He also serves as the Mayor of Wyoming, PA.

Mary Brewster is a Professor and Chair of Criminal Justice at West Chester University of Pennsylvania. She earned her Ph.D. at Rutgers School of Criminal Justice. Her research interests include victimology, intimate partner violence and stalking, animal cruelty, specialized courts, and juvenile drug and alcohol prevention.

John T. Conlon is an Adjunct Professor of Criminal Justice at the University of Scranton. He received his MPA with a concentration in criminal justice from Marywood University. He is the former director of Adult Probation and Parole of Lackawanna County, PA, and currently serves as a consultant in issues related to sentencing and community-based corrections.

Harry R. Dammer is a Professor and Chair of the Sociology, Criminal Justice and Criminology Department at the University of Scranton. He received his Ph.D. from the Rutgers School of Criminal Justice. He is a former juvenile counselor and high school teacher. His teaching and research interests include corrections, comparative criminal justice, and religion in prison.

Maria L. Garase is an Associate Professor of Criminal Justice at Mercyhurst University, Erie, PA. She received her Ph.D. from Indiana University of Pennsylvania. Prior to becoming an academic she was a counselor specialist at a day/evening treatment facility for delinquent females in Pittsburgh, PA. Her research and teaching interests include juvenile justice, women and crime, and ethics in criminal justice.

Shannon Grugan is a doctoral student at Rutgers University and an environmental policy and data consultant at Booz Allen Hamilton. Her research and teaching interests include crime theory, environmental crime, cybercrime, and animal cruelty.

Michael J. Jenkins is an Assistant Professor of Criminal Justice at the University of Scranton. He received his Ph.D. from Rutgers School of Criminal Justice. He has worked as a Case Manager for adult parolees. His scholarly interests include police organizations, police-community collaborations and technology in police operations.

Jerry Morano is an Assistant District Attorney for the Chester County, Pennsylvania, District Attorney's Office. He is also an adjunct faculty at the Widener School of Law and West Chester University. He received his Juris Doctorate from the Dickinson School of Law of the Pennsylvania State University.

Jana Nestlerode is a Professor of Criminal Justice at West Chester University. She received her Juris Doctorate from Widener University School of Law. Prior to joining West Chester University, she was an Assistant District Attorney in Delaware County, Pennsylvania, responsible for prosecuting criminal jury trials. Her research interests include the Fourth Amendment, election fraud, pharmaceutical battery, and whistleblowers.

James C. Roberts is an associate professor of criminal justice at the University of Scranton, Scranton, PA. His research interests include alcohol and aggression, drugs and crime, and intimate partner violence. He holds a doctorate in criminal justice from Rutgers University.

Jenny P. Roberts is an assistant district attorney and head of the special victims unit in the Luzerne County District Attorney's Office, Wilkes-Barre, PA. She holds a master's degree in criminal justice from Rutgers University and a juris doctorate from Villanova University.

Timothy Robicheaux is a Lecturer of Sociology and Criminology at the Pennsylvania State University, University Park, PA. He received his M.A. in Psychology at the University of Nebraska-Lincoln and his Masters of Legal Studies (MLS) at the University of Nebraska College of Law. He regularly teaches a variety of criminology courses. He currently is completing his Ph.D. in law and psychology at the University of Nebraska-Lincoln and studies jury decision making and eyewitness memory.

Jane M. Tucker is an Assistant Professor of Criminal Justice at West Chester University of Pennsylvania. Her research interests include police subculture and stress, police agency policy and practice, and victimology.

Pennsylvania's Criminal Justice System

Chapter 1

Crime Trends in Pennsylvania

Shannon T. Grugan

Learning Objectives

After reading the chapter, students will be able to:

- Describe the FBI's Uniform Crime Report, its purpose, and its limitations.
- Describe how crime data are collected and converted to crime rates.
- Describe official definitions of Part I violent and property offenses.
- Summarize recent rates of crime and current crime problems in Pennsylvania.
- Describe and compare trends for specific crimes in Pennsylvania and nationally over the last 50 years.
- Explain the direction in which most crimes are currently trending both nationally and in Pennsylvania.
- Describe current rates of drug abuse offenses in Pennsylvania and compare these to current national rates.

Key Terms

Aggravated Assault	Motor Vehicle Theft
Burglary	Murder/Non-Negligent Homicide
Crime	Part I Index Crimes
Crime Drop	Property Crime
Crime Rate	Robbery
Drug Abuse	Uniform Crime Report Program
Larceny-Theft	Violent Crime

Introduction

Crime: Definitions, Perceptions, and Realities

When trying to understand crime and the justice system, it is important to first examine the nature and extent of crime in a state. The unfortunate reality is that while many people believe they have an accurate and informed understanding of the extent of crime, research has shown otherwise. Most Americans believe that crime has been increasing over the last 20 years, when the reality is that crime has generally been in decline or is at least much lower than peak rates seen in the 1970s, 1980s, and, in the case of some types of crime, the 1990s (Gallup, 2011a). Why would perceptions of crime be so far from the reality of crime? The public's fear of crime is a likely reason for this inaccurate view. In a recent survey of Americans, nearly half of respondents expressed some sort of concern about the potential for crime victimization (Gallup, 2011b). While many of these individuals will never fall victim to crime, their fear is very real and shapes the way in which crime is perceived as a phenomenon.

People fear it and believe it is on the rise, but what is crime? Crime and deviance can be defined differently within a number of different contexts: political, social, legal, psychological, etc. In this chapter, crime is considered within its legal context because the goal here is to examine the extent of crime in Pennsylvania. The best way to do this is to look at official crime statistics that contain counts of criminal law violations. Therefore, crime is defined as any act or omission that is prohibited by law. This chapter is intended to provide an understanding of crime trends in Pennsylvania through a thorough and accurate review of state and national crime data. The chapter begins with a description of the source of the crime data presented throughout, the Uniform Crime Report (UCR), and addresses the need for use of crime rates as opposed to crime counts. The chapter continues with a summary of crime in Pennsylvania over the last 50 years, comparison to national crime trends over the same time period, and brief discussion of drug offenses in the state. Conclusions about the realities of crime in Pennsylvania will then be discussed.

Crime Statistics: The FBI's Uniform Crime Report

In order to track crime trends, it is important for police departments and law enforcement agencies to maintain data on the number of crimes that occur within their jurisdictions. The Uniform Crime Report (UCR), which is published by the Federal Bureau of Investigation (FBI), has become a primary tool for recording and reporting crime in the United States. The UCR Program was implemented in 1929, and since then, most law enforcement organizations in the United States have submitted crime counts and clearance rates to the FBI on a monthly basis. The data are compiled by the FBI and a full report of the number of crimes is released to the public annually. Most states also provide full reports of UCR crimes that have occurred within that state on an annual basis. While these reports are helpful in identifying and analyzing crime trends, it should be noted that the UCR does not include data on all crimes. The UCR is divided into two sections, Part I and Part II crimes. Part I includes serious felonies, often referred to as "Index crimes" because these crimes are generally reported more reliably and at a higher rate than less serious offenses. These Part I Index crimes include murder and non-negligent homicide, forcible rape, robbery, aggravated assault, burglary, larceny-theft, motor vehicle theft, and arson.[1] Part II of the UCR includes the lesser offenses of simple assault, public drunkenness, disorderly conduct, vagrancy, loitering, white collar crimes (embezzlement and fraud), driving under the influence, drug offenses, fraud, gambling, liquor offenses, offenses against the family, prostitution, runaways, sex offenses, stolen property, vandalism, and weapons possession offenses. This chapter will focus on Part I offenses in Pennsylvania due to the fact that, despite some of these crimes occurring less frequently, these very serious crimes are generally reported to police at a much higher rate than are other crimes and will therefore provide a more accurate picture of crime trends.

While the UCR is an important resource for law enforcement agencies, social science scholars, politicians, and the public, there are some limitations to these reports. First of all, not all occurrences of crime are captured in the UCR. As with any official or administrative data, the crime counts only reflect those crimes that have been reported to the police or that have been discovered by the police in some other way. There are many crimes that are never reported to or discovered by the police that go undocumented. Secondly, the overall counts are dependent on how crimes are defined in statutes as well as the procedures and arrest policies of each police department and law enforcement agency that reports data. A good example of this is the recent change to the UCR definition of forcible rape. Until 2013, rape was defined as "the carnal knowledge of a female through the use of force or the threat of force" (Federal Bureau of Investigation, 2004, p.19). The updated definition is gender neutral, meaning that males who are subject to nonconsensual sex acts are now recognized as rape victims for the first time in the history of the UCR. This new definition also includes language that specifies the "carnal knowledge" that

---

1. Trend data for arson are not available. Arson data are not reported in this chapter.

qualifies as rape and does away with the provision that force must be involved, instead identifying lack of consent as the key factor in qualifying a sex act as rape. These types of administrative changes challenge accurate tracing of trends and crime patterns over time because it can be difficult to determine if changes in crime rates are a result of actual changes in the amount of crimes committed or are merely a result in defining the crime differently. The FBI has already anticipated that 2013 rape rates will increase due to the specificity of the acts identified and the inclusion of male victims in the new definition (Federal Bureau of Investigation, 2012b). Thirdly, with these reports coming from police, further judgment of the acts in the justice system (i.e., court decisions in the form of guilty or not guilty) are not taken into account. By collecting data from police reports, there may be cases included that ultimately are determined not to be crimes. Fourthly, the UCR allows for the reporting of only one crime type in an incident. This may obscure any additional crimes which may have occurred at the same time involving the same victim and perpetrator. Reporting requirements for these situations follow the "Hierarchy Rule," which calls for the reporting police department to "locate the offense that is highest on the hierarchy list [in terms of seriousness] and score that offense involved and not the other offense(s) in the multiple-offense situation" (Federal Bureau of Investigation, 2004, p.10). For example, in a situation where a burglary and a murder occurred, only the murder would be included in the UCR counts for that crime event. Even with these limitations, the UCR is an invaluable resource of data on crime in each of the states, as well as the nation as a whole. Additionally, since these data have been recorded over a long period of time, the UCR is very helpful when it comes to evaluating and comparing crime trends at the local, state, and national levels. UCR data reported by the Commonwealth of Pennsylvania as well as the nation as a whole will be used below to discuss crime and crime trends in the state over the last 50 years.

Crime Counts Versus Crime Rates: The Need for Standardization

The UCR provides crime counts and crime rates for each of the recorded offenses and both will be presented in discussions of crime in Pennsylvania below. Crime counts are important in providing an overall number of offenses committed, but are not very useful when it comes to looking at trends over time or in making comparisons across states or to national levels due to differences in population. Crime rates take care of this problem. A crime rate is calculated by converting true counts of crime into standardized crime rates per a certain number of residents in the population. In many cases, crime rates are calculated as the number of crimes occurring for every 100,000 people in the population. Comparisons of crime become possible when looking at the number of crimes in this standardized manner.

Crime in Pennsylvania

Recent Data: Crime in Pennsylvania in 2011

A total of 329,627 Part I Index crimes were reported to police in Pennsylvania in 2011, at a rate of 2,586.9 crimes per 100,000 residents. This number marked an overall increase of 2.1% in reported crimes over the previous year. This increase is notable because it is inconsistent with national trends. Overall, violent crimes per 100,000 people dropped by 3.8% and property crimes dropped .5% nationally from 2010 to 2011 (Federal Bureau of Investigation, 2012a).

The frequencies, percentages, and rates for each of the Index crimes in 2011 are provided in Table 1.1. Not surprisingly, there were many more reported property crimes (2,226 per 100,000 population or 86.1% of all crimes) than vi-

Table 1.1 Frequency, Percentage, and Rate for Crimes in Pennsylvania in 2011 by Crime Type

	N	%	Rate[a]
Total	329,627	100%	2,586.9
Violent	45,967	13.9%	360.7
Murder	638	.2%	5.0
Forcible Rape[b]	3,320	1.0%	26.1
Robbery	16,117	4.9%	126.5
Aggravated Assault	25,892	7.9%	203.2
Property	283,660	86.1%	2,226.0
Burglary	57,675	17.5%	452.6
Larceny-Theft	207,398	62.9%	1,627.6
Motor Vehicle Theft	16,812	5.1%	131.9
Arson	1,775	.45%	13.9

Source: Pennsylvania Uniform Crime Reporting System 2011 Annual Report (2012a).
Note: Percentages may not add up to 100% and rates may not add up to their respective totals due to rounding.

[a] Rates are based on population estimates provided by the United States Census Bureau (2013).

[b] Forcible rape in 2011 was still considered an act perpetrated against women only. Because of this, rape calculations are based on female population totals only.

olent crimes (360.7 per 100,000 population or 13.9% of all crimes). Additionally, the rates for violent crimes committed in 2011 had an inverse relationship to the seriousness of the offense, with murder and forcible rape the most serious, yet the least common violent offenses (with rates of 5 and 26.1 per 100,000 population, respectively). Robbery and aggravated assault, which are comparatively less serious in nature than murder and rape, were reported more frequently (with rates of 126.5 and 203.2 per 100,000 population, respectively). This trend of more serious crimes occurring less frequently has generally been consistent in Pennsylvania over time (as will be discussed later in this chapter) and across the United States. When it comes to property crimes, however, it is not unusual to find that there is no discernible pattern or relationship between seriousness and rate of occurrence. Pennsylvania's data for 2011 seem to be no exception. In 2011, larceny-theft (1,627.6 per 100,000 population) topped property crimes in terms of frequency, followed by burglary (452.6 per 100,000 population), motor vehicle theft (131.9 per 100,000 population), and arson (13.9 per 100,000 population).

It is important to look at the differences in rural and urban crime rates in a state like Pennsylvania because of the large disparity in population density throughout the state. Over 12.7 million people live in Pennsylvania, making it the 6th largest state in terms of population (United States Census Bureau, 2013). Higher concentrations of people live in and around the urban centers of Philadelphia and Pittsburgh, with nearly 2.7 million, or 21% of the state's population residing in these cities, with the remaining 10 million residents spread across the state in suburban and rural communities (Pennsylvania Uniform Crime Reporting System, 2012b). Differences in crime occurring in urban, suburban, and rural areas of Pennsylvania are provided in Table 1.2. More Part I offenses occur in suburban areas (49.9%) than do in urban and rural areas (38.2% and 11.9%, respectively). However, when factoring in population density, the crime rate was highest in the cities with 4,677.5 crimes per 100,000

Table 1.2 Frequency, Percentage, and Rate for Crimes in Pennsylvania by Metropolitan Statistical Area Classification

	N	%	Rate
Total	329,627	100%	2586.9
Urban	126,013	38.2%	4677.5
Suburban	164,515	49.9%	2060.6
Rural	39,099	11.9%	1893.5

Source: Pennsylvania Uniform Crime Reporting System 2011 Annual Report (2012a).

residents and lower in suburban and rural areas of the state, with 2,060.6 crimes per 100,000 residents in suburban areas of the state, and as low as 1,893.5 per 100,000 residents in rural areas. This means that, not surprisingly, cities in Pennsylvania have larger problems with serious crime than do the less populated areas.

Part I Crimes in Pennsylvania in Detail

While having an understanding of the most recent data and rates available from official reports of crime in Pennsylvania is important in understanding crime in Pennsylvania, it is perhaps even more important to look at Pennsylvania crime trends over time and in comparison to the whole of the United States. We will now take a more detailed look at Part I Index crimes in Pennsylvania, trends in these crimes over time, and a comparison of these trends with national crime trends. This section is divided into violent crimes and property crimes.

Violent Crime

Murder, forcible rape, robbery, and aggravated assault make up the violent crimes recorded in UCR data. We will be discussing each of these individually later in the chapter. Figure 1.1 provides a comparison of national and Pennsylvania rates of all violent crimes from 1960 through 2010. The first thing

Figure 1.1 Rates of Violent Crime in Pennsylvania Compared to National Rates, 1960–2010

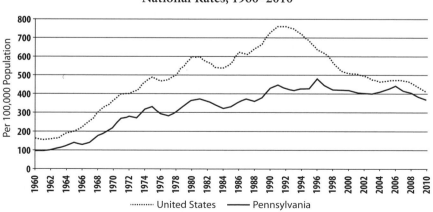

Source: Federal Bureau of Investigation, Uniform Crime Reporting Statistics (2010).

that is apparent in this comparison is that Pennsylvania's rate of violent crime has historically been lower than that of the national average. Even with the lower overall rates of violent crime over time, the national and Pennsylvania rates have generally followed a similar pattern—increasing from 1960, with some fluctuation, through to the 1990s. Violent crime peaked nationally in 1991 at 758.2 per 100,000 population. Since this time, the national rate has been in a steep decline, with the violent crime rate falling to 403 per 100,000 population in 2010, a rate not seen since the 1970s. Violent crime peaked in Pennsylvania in 1996 at 480.3 per 100,000, went into a shallow decline over the next 8 years but then rose again for three years starting in 2004. By 2007 violent crime rates began declining again but the gap between Pennsylvania and national rates of violent crime has quickly become much smaller. Pennsylvania ended 2010 with a violent crime rate of 366.2 per 100,000 population and the national rate was 403.6 per 100,000 population.

Murder

According to the UCR Handbook (2004), murder and non-negligent manslaughter are defined as the willful killing of a human being by another. The statute does not include manslaughter by negligence or justifiable homicides. Figure 1.2 shows the annual murder rate in Pennsylvania and the United States from 1960 to 2010. There are some interesting trends that emerge from comparison of the local and national murder rates during this period. From

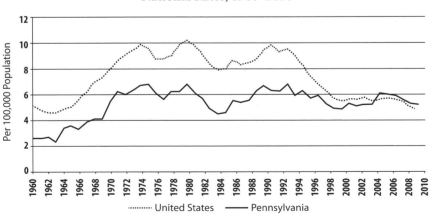

Figure 1.2 Rates of Murder in Pennsylvania Compared to
National Rates, 1960–2010

Source: Federal Bureau of Investigation, Uniform Crime Reporting Statistics (2010).

the beginning of this time frame in 1960 through 2004, the murder rate in Pennsylvania was lower than the national rate. From 2005 through 2010, Pennsylvania's murder rate has surpassed that of the national rate, starting with an increase in 2005. The murder rate still remains higher in Pennsylvania than it is in the nation as a whole, but only slightly. Additionally, the murder rate has dropped every year since the initial spike in murders in Pennsylvania in 2005. So while the state rate is still higher than the national rate, the murder rate in Pennsylvania is currently on a downward trend.

There are some other notable trends in both the national and Pennsylvania rates of murder when looking at data from 1960 through 2010. Throughout most of this time period, the national and state murder rates followed the same general pattern, even with Pennsylvania's rate lower than that of the United States. First of all, there was an increase in murders from 1960 through 1980 both nationally and in Pennsylvania. Pennsylvania's rate, however, stayed well below the national rate throughout this twenty-year span of time. Murder rates peaked both nationally and in Pennsylvania in 1980. That year, the national rate hit 10.2 per 100,000 population and Pennsylvania saw a rate of 6.8 murders per 100,000 population. After this peak, rates began decreasing nationally and locally, but then rose again from the mid-1980s through the early 1990s. This same pattern can be seen in both the overall United States rate and the Pennsylvania rate. From the early to mid-1990s, the national murder rate dipped steadily through 2010.

However, as also noted in Figure 1.2, the murder rate in Pennsylvania (6.1 per 100,000 population) spiked higher than the national rate (5.6 per 100,000 population) in 2005 and, although it has decreased every year since then, it has remained higher than the national murder rate which has continued to decline. As of 2010, murder nationally and in Pennsylvania remain much lower than the peak murder rates reached in 1980 and are closer to rates seen in the mid to late 1960s nationally and in 1970 in Pennsylvania (4.8 and 5.2 per 100,000 population respectively).

While discussion of the murder rate is important, there is a great deal of additional information on the nature and circumstance of murder that are recorded in the UCR. These include discussion of murder victims, types of weapons used, the relationship between the offender and the victim, and the distribution and rates of murder per county. Table 1.3 provides information on the gender, ethnicity, and age of murder victims in Pennsylvania in 2011. This table includes the number and percentage of victimizations, the percentage of each one of these demographic attributes in Pennsylvania's population (looking at total population of the state, not just those victimized), and the rate of victimization within these demographic categories. Of the 638 mur-

**Table 1.3 Demographic Characteristics of Murder
Victims in Pennsylvania in 2011**

	Number of Victims	% of Total Victims	% of This Demographic within the PA Population	Rate*
Total	638	100%	100%	5.2
Gender				
Male	521	81.7%	47.8%	8.6
Female	117	18.3%	52.2%	1.8
Race/Ethnicity				
White	224	31.5%	79.2%	2.2
Non-White	414	64.9%	20.8%	15.7
Age				
Under 18	59	9.2%	21.7%	2.1
18–29	305	47.8%	16.3%	14.7
30–39	105	16.5%	11.7%	10.1
40 and Over	169	26.5%	50.3%	2.7

Source: Pennsylvania Uniform Crime Reporting System 2011 Annual Report (2012a). U.S. Census Bureau Pennsylvania Quick Facts.

* Rate based on total number of people in the PA population that align to that attribute.

ders committed in 2011, 81.7% involved male victims. Consistent with other states and national data, males (8.6 per 100,000) were murdered at a higher rate than were females (1.8 per 100,000).

Almost two-thirds (64.9%) of all murders in Pennsylvania in 2011 were committed against non-White victims.[2] This is notable because non-White individuals make up a much smaller percentage of Pennsylvania's population than do Whites. Non-Whites made up only 20.8% of Pennsylvania's population in 2011, but were murder victims at a rate of 15.7 per 100,000 non-Whites in the population. Whites made up 79.2% of the Pennsylvania's population in 2011 and were murdered at a rate of 2.2 per 100,000 Whites in the population. This leaves the rate of non-Whites murdered over seven times that of Whites in Pennsylvania in 2011. This is notable but not surprising based on national trends in murder. According to Fox and Zawitz (2005), the rate of murder vic-

---

2. Available data only specifies victims as White or non-White, so numbers for specific races and ethnicities other than White are not included here.

timization among non-Whites is also much higher than that of Whites. It should be noted that more non-Whites than Whites commit murder, both nationally and in Pennsylvania, with black on black crime occurring frequently (Fox & Zawitz, 2005). In 2011, 59.7% of murders in Pennsylvania were committed by non-Whites, while 40.3% were perpetrated by Whites (Pennsylvania Uniform Crime Reporting System, 2012a). Nearly half of all of those murdered in Pennsylvania in 2011 were between the ages of 18 and 29 (47.8%). Victimization rates are also highest among this group (14.7 per 100,000 population). Just over one-quarter of victims were over the age of 40, though the rate of victimization in this group was fairly low (26.5% of all murder victimizations, 2.7 per 100,000 over 40 in the population). While 30–39-year-olds made up a relatively small percentage of all Pennsylvania murder victims in 2011, the rate of murder among this group was high (16.5% of murder victimizations, 10.1 per 100,000 30–39 in the population). Finally, murder of those under 18 made up the lowest percentage and lowest rate of all murder victimizations (9.2% of murder victimizations, 2.1 per 100,000 under 18 in the population.

Weapon or method used to commit the offense and the relationship between the offender and the victim are additional important aspects of murder that are reported in the UCR. When looking at weapons used in the commission of murders in Pennsylvania, use of firearms was the most popular. Table 1.4 summarizes the weapons and methods used in murders in Pennsylvania in 2011. Almost three-fourths of these murders (73.8%) involved firearms, with most of these crimes committed using handguns (59.6%). When guns and firearms were not involved, other weapons included knives and other sharp objects (11.9%), blunt instruments (2.6%), personal weapons such as hands and feet (4.3%), strangulation (1.3%), and fire (.4%).

Table 1.5 shows the known victim-offender relationships for 2011 Pennsylvania murders. Out of the 638 murders that took place, the relationship between the offender and the victim was established in 362 (56.7%) cases. Of those in which the relationship between the offender and the victim was identified, nearly three-fourths involved a friend or acquaintance (73.3% of known relationships) while 16.4% involved family members or spouses. An additional 10% of the murders in which victim-offender relationship had been established involved strangers with no relationship to one another.

Distribution of murder varies widely across the state. Table 1.6 lists the counties with more than 10 murders reported and their respective murder rates for 2011. Not surprisingly, Philadelphia County had the highest number of murders, accounting for just over half of all murders in Pennsylvania in 2011 (324 total, 50.8% of all murders in the state). Allegheny County had ap-

Table 1.4 Number and Percentage of Murders in Pennsylvania According to Weapon Type in 2011

	N	%
Total	638	100%
Firearm	471	73.8%
Handgun	380	59.6%
All other firearms	91	14.2%
Non-Firearm	167	26.2%
Stabbing	75	11.9%
Blunt Instrument	16	2.6%
Personal Weapons	27	4.3%
Strangulation	8	1.3%
Fire	2	0.4%
All Other Non-Firearms*	36	5.7%

Source: Pennsylvania Uniform Crime Reporting System 2011 Annual Report (2012a).
   * All other non-firearms include asphyxiation, drowning, drugs/narcotics/sleeping pills, explosives, and unknown methods.

Table 1.5 Number and Percentage of Murders in Pennsylvania According to Victim-Offender Relationship in 2011

	N	%
Total	362	100%
Friend/Acquaintance	265	73.3%
Stranger	37	10.3%
Immediate Family	30	8.2%
Spouse	15	4.1%
Other Family	15	4.1%

Source: Pennsylvania Uniform Crime Reporting System 2011 Annual Report (2012a).

proximately one-fifth the number of murders as Philadelphia County, with 67 reported for the year (10.5% of all reported murders in the state). The murder totals in other counties continue to decrease from there, with only 7 out of all 67 counties having recorded 10 or more murders in 2011. It is notable that two of the three counties with the top murder totals, Philadelphia and Delaware, are adjacent to one another and are both considered part of the Greater Philadelphia Metropolitan Area. The second half of Table 1.6 looks at

Table 1.6 Frequencies, Percentages, and Rates of Murder in
Pennsylvania by Select Counties in 2011

County	N	%	Rate*
Total	638	100%	5.2
Philadelphia	324	50.8%	21.1
Allegheny	67	10.5%	5.4
Delaware	31	4.9%	5.5
York	20	3.1%	4.6
Berks	19	3%	4.6
Lehigh	16	2.5%	3.5
Montgomery	16	2.5%	2.0
Dauphin	14	2.2%	5.2
Luzerne	12	1.9%	3.8

Source: Pennsylvania Uniform Crime Reporting System 2011 Annual Report (2012a).
  * Rate based on total number of people living in each county as of 2011.

the murder rates within these counties. While the murder *counts* per county
provide an interesting look at concentrations of murder, the murder *rate* per
county provides a more accurate picture of murder in Pennsylvania counties.
In this regard, Philadelphia still holds the top spot with an extremely high rate
of 21.1 murders per 100,000. The rest of the counties with the highest counts
of murder have rates that range from 2 to 5.5 murders per 100,000. As the
largest urban center in the state, Philadelphia County clearly has a serious murder problem.

Forcible Rape

Forcible rape is defined as "the carnal knowledge of a female through the use
of force or the threat of force" (Federal Bureau of Investigation, 2004).[3] Forcible
rape also includes rape of victims unable to give consent due to age or mental
disability and attempted rape and related assaults. Additionally, Pennsylvania
does not include statutory rape, incest, or sodomy as forcible rape unless force
or lack of consent is involved. It should be noted that since the definition of
forcible rape in 2011 applied only to cases in which a female victim was involved, rates of this crime are based on number of incidents per 100,000 women,
not per 100,000 of the total population.

---

3. Please note that the definition of forcible rape here remains "carnal knowledge of a
female ..." because the data used are from 2011 when this definition still applied.

Figure 1.3 Rates of Forcible Rape in Pennsylvania Compared to National Rates, 1960–2010

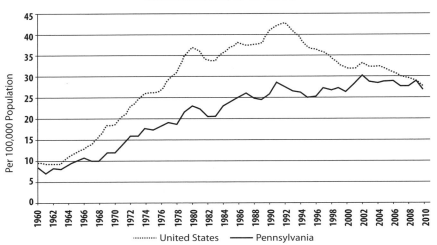

Source: Federal Bureau of Investigation, Uniform Crime Reporting Statistics (2010).

Figure 1.3 provides both the national and Pennsylvania rates of forcible rape from 1960 through 2010. Throughout most of the 50-year time period, Pennsylvania has trailed the nation in rates of this crime. Nationally, rape rates peaked in 1992 (43 per 100,000 females in the population) and then began a general, though not constant, downward trend since that time. The Pennsylvania rate also hit a high in 1992 (28.7 per 100,000 females in the population) but did not peak until almost 15 years later, in early 2006 (26.1 per 100,000 females in the population). There are three notable trends in these data when comparing the national and Pennsylvania rates. First of all, from 1960 through the mid-1990s, the national and state rape rates followed a similar pattern of increases and decreases. Secondly, it is important to note that while the national rate and Pennsylvania's rate followed these similar patterns, the rate in Pennsylvania remained lower than the national rate. This difference in rates became much larger by the late 1970s, when the national rape rate rose rapidly while increases in the Pennsylvania rate were more modest. The third trend in these data begins in the mid-1990s, when the national rape rate continued to decline, while Pennsylvania's rate began increasing. By the late 2000s the Pennsylvania forcible rape rate had begun declining again, as did the national rate. By 2010, both rates continued to decline but Pennsylvania had almost met the national rate of forcible rape (with rape hitting 26.6 rapes per 100,000 nationally and 27.1 rapes per 100,000 in Pennsylvania).

Figure 1.4 Rates of Robbery in Pennsylvania Compared to the
National Rates, 1960–2010

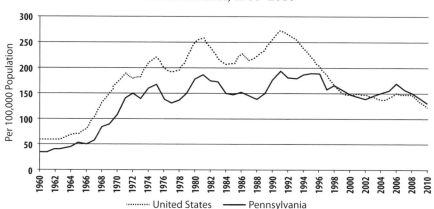

Source: Federal Bureau of Investigation, Uniform Crime Reporting Statistics (2010).

Robbery

Robbery is "the taking or attempting to take anything of value from the care, custody, or control of a person or persons by force or threat of force or violence and/or by putting the victim in fear" (Federal Bureau of Investigation, 2004 p. 21). Data on robberies include robberies involving weapons (armed robbery), strong-arm robberies (muggings), assaults that involve the taking of the victim's property, and all robbery attempts (Federal Bureau of Investigation, 2004). Figure 1.4 provides Pennsylvania's robbery rates in comparison to the national rates from 1960 through 2010. Pennsylvania has generally had lower rates of robbery than has the nation. However, even with rates decreasing since 2004, Pennsylvania's robbery rate has remained higher than the national rate since 2003. Before this turning point, robbery rates in Pennsylvania, while lower than the national rates, maintained a remarkably similar pattern of national robbery rates. There was a marked increase in robbery rates both nationally and in Pennsylvania in the late 1960s through the early 1970s. The rates then became variable, with decreases in some periods (ex: 1975 through 1977) and notable increases in others (ex: 1978 through 1981) at both the national and state level. Robbery rates peaked in the nation and Pennsylvania in 1991 (272.7 and 193.9 per 100,000 population, respectively). As of 2010, Pennsylvania's robbery rate remains higher than the national rate but both of these rates are at levels that have not been seen since the late 1960s nationally and the mid-to-late 1970s in Pennsylvania.

**Table 1.7 Number and Percentage of Robberies in Pennsylvania
According to Weapon Type and Location in 2011**

	N	%
Total	16,117	100%
Armed Robberies	8,947	55.5%
Strong-Arm	7,170	44.5%
Armed	8,947	100%
Firearms	6,805	76.0%
Knife or Cutting Instrument	1,162	13.0%
Other Weapon[a]	980	11.0%
Location		
Highway	9,902	61.4%
Residences	1,741	10.8%
Commercial House	1,002	6.2%
Convenience Stores	912	5.7%
Banks	249	1.7%
Miscellaneous	1968	12.2%

Source: Pennsylvania Uniform Crime Reporting System 2011 Annual Report (2012a).
 [a] Other weapons include clubs, acid, explosives, brass knuckles, Mace, pepper spray, or other dangerous weapons.

The UCR provides additional information regarding specific details of robberies in Pennsylvania. Table 1.7 shows details of armed and unarmed/strong-arm robberies in Pennsylvania in 2011, including the number and percentages of each type of robbery and the location in which these robberies took place. Just over half (8,947 total, 55.5%) involved use of a weapon. Of these armed robberies, firearms were the most popular weapons used (6,805 total, 76% of armed robberies).

Most robberies occurred in public spaces, such as streets, parks, and parking lots (9,902 total, 61.4%). A large number of robberies occurred on unspecified miscellaneous properties (1,968 total, 12.2%), in private residences (1,741 total, 10.8%), in commercial spaces like supermarkets, department stores, malls, and restaurants (1,002 total, 6.2%), and in convenience stores (912 total, 5.7%). Banks accounted for a small number of all robberies (249 total, 1.7%). Robberies are one of the few crimes for which Pennsylvania currently has a higher rate than the national average.

Figure 1.5 Rates of Aggravated Assault in Pennsylvania Compared to National Rates, 1960–2010

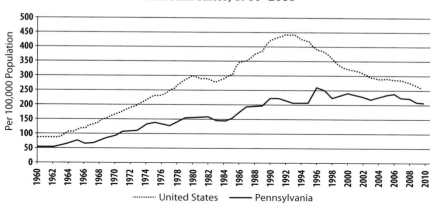

Source: Federal Bureau of Investigation, Uniform Crime Reporting Statistics (2010).

Aggravated Assault

Aggravated assault is defined as "the unlawful attack by one person upon another with the intent to inflict great bodily injury, usually accomplished by the use of a weapon or other means likely to produce death or serious bodily harm" (Federal Bureau of Investigation, 2004). Aggravated assault includes attempted murder and attempted assault involving a deadly weapon. The use of a deadly weapon or the high level of severity of a victim's injuries distinguishes aggravated assault from simple assault. Figure 1.5 presents rates of aggravated assault in Pennsylvania in comparison to the national values from 1960 to 2010. As with many of the crimes discussed thus far, the Pennsylvania rates of aggravated assault have remained lower than the national average rates. Rates of aggravated assault followed a generally upward trend both nationally and in Pennsylvania from 1960 through the early 1990s. The national rate peaked in 1992 at 440.5 per 100,000 and Pennsylvania peaked 5 years later in 1996 at 260.5 per 100,000. In 1993, the national rate began dropping and, while Pennsylvania saw a small drop this same year, the rate of aggravated assault in Pennsylvania continued on a generally upward, though volatile, trend until the end of the period reported here in 2010.

The UCR provides additional information on the types of weapons used in armed robberies. A summary of the weapons used during the commission of

Table 1.8 Number and Percentage of Aggravated Assault Crimes by Weapon Type in Pennsylvania in 2011

	N	%
Total	25,892	100%
Firearm	4,992	19.3%
Knife of Cutting Instrument	3,814	14.7%
Other Dangerous Weapon*	5,946	23.0%
Hands, Fist, Feet, etc.	11,140	43.0%

Source: Pennsylvania Uniform Crime Reporting System 2011 Annual Report (2012a).

* Other dangerous weapons include Mace, pepper spray, clubs, bricks, jack handles, tire irons, bottles, other blunt instruments, explosives, acid, lye, poison, scalding, and burnings.

armed robbery in Pennsylvania in 2011 is listed in Table 1.8. A weapon, besides hands and feet, was used in 57% of all aggravated assaults. Firearms (19.3%) and knives or other cutting objects (14.7%) were commonly seen in aggravated assaults. A large number of these crimes were committed using a variety of other dangerous weapons including Mace, pepper spray, clubs, bricks, jack handles, tire irons, bottles, other blunt instruments, explosives, acid, lye, poison, scalding, and burnings (43%).

Property Crime

Property crimes included here are burglary, motor vehicle theft, and larceny-theft. Figure 1.6 provides a comparison of the rates of all property crime in Pennsylvania to those of the national average from 1960 through 2010. Again, just as with the overall rates for violent crimes, Pennsylvania property crime rates have remained lower than the national rate throughout this time period. Just as with many violent offenses already discussed, even with these lower rates of property crime, the Pennsylvania rate has maintained a similar pattern to the national rate in terms of the increases and decreases over time. Just like violent crimes, property crime rates began increasing in the 1960s. Nationally, the property crimes peaked in 1980 at 5353.3 per 100,000 population. Pennsylvania rates of property crime also peaked in 1980 at 3372.4 per 100,000 population. The national and Pennsylvania rates then declined throughout the rest of the 1980s. After some fluctuation in the 1990s, property crime has been on the decline both nationally and in Pennsylvania. As of 2010, property crime dropped to levels not seen since the 1960s nationally (2941.9 per 100,000 population) and the 1970s in Pennsylvania (2173 per 100,000 population).

Figure 1.6 Rates of Property Crime in Pennsylvania Compared to National Rates, 1960–2010

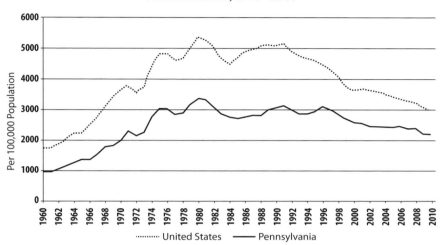

Source: Federal Bureau of Investigation, Uniform Crime Reporting Statistics (2010).

Burglary

Burglary is defined as the unlawful entry of a structure, with or without force, to commit a felony or theft (Federal Bureau of Investigation, 2004). As with other crimes described here, data on burglaries include all attempted burglaries. Structures include commercial, industrial, and residential buildings (Federal Bureau of Investigation, 2004).

As is the case with most of the Part I crimes discussed thus far, Pennsylvania has generally had lower than average rates of burglary over the last 50 years (see Figure 1.7). However, the patterns of both the national and state rates over time have tended to trend in the same direction at the same time. Burglary rates increased dramatically from 1960 to 1975 in the nation as well as in Pennsylvania. In 1960, the national burglary rate was 508.6 per 100,000 population, while Pennsylvania's rate was 297.8 per 100,000 population. By 1975, the national rate of burglaries hit 1532.1 per 100,000 population and in Pennsylvania, there were 983.3 burglaries per 100,000 population. After a slight dip in burglaries both nationally and in Pennsylvania, from 1976 to 1979, burglary hit its peak rate in 1980 in Pennsylvania (1038.5 per 100,000 population) and the nation (1684.1 per 100,000 population). Since 1980, burglaries have generally followed a decreasing trend. As of 2010, the rates of burglary in both the United States and Pennsylvania had fallen to levels not seen since the late 1960s (669.6 and 434.3 per 100,000 population, respectively).

**Figure 1.7 Rates of Burglary in Pennsylvania Compared to
National Rates, 1960–2010**

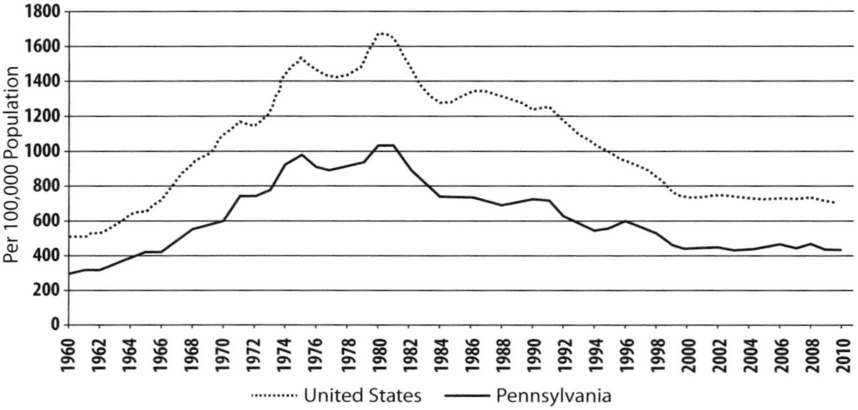

Source: Federal Bureau of Investigation, Uniform Crime Reporting Statistics (2010).

Motor Vehicle Theft

Motor vehicle theft is defined as the illegal taking or attempted taking of a motor vehicle without the owner's consent (Federal Bureau of Investigation, 2004). Motor vehicles include automobiles, tractor trailers, buses, motorcycles, motor scooters, and snowmobiles. Theft of motor vehicles includes only those offenses involving the entire vehicle. Theft of motor vehicle parts and accessories is considered larceny-theft and will be discussed below. Like many of the other crimes discussed here, rates of motor vehicle theft in Pennsylvania over the last 50 years have been lower than the national average but national and Pennsylvania rates have followed very similar trend lines (see Figure 1.8). Both nationally and in Pennsylvania, motor vehicle theft rates have fluctuated since 1960. Like many of the other crimes discussed here, rates of motor vehicle theft increased fairly steadily from 1960 through the mid-1970s in both the nation and Pennsylvania. Motor vehicle thefts in Pennsylvania increased from 122.4 per 100,000 population in 1960 to 375.7 per 100,000 population by 1974. Nationally, rates increased from 183 per 100,000 population in 1960 to 462.2 per 100,000 population in 1974. From the mid-1970s through the mid-1980s, rates fluctuated. The rate of motor vehicle thefts peaked in the early 1990s both nationally (655.8 per 100,000 population in 1991) and in Pennsylvania (505.5 per 100,000 population in 1990). The rates of motor vehicle theft have been trending downward both nationally and in Pennsylvania since this time, with 2010 rates for both the lowest they have been since the early 1960s.

Figure 1.8 Rates of Motor Vehicle Theft in Pennsylvania Compared to National Rates, 1960–2010

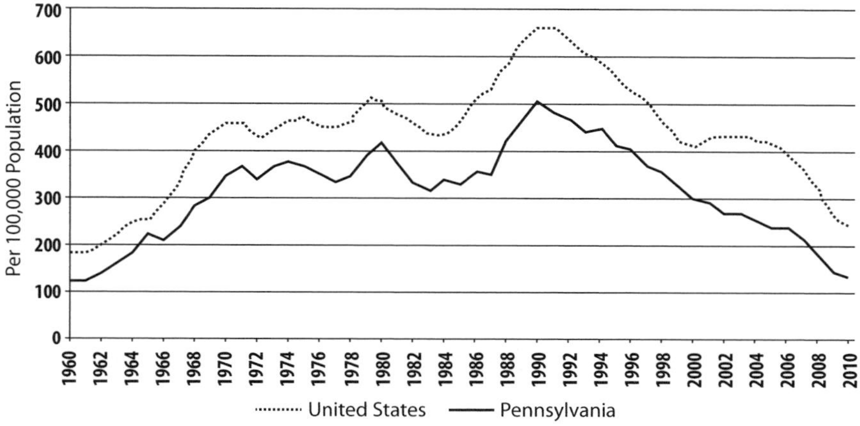

Source: Federal Bureau of Investigation, Uniform Crime Reporting Statistics (2010).

Larceny-Theft

Larceny-theft is defined as "the unlawful taking, carrying, leading, or riding away of property from the possession or constructive possession of another" and includes shoplifting, pick-pocketing, purse snatching, thefts from autos, theft of auto parts and accessories, and bicycle theft (Federal Bureau of Investigation, 2004 p. 31). Embezzlement, confidence schemes, other types of white collar frauds, and, of course, theft of motor vehicles (which is its own Part I offense and is discussed above) are not counted as larceny-theft. All other thefts, regardless of the value of the object or dollar amount lost, are counted in the larceny-theft rate.

Rates of larceny-theft are presented for Pennsylvania and the United States from 1960 through 2010 in Figure 1.9. Again, as with many of the crimes discussed in this chapter, the Pennsylvania rate of larceny-theft has historically been much lower than the national average but has followed a similar pattern in terms of increases and decreases over time. Also following the trends of other crimes here, national and Pennsylvania rates of larceny-theft increased from 1960 through the 1980s, with some minor fluctuations. The national larceny-theft rate peaked in 1991 at 3229.1 per 100,000 population and Pennsylvania peaked five years later, in 1996, at 2079.9 per 100,000 population. Rates have been on a shallow decline since these peaks.

Figure 1.9 Rates of Larceny-Thefts in Pennsylvania Compared to the
National Rates, 1960–2010

Source: Federal Bureau of Investigation, Uniform Crime Reporting Statistics (2010).

Table 1.9 Number and Percentage of Larceny-Thefts in Pennsylvania
According to Dollar Amount and Location in 2011

	N	%
Total	207,398	100%
Dollar Amount		
Under $50	59,834	28.8%
$50–$200	55,533	26.8%
Over $200	92,031	44.4%
Location/Circumstance		
Pickpocketing	1,309	.6%
Purse Snatching	1,441	.7%
Shoplifting	38,243	18.4%
From Motor Vehicles	48,790	23.5%
Motor Vehicle Parts and Accessories	9,701	4.7%
Bicycles	7,891	3.8%
From Buildings	31,193	15.0%
From Coin Operated Machines	973	.5%
All Other	67,858	32.7%

Source: Pennsylvania Uniform Crime Reporting System 2011 Annual Report (2012a).

Two important factors related to larceny-theft are the amounts stolen and location/circumstances in which the theft occurred. Table 1.9 provides information on both of these factors for larceny-thefts in 2010. More than half (55.6%) of the larceny-thefts in Pennsylvania in 2011 involved stolen property equaling less than $200. With the exception of "all other" larcenies, theft from motor vehicles accounted for the highest number of thefts (23.5%) with shoplifting (18.4%) and theft from buildings (15%) also accounting for a high portion of thefts in the state.

Drug Abuse Crimes

Drug abuse offenses are defined as "all violations of state and local ordinances related to the unlawful possession, sale, use, growing, manufacture, and making of narcotics" (Pennsylvania Uniform Crime Reporting System 2012a). Though not one of the serious Part I index offenses, drug abuse offenses are a large problem and are sometimes related to other types of crimes that are considered Part I offenses, including murder, aggravated assault, and various property offenses (Dorsey & Middleton, 2008). As with many of the Part I offenses discussed above, the rate of drug abuse crimes reported in Pennsylvania is lower than the national rate.[4] In 2011, there were 52,013 drug abuse offenses reported in Pennsylvania resulting in a rate of 408.2 per 100,000 population. Nationally, there were 1,531,251 drug abuse offense arrests in 2011 resulting in a rate of 493.2 per 100,000 population. Although long-term trends are not available, drug offenses are on the decline. The Pennsylvania Uniform Crime Reporting System (2012a) reports that the number of drug offenses in Pennsylvania have been decreasing since 2008 and the FBI (2012a) reports decreases in drug offenses nationally since 2002. A majority of offenses involve possession of drugs as opposed to sale or manufacturing and most cases of possession involve marijuana (FBI 2012a).

Summary and Conclusions:
Overall Crime Trends

What does all of the information presented above tell us about crime in Pennsylvania? What does it tell us about crime trends in Pennsylvania in comparison to the whole of the United States? When looking at all of the data pre-

---

4. Only the most recent data on drug offenses are presented here because trend data for drug abuse offenses are not available.

sented above, it is clear to see that certain patterns in crime emerge. First of all, with the notable exceptions of the violent crimes of murder and robbery, Pennsylvania has had and continues to have lower than average rates of crime than the nation. However, with recent increases in violent crime, future crime rates should be watched closely. Secondly, crime in the whole of the United States and in Pennsylvania has followed two general trends over the last 50 years. The first is an upward trend beginning in 1960. Crime rates increased both nationally and in Pennsylvania, with many of the crime types discussed above continuing to increase through the 1970s, 1980s, or even into the early 1990s, depending on the specific type of crime. By the mid-1990s, overall rates of crime were decreasing fairly rapidly in both Pennsylvania and nationally, in a phenomenon commonly referred to as the "crime drop." However, the gap between the higher national rates of crime and Pennsylvania's lower rates of crime, particularly for violent offenses, has been closing (see Figure 1.1). This means that crime is decreasing at a faster rate nationally than it is in Pennsylvania. Additionally, rates of some violent offenses have increased in Pennsylvania in recent years, while continuing to decrease nationally. Pennsylvania rates of murder and robbery are now trending downward after increasing in the early 2000s and surpassing the national rates for the first time in the last 50 years but still remain higher than the national rates. Thirdly, despite this recent uptick in violent crimes in Pennsylvania, and overall differences in the volume of crime, it is notable that violent and property crimes in Pennsylvania have followed very similar patterns over the past 50 years.

This chapter has presented information on the nature and extent of crime in Pennsylvania and a comparison of trends and patterns seen over the last 50 years between Pennsylvania and the whole of the United States. While the detailed information on rates of crime discussed here is extremely important, there are four major points to keep in mind from this chapter as you read the rest of this book. First, crime rates tend to be lower in Pennsylvania in comparison to the national rates of crime. Second, as a notable exception to this first point, Pennsylvania has seen higher than national rates of some violent offenses in recent years. Third, even with these recent discrepancies, Pennsylvania crime has generally trended in the same way national crime rates have in terms of increases and decreases over time. Fourth, the so called "crime drop" that occurred in the mid-1990s is readily apparent in rates of crime in Pennsylvania even though more recent years have seen increases in crime that are not typical of national trends.

Key Terms and Definitions

Aggravated Assault: The unlawful attack by one person upon another with the intent to inflict great bodily injury, usually accomplished by the use of a weapon or other means likely to produce death or serious bodily harm.

Burglary: The unlawful entry of a structure, with or without force, to commit a felony or theft.

Crime: Any act or omission of an act that is prohibited by law.

Crime Drop: A notable decrease in crime throughout the United States that took place in the 1990s. Prior to this drop, crime had generally been in an upward trend since the middle of the 20th century.

Crime Rate: A standardized measure of crime calculated by dividing true counts of crime into a certain number of residents in the population (typically 100,000 residents) that is used to evaluate trends and make comparisons about the prevalence of crime in different areas.

Drug Abuse: A violation of state and local ordinances related to the unlawful possession, sale, use, growing, manufacture, and making of narcotics.

Larceny-Theft: The unlawful taking or stealing of property or articles of value without the use of force, violence, or fraud.

Motor Vehicle Theft: The illegal taking or attempted taking of a motor vehicle without the owner's consent.

Murder/Non-Negligent Homicide: The willful killing of a human being by another.

Part I Index Crimes: A group of serious crimes that are collected and reported in the Uniform Crime Report. These crimes include murder/non-negligent homicide, forcible rape, robbery, aggravated assault, burglary, motor vehicle theft, larceny-theft, and arson.

Property Crime: Crimes that involve unlawful taking or damaging the property of one person by another. UCR Part I Property crimes include burglary, motor vehicle theft, and larceny-theft.

Robbery: The taking or attempting to take anything of value from the care, custody, or control of a person or persons by force or threat of force or violence and/or by putting the victim in fear.

Uniform Crime Report Program: A national data collection initiative developed and managed by the Federal Bureau of Investigation that provides annual reports on crime as recorded by local police departments across the country.

Violent Crime: Crimes intended to physically harm or otherwise violate a person. UCR Part I Violent crimes include murder/non-negligent homicide, forcible rape, robbery, and aggravated assault.

Websites

Federal Bureau of Investigation Uniform Crime Report: http://www.fbi.gov/ about-us/cjis/ucr/ucr.

Federal Bureau of Investigation Uniform Crime Reporting Statistics: http:// ucrdatatool.gov/.

Federal Bureau of Investigation Uniform Crime Report Handbook: http:// www2.fbi.gov/ucr/handbook/ucrhandbook04.pdf.

Pennsylvania Uniform Crime Report System: http://www.paucrs.pa.gov/UCR/ Reporting/RptMain.asp.

Gallup—Crime in the United States: http://www.gallup.com/poll/1603/crime. aspx.

United States Census Bureau American Fact Finder: http://factfinder2.census. gov/faces/tableservices/jsf/pages/productview.xhtml?src=bkmk.

United State Census Bureau Pennsylvania Quick Facts: http://quickfacts.census. gov/qfd/states/42000.html.

Review Questions

1. What is the Uniform Crime Report (UCR) Program? What agency oversees the program? How are data collected for the UCR? What are some of the limitations to UCR data?
2. What is a crime rate? Make sure to include how rates are calculated and why crime rates are of better use than crime counts when describing trends over time or making comparisons.
3. Identify and define each of the Part I Index Crimes. Include discussion of the general trend for each in Pennsylvania since 1960.

Critical Thinking Questions

1. Discuss the two UCR definitions that have been used over time for forcible rape. What are the implications of making this type of change to official

crime definitions when analyzing trends in crime over time? What has been/could be done to ensure that the crime rates that result from these types of definitional changes to Part I crimes are not misconstrued as sharp changes in actual amounts of crime?

2. Throughout this chapter, rates of crime over the last 50 years have been discussed for all of the UCR Part I offenses. Why is it important to review these data when looking at the justice system in Pennsylvania? For that matter, why is it important to have a program like the UCR in place? Make sure to discuss the implications for policy, including policing, the courts, and the correctional system.

3. Since the mid-2000s, rates of murder and robbery in Pennsylvania have increased or remained higher than the national average, while national rates of these crimes have continued to decline. Discuss some potential reasons for this shift in Pennsylvania.

4. As presented in Table 1.6, the murder rate in Philadelphia County, the largest urban center in the state, was over 4 times higher than other Pennsylvania counties with large number of murders in 2011. What are some explanations for this?

References

Federal Bureau of Investigation. (2004). *Uniform Crime Report Handbook.* Washington, D.C.: U.S. Department of Justice.

Federal Bureau of Investigation. (2010). Reported crime by locality (city, county), state, and Nation [data file]. *Uniform Crime Reporting Statistics.* Retrieved from: http://ucrdatatool.gov/Search/Crime/Crime.cfm.

Federal Bureau of Investigation. (2012a). *Crime in the United States 2011.* Retrieved from: http://www.fbi.gov/about-us/cjis/ucr/crime-in-the-u.s/2011/crime-in-the-u.s.-2011/tables/table-1.

Federal Bureau of Investigation. (2012b). UCR program changes rape definition. *Criminal Justice Information Services Link* [Newsletter]. Retrieved from: http://www.fbi.gov/about-us/cjis/cjis-link/march-2012/ucr-program-changes-definition-of-rape.

Fox, A. & Zawitz, M. (2005). *Homicide trends in the United States.* Washington, D.C: Bureau of Justice Statistics. Retrieved from: http://www.bjs.gov/content/pub/pdf/htius.pdf.

Gallup. (2011a). Most Americans believe crime in the United States is worsening. Gallup Wellbeing Retrieved from: http://www.gallup.com/poll/150464/americans-believe-crime-worsening.aspx.

Gallup. (2011b). *Crime*. Retrieved from http://www.gallup.com/poll/1603/ crime.aspx.

Pennsylvania Uniform Crime Reporting System. (2012a). *Crime in Pennsylvania Annual Uniform Crime Report*. Harrisburg, PA: Pennsylvania State Police. Retrieved from: http://www.paucrs.pa.gov/UCR/Reporting/Annual/ AnnualFrames.asp?year=2011.

Pennsylvania Uniform Crime Reporting System. (2012b). *Executive Summary Crime in Pennsylvania Annual Uniform Crime Report*. Harrisburg, PA: Pennsylvania State Police. Retrieved from: http://www.paucrs.pa.gov/UCR/ Reporting/Annual/pdf2011/2011ExecutiveSummary.pdf.

United States Census Bureau. (2013). State and county quickfacts: Pennsylvania. Retrieved from: http://quickfacts.census.gov/qfd/states/42000.html.

Chapter 2

Pennsylvania Criminal Law

Jerry Morano and Jana Nestlerode

Learning Objectives

After reading this chapter students will be able to:

- Describe how criminal statutes are enacted in Pennsylvania.
- Explain the differences between criminal laws and civil laws.
- Define and distinguish the terms "mens rea" and "actus reus."
- Describe the statutory limitations on filing charges and prosecuting crimes.
- Define and distinguish the inchoate crimes of attempt, conspiracy, and solicitation.
- Define and explain the major violent crimes against persons.
- Identify and define the various defenses to criminal prosecution.

Key Terms

Accomplice liability
Affirmative defense
Aggravated assault
Burglary
Civil law
Competence
Criminal law
Felony
Inchoate crimes
Insanity

M'Naghten
Misdemeanor
Murder
Preponderance of evidence
Presumption of innocence
Rape
Robbery
Substantial capacity
Summary offense
Theft

Introduction

The legal system can be separated into two arenas: the civil arena and the criminal arena. The civil arena provides for litigation of disputes between private parties. Examples include suing another for breach of contract, wrongful termination, defamation, and wrongful death. Civil wrongdoings are called "torts."

By contrast, criminal wrongdoings are called "crimes." State and federal legislatures pass laws that permit the punishment of individuals for the commission of certain defined acts. Through our legislatures we, as a society, determine what behavior we want our government to forbid. Those determinations may vary from jurisdiction to jurisdiction. For instance, prostitution is illegal in nearly every state. The exception is Nevada, which has legalized prostitution in certain counties (NRS 244.345). Recently, several states have decriminalized the possession of marijuana for personal use and/or for medical use (Knowles, 2013). Yet possession of marijuana remains a serious crime under the laws of the federal government and the laws of many other states.

A distinction must also be made between moral wrongdoings and criminal wrongdoings. Moral wrongdoings can be subject to individual opinion. Acts considered to be moral wrongdoings may or may not be criminalized. For instance, some may consider prostitution to be a moral wrongdoing. But as noted above, prostitution is lawful in some jurisdictions. Likewise, not all criminal wrongdoings are necessarily moral wrongdoings. Failure to wear a seatbelt may be a criminal wrongdoing, but few would consider it to be a moral wrongdoing.

As most students of criminal justice know, the executive branch of our government is charged with enforcing the laws. The judicial branch is charged with interpreting the laws. It is the responsibility of the legislature, however, to enact the laws. In Pennsylvania, the legislature is referred to as the General Assembly. The members of the General Assembly are charged with creating, reviewing, and passing legislation that serves the citizens of the Commonwealth of Pennsylvania.

Enacting a Criminal Law

The Pennsylvania General Assembly is composed of a House of Representatives and a Senate. The members of each are elected by the voters of the Commonwealth (Pa. Constitution Article II, 1874). A law may be proposed by a member (or members) of either house, or by the Governor. The written proposal is submitted to the Legislative Reference Bureau.

The LRB was created in 1909 to assist members of the legislature and others in the preparation of bills and resolutions for introduction to the General Assembly (Legislative Reference Bureau of Pennsylvania). Upon request, the Bureau prepares a properly worded "bill" for the legislator to submit to the General Assembly for consideration. A bill may be sponsored by one or several members of the House of Representatives or of the Senate, and may be introduced in either chamber. (It is more likely that the bill will be voted into law if it has many sponsors.) The bill is given a number, a printer's number, and a title. When the bill is amended, only the printer's number changes (The Pennsylvania Capitol, Making Law Pennsylvania).

The numbered and titled bill is then referred to the appropriate committee in the Pennsylvania Senate. The members of the committee review the bill, and may even hold public hearings on the matter. The committee may propose amendments to the bill. After sufficient review, the committee then decides whether the bill should proceed to the full Senate for consideration. If the committee does not refer the bill to the full Senate, it is said to have "died in committee" (The Pennsylvania Capitol, Making Law Pennsylvania).

Article III, Section 4 of the Pennsylvania Constitution requires that a bill be considered on three separate days in each House. The first of the three days is the day the bill is referred to the committee. The second day of consideration occurs when and if the bill is referred from the committee to the full Senate. At this time, further amendments may be proposed by Senators who were not on the reviewing committee. The third day of consideration occurs when the bill is debated on the floor of the Senate and a final vote is taken. Amendments may be made to the bill at this time only by a unanimous vote of the Senate. A majority of Senators must vote in favor of the bill for it to pass (The Pennsylvania Capitol, Making Law Pennsylvania).

After passage by the Senate, the bill is referred to the appropriate committee in the House of Representatives. This committee, like the Senate committee, reviews the bill, after which it either refers the bill to the full House for a vote, or lets the bill die in committee. The referred bill must then go through two further days of consideration in the House. A majority of the members of the House must support the bill for it to pass. If the passed bill contains amendments that were not part of the original Senate bill, it must go back to the Senate for a new vote. If there is disagreement between the Houses, the bill may be referred to a conference committee. The conference committee is composed of three members from each chamber, and is tasked with reconciling the differences between the two versions of the bill. The reconciled bill is then returned to both chambers for reconsideration (Pennsylvania Constitution, Article III, §4).

A bill that has been approved by a majority of the members of both legislative chambers is sent to the Governor. If the Governor signs the bill, it becomes law. If the Governor takes no action within ten calendar days of the legislative session (or thirty days if the legislature is not in session), the bill automatically becomes law. If the Governor vetoes the bill, it is returned to the legislature for further consideration. The legislature can override a gubernatorial veto if two-thirds of the members of each chamber vote for the bill (Pennsylvania Constitution, Article IV, §14).

The criminal and civil laws of the Commonwealth of Pennsylvania are printed in Purdon's Pennsylvania Consolidated Statutes (Pa. C.S.). The annotated version (Pa. C.S.A.) includes cross-references, footnotes and commentary. Thomson West, with the agreement of the Pennsylvania legislature, offers the unofficial version of the Pennsylvania statutes on line for free (Pennsylvania General Assembly Home). Proscribed and punishable acts and their defenses are found in multiple titles of Purdon's Pennsylvania Consolidated Statutes.

Crimes in Pennsylvania

Statutory Crimes

In Pennsylvania, only conduct defined as criminal under the Crimes Code or another statute or ordinance can constitute a crime. Prior to the enactment of the Crimes Code, crimes were primarily defined by the common law. Pennsylvania's Crimes Code became effective June 6, 1973 (18 Pa.C.S.A. §§101-9183). Since its effective date, Pennsylvania recognizes no common law crimes [18 Pa.C.S.A. §107(b)]. Thus, Pennsylvania is a code jurisdiction.

The legislature has the sole power to pronounce which acts are crimes, to define crimes, and to set the punishment for all crimes. The legislature also has the sole power to classify crimes and to designate rules of procedure (Pennsylvania Constitution, Article II, §1). The legislative power to enact statutes for the health, welfare, and safety of the community flows from the general power.

Pennsylvania criminal laws and rules of procedure are located in multiple titles of Purdon's. Title 18 contains the Crimes Code. The Crimes Code defines the commonly known offenses such as murder, robbery and burglary. Title 35 contains The Controlled Substance, Drug, Device and Cosmetic Act. This title contains the laws pertaining to the possession, manufacture, and trafficking of controlled substances. Title 42 contains the Juvenile Act which defines procedures for prosecuting those under the age of eighteen. Title 42 also contains the

Table 2.1 Purdon's Consolidated Statutes
Titles Relevant to Criminal Law

Title 18	Crimes Code
Title 35	Controlled Substance, Drug, Device and Cosmetic Act
Title 42	Juvenile Act
Title 42	Rules of Criminal Procedure
Title 75	Vehicle Code

Rules of Criminal Procedure. Title 75 contains the Vehicle Code. This title contains the laws that define crimes pertaining to the operation of vehicles.

Title 18 is generally divided into three parts. Each of those parts is, in turn, divided into chapters. The first part delineates preliminary matters and includes criminal culpability, defenses to crimes, and inchoate offenses. The second part provides the elements and definitions of each offense listed in the Crimes Code. The third part concerns miscellaneous provisions including criminal history information and crime victims' rights. (See Appendix A.)

General Provisions of the Crimes Code

The first chapter of Title 18 provides the basic definitions that are used throughout the remainder of the title. Definitions found in 18 Pa.C.S.A. § 103 include the following:

- **Act**: a bodily movement whether voluntary or involuntary.
- **Actor**: includes, where relevant, a person guilty of an omission.
- **Acted**: includes, where relevant, "omitted to act."
- **Conduct**: an action or omission and its accompanying state of mind, or, where relevant, a series of acts and omissions.
- **Element of an offense**: such conduct or such attendant circumstances or such a result of conduct as: (1) is included in the description of the forbidden conduct in the definition of the offense; (2) establishes the required kind of culpability; (3) negatives an excuse or justification for such conduct; (4) negatives a defense under the statute of limitation; or (5) establishes jurisdiction or venue.
- **Intentionally**: with intent or with design.
- **Knowingly**: knowing or with knowledge.
- **Material element of an offense**: an element that does not relate exclusively to the statute of limitations, jurisdiction, venue or to any other matter similarly unconnected with: (1) the harm or evil incident to con-

duct, sought to be prevented by the law defining the offense; or (2) the existence of a justification or excuse for such conduct.

- **Negligently**: with negligence.
- **Omission**: a failure to act.
- **Police officer**: includes the sheriff and deputy sheriffs who have successfully completed the requirements under the Municipal Police Education and Training Law.
- **Purposely** or **with purpose**: intentionally.
- **Reasonably believes** or **reasonable belief**: a belief which the actor is not reckless or negligent in holding.
- **Recklessly**: with recklessness.
- **Statute**: includes the Constitution of Pennsylvania and a local law or ordinance of a political subdivision.

In addition, the Crimes Code indicates that the general purposes of criminal legislation are:

(1) to forbid and prevent conduct that unjustifiably inflicts or threatens substantial harm to individual or public interest;

(2) to safeguard conduct that is without fault from condemnation as criminal;

(3) to safeguard offenders against excessive, disproportionate or arbitrary punishment;

(4) to give fair warning of the nature of the conduct declared to constitute an offense, and of the sentences that may be imposed on conviction of an offense; and

(5) to differentiate on reasonable grounds between serious and minor offenses, and to differentiate among offenders with a view to a just individualization in their treatment (18 Pa.C.S.A. § 104).

Further, the Crimes Codes establishes the four classifications of crimes as: murder, felony, misdemeanor, and summary offense (18 Pa.C.S.A. § 106). Table 2.2 depicts the relative seriousness of each category of offense, along with the maximum penalties.

Although, the Crimes Code does not specifically define the term "crime," Pennsylvania law states that a person cannot be guilty of a crime unless he violates a specific statute (*Kendrick v. District Attorney of Philadelphia County*, 2007). The law specifically states: "A person is not guilty of an offense unless his liability is based on conduct which includes a voluntary act or the omission to perform an act of which he is physically capable" [18 Pa.C.S.A. § 301(a)]. In order to be held liable for an offense based on a failure to act, the omission must be expressly made sufficient to constitute an offense by the law defining the offense;

Table 2.2 Classifications of Crimes

Classifications of Crimes	Maximum Penalty
Murder in the First Degree	Life or death
Murder in the Second Degree (felony murder)	Automatic life
Felony of the First Degree	20 years
Felony of the Second Degree	10 years
Felony of the Third Degree	7 years
Misdemeanor of the First Degree	5 years
Misdemeanor of the Second Degree	2 years
Misdemeanor of the Third Degree	1 years
Summary Offense	90 days

in the alternative, the actor must have failed to perform a duty imposed by law [18 Pa.C.S.A. § 301(b)]. The criminal act, or the failure to act when there is a legal duty to act is called the *actus reus*.

Following the concept of innocent until proven guilty, the Crimes Code sets forth the general requirements of culpability. For example, a person is not guilty of an offense unless he acted intentionally, knowingly, recklessly, or negligently, as the law may require, with respect to each material element of the offense [18 Pa.C.S.A. § 302(a)]. Section 302 of Title 18 defines the kinds of culpability required to establish the requisite intent for each crime. This culpability requirement is known as *mens rea*—the state of mind a defendant must possess to commit a crime. The term *mens rea* is Latin for guilty mind and is defined as "[t]he state of mind that the prosecution, to secure a conviction, must prove that a defendant had when committing a crime" (Garner, 2009).

As stated above, the Crimes Code specifically identifies four possible mental states: intentional, knowing, reckless and negligent. Generally, a person acts intentionally if it is his conscious object or purpose to cause the result. A person acts knowingly if he is practically certain that his conduct will cause the result. A person acts recklessly when he consciously disregards a substantial and unjustifiable risk that his conduct will result in the proscribed harm; the risk must be of such a nature and degree that its disregard involves a gross deviation from the standard of conduct that a reasonable person would observe in the actor's situation. A person acts negligently when he should be aware of a substantial and unjustifiable risk that the proscribed harm will result from his conduct. The risk must be of such a nature and degree that the actor's failure to perceive it is a gross deviation from the standard of care that a reasonable person would observe in the actor's situation [18 Pa.C.S.A. §302(b)].

Interestingly, a crime might not list a particular mental state but instead might provide for absolute or strict liability. In such cases, the prosecution is not required to prove a *mens rea*. Absolute liability is imposed because the proscribed conduct is subject to stringent public regulation and may seriously threaten the community's health or safety. Such statutes are in the nature of police regulations, and the legislature may, for the protection of all the people, punish their violation without regard to guilty knowledge (*Appeal of DaPra*, 1967).

According to Pennsylvania law, "A person is guilty of an offense if it is committed by his own conduct or by the conduct of another person for which he is legally accountable, or both" [18 Pa.C.S.A. §306(a)]. Every person who is connected with the commission of a crime may be charged and convicted of that crime if 1) the person directly commits the crime; 2) the person promotes or facilitates the crime; 3) the person solicits, aids or agrees to commit the crime; or (4) the person attempts to aid another person in the planning or commission of the crime [18 Pa.C.S.A. §306(b)]. Such persons are referred to as "accomplices," and their culpability is argued under the theory of "accomplice liability." In addition, any person who is connected with the commission of a crime may be convicted even if that person did not directly commit the crime, and even if the person who directly committed the crime was not prosecuted or convicted, or was acquitted.

Pennsylvania law also requires that the prosecution prove a causal relationship between the actor's conduct and the result that occurs from such conduct (18 Pa. C.S.A. §303). This requirement is more stringent than the civil notion of "proximate cause." Pennsylvania prosecutors must go a step beyond and prove that the actions of the defendant were a direct and substantial factor in causing the harm to the victim (Commonwealth v. Evans, 1985).

Inchoate Crimes

"Inchoate" means partially completed, imperfectly formed, just begun, or undeveloped (Garner, 2009). The Pennsylvania Crimes Code identifies three inchoate crimes: criminal attempt, criminal solicitation, and criminal conspiracy. An actor may be found guilty of an inchoate crime even though the underlying offense might not have been successfully completed (Ashworth & Horder, 2013). Pennsylvania law criminalizes the steps taken toward the commission of the crime, regardless of whether the crime is actually completed.

Criminal attempt occurs when an accused has intent to commit a specific crime, and he does any act which constitutes a substantial step toward the commission of that crime (18 Pa.C.S.A. §901). Criminal solicitation occurs when an accused intentionally commands, encourages, or requests another person to engage in a crime (18 Pa.C.S.A. §902). Criminal conspiracy occurs when an accused intentionally enters into an agreement with one or more persons to commit an unlawful act, and then engages in an overt act in furtherance of that agreement (18 Pa.C.S.A. §903).

An accused may not be convicted of more than one of the inchoate crimes for conduct stemming from same crime (18 Pa.C.S. §906). Renunciation is a defense to all three inchoate offenses. Renunciation is a complete and voluntary abandonment of the criminal purpose before a crime is committed (Garner, 2009). To use the defense of renunciation against the charge of criminal conspiracy, the accused must also thwart the conspiracy's success [18 Pa.C.S.A. §903(f)].

Major Crimes

The majority of the commonly prosecuted crimes are located in Part II of the Crimes Code. Those crimes are broadly organized according to the nature of the harm caused (See Table 2.3).

Table 2.3 Categories of Commonly Prosecuted Crimes

Offenses Involving Danger to the Person	Criminal homicide, crimes against unborn children, robbery, assault, kidnapping, trafficking of persons, sexual offenses, abortion
Offenses Against Property	Arson, criminal mischief, burglary, criminal trespass, theft, forgery
Offenses Against the Family	Bigamy, incest, endangering the welfare of children, concealing death of a child
Offenses Against Public Administration	Bribery, perjury, victim and witness intimidation, obstructing governmental operations, escape, abuse of office
Offenses Against Public Order and Decency	Riot, disorderly conduct, harassment, public drunkenness, cruelty to animals, public indecency
Miscellaneous Offenses	Computer offenses, internet child pornography, firearm offenses, corruption of minors

Offenses Involving Danger to the Person

The Crimes Code provides key definitions which are used throughout this category. For example, "bodily injury" is defined as an "impairment of physical condition or substantial pain." "Serious bodily injury" is defined as "bodily injury which creates a substantial risk of death or which causes serious permanent disfigurement, or protracted loss or impairment of any bodily member or organ." "Deadly weapon" is defined as "any firearm, whether loaded or unloaded, or any device designed as a weapon and capable of producing death or serious bodily injury." "Serious provocation" is defined as "conduct sufficient to incite intense passion in a reasonable person" (18 Pa.C.S.A. § 2301).

Criminal Homicide

Criminal homicide is defined as intentionally, knowingly, recklessly, or negligently causing the death of another human being. Pennsylvania law classifies criminal homicide into three categories: Murder, Voluntary Manslaughter and Involuntary Manslaughter (18 Pa.C.S.A. § 2501).

Murder is broken down into three degrees: first, second, and third. Murder of the first degree is defined as an intentional killing [18 Pa.C.S.A. § 2502(a)]. An intentional killing is a killing "by means of poison, or by lying in wait, or by any other kind of willful, deliberate and premeditated killing" [18 Pa.C.S.A. § 2502(d)].

Murder of the second degree is a killing committed while the defendant was engaged as the main actor or as an accomplice in the perpetration of a felony [18 Pa.C.S.A. § 2502(b)]. To be guilty of this offense, the killing may have occurred during the attempted commission or actual commission of a felony, or during the flight thereafter. The statute identifies six felonious offenses which may trigger this statute: robbery, rape, deviate sexual intercourse by force or threat of force, arson, burglary or kidnapping. Murder of the second degree is commonly referred to as a felony murder.

Murder of the third degree is a felony of the first degree, and is defined as "all other kinds of murder" [18 Pa. C.S.A. § 2502(c)]. All murders, whether first, second or third degree, require the prosecution to prove that the defendant acted with malice.

Voluntary manslaughter is an intentional killing done while the accused: (1) acts under a sudden and intense passion resulting from serious provocation by the individual killed (known as "heat of passion"); or (2) acts with an unreasonable belief that would justify the killing, (known as "imperfect self-defense") [18 Pa.C.S.A. § 2503(a)(b)]. Voluntary manslaughter is a felony of the first degree. Involuntary manslaughter is an unintentional killing resulting from doing a lawful or an unlawful act in a reckless or grossly negligent manner that causes another person's death. Involuntary manslaughter is a misdemeanor of the first degree (18 Pa.C.S.A. §2504).

Assault

Under Pennsylvania law, there are twenty-two separate and distinct crimes of assault. An assault, generally, is the threat of force or the use of force against another causing that person to have a reasonable apprehension of imminent harmful or offensive contact (Garner, 2009). Pennsylvania law provides statutes for simple assault, aggravated assault, recklessly endangering another person, and terroristic threats. Simple assault and recklessly endangering another person are misdemeanors (18 Pa.C.S.A. §§2701, 2705). Terroristic threats are generally a misdemeanor but may constitute a felony if the threat causes the public to be diverted from their normal or customary operations (18 Pa.C.S.A. §2706). Aggravated Assault is a felony (18 Pa.C.S.A. §2702). Generally, aggravated assault requires "serious bodily injury," or an attempt to cause "serious bodily injury." However, Pennsylvania law provides a list of thirty-seven protected classes of individuals whereby an assault either attempting to cause or causing only "bodily injury" suffices for aggravated assault. That enumerated list includes police officers, firemen, teachers, and a variety of court personnel [18 Pa.C.S.A. §2702(c)].

Robbery

Robbery is a theft or an attempted theft conducted by force or threat of force. The force or threat of force may occur during the theft or attempted theft, or in the flight thereafter (18 Pa.C.S.A. §3701). Robbery can be a felony of the first, second, or third degree depending on the amount of force used and the harm or injury caused. Pennsylvania also recognizes "robbery of a motor vehicle." Under the Pennsylvania statute, "robbery of a motor vehicle" is the "theft of a vehicle from another person in the presence of that person or any other person in lawful possession of the motor vehicle" (18 Pa. C.S.A. §3702). As Pennsylvania's "carjacking" statute, it is a felony of the first degree.

Sexual Offenses

Pennsylvania law delineates ten sexual crimes which constitute either misdemeanors or felonies. These crimes include, inter alia, rape, statutory sexual assault, involuntary deviate sexual intercourse, and aggravated indecent assault. The age of the victim is an element of the offense in several of these crimes. The defendant's mistake as to the age of the child may be a defense, but it is not a defense if an element of the crime requires the child victim to be below 14 years of age. The crimes vary concerning sexual activities between both consenting and non-consenting partners. Generally, a child 16 or under cannot legally consent. For example, a person commits a felony of the second degree when he engages in sexual intercourse with a victim under the age of 16 years and that person is four or more years older than the complainant and they are not married to each other (Pa. C.S.A. § 3101 et seq.).

Offenses against Property

Arson

Arson can be a felony of the first degree, a felony of the second degree, or may constitute a murder of the second degree. Arson is a felony of the first degree if a person intentionally starts a fire or causes an explosion on any property where he recklessly places another person in danger of death or bodily injury or he destroys or damages an inhabited building or occupied structure [18 Pa.C.S.A. § 3301(a)(1)(i)(ii)]. Arson is a felony of the second degree if a person intentionally starts a fire or causes an explosion on any unoccupied structure [18 Pa.C.S.A. § 3301(c)(1)(2)]. Arson constitutes murder of the second degree and carries a sentence of life imprisonment if the fire or explosion causes the death of any person and was set with the purpose of causing the death of another person [18 Pa.C.S.A. § 3301(a)(2)].

Criminal Mischief

Criminal mischief ranges in punishment from a felony of the third degree to a summary offense depending on the nature and value of the property damaged. A person is guilty of criminal mischief when he intentionally or recklessly (1) damages tangible personal or public property; (2) causes another to suffer pecuniary loss by deception or threat; (3) damages real or personal property of another; or (4) defaces personal, private or public property with graffiti by using a paintball gun or indelible marking device [18 Pa.C.S.A. § 3304(a)(1)(2)(3)(4)(5)].

Burglary and Criminal Trespass

Burglary and criminal trespass share the basic element of unprivileged entry into buildings, occupied structures, or other premises, but burglary is a more serious offense and requires the added element of intent to commit a crime while inside the building or occupied structure. An occupied structure is "any structure, vehicle or place adapted for overnight accommodation of persons, or for carrying on business therein, whether or not a person is actually present" (18 Pa.C.S.A. §3501). Burglary can be one of four separate offenses depending on the type of building the burglar enters and whether there are any people present in the structure [18 Pa.C.S.A. §3502(a)(1)(2)(3)(4)]. There are three statutorily acknowledged defenses to the charge of burglary: 1) that the building or structure was abandoned, 2) that the premises were open to the public or 3) that the actor was licensed or privileged to enter [18 Pa.C.S.A. §3502(b)]. Burglary is generally graded as a felony of the first degree. However, if the entry is into a dwelling not adapted for overnight accommodations and no one is present, the burglary is a felony of the second degree [18 Pa.C.S.A. §3502(c)].

Four varieties of criminal trespass are set forth in the statute: 1) criminal trespass into buildings and occupied structures, 2) defiant trespass, 3) simple trespass, and 4) agricultural trespass [18 Pa.C.S.A. §3503(a)(b)]. The three defenses to criminal trespass are: 1) proof that the property was abandoned, 2) proof that the property was open to the public, or 3) the defendant's reasonable belief that the owner would have given him permission to enter [18 Pa.C.S.A. §3503(c)].

Theft and Related Offenses

Generally, a theft is the unlawful taking or exercise of unlawful control over property of another [18 Pa.C.S.A. §3921(a)]. Pennsylvania law delineates sixteen theft related crimes. The theft offenses are: theft by unlawful taking or disposition; theft by deception; theft by extortion; theft of property lost, mislaid, or delivered by mistake; receiving stolen property; theft of services; theft by failure to make required disposition of funds; unauthorized use of automobiles and other vehicles; retail theft; library theft; unlawful possession of retail or library theft instruments; organized retail theft; theft of trade secrets; theft of unpublished dramas and musical compositions; theft of leased property; and theft from a motor vehicle (18 Pa.C.S.A. §§3931–3934). The most common of these crimes is theft by unlawful taking, which occurs when a person unlawfully takes, transfers, or exercises unlawful control over movable or immovable property of another with intent to deprive the true owner or to benefit himself [18 Pa.C.S.A. §3921(a)(b)]. The grading of the various crimes of theft range from summary offenses to felonies of the first degree depending on the nature and value of the item taken (18 Pa.C.S.A. §3903).

Vehicle Code

Title 75 of Purdon's Pennsylvania Statutes contains the Vehicle Code. Generally, the Vehicle Code addresses matters involving drinking and driving, driver licensing, automobile insurance, automobile registration and titling, operation of vehicles (road rules), leaving the scene of an accident, mechanical violations, use of seat belts, child restraints, unlawful vehicle modifications, accident reporting, odometer tampering, and commercial driver regulations. Driving offenses may range from summary offenses such as speeding or careless driving, to misdemeanors such as driving under the influence of alcohol or controlled substance (DUI) to felonies such as DUI-related vehicular homicide [75 Pa. C.S.A. §3735(1)].

Driving Under the Influence

One of the more serious crimes under the Vehicle Code is Driving Under the Influence of Alcohol or Controlled Substance (DUI) (75 Pa.C.S.A. §3802). In 2003, Pennsylvania lowered its threshold blood alcohol concentration (BAC) from 0.10% to 0.08%. The current DUI law provides that a person "may not drive, operate or be in actual physical control of the movement of a vehicle after imbibing a sufficient amount of alcohol such that the individual is rendered incapable of safely driving, operating or being in actual physical control of the movement of the vehicle" [75 Pa.C.S.A. §3802(a)]. Pennsylvania adopted a three-tiered approach to alcohol-related DUI offenses based upon the alcohol concentration in an offender's breath or blood. The BAC levels do not relate to the time of driving, but instead relate to the BAC level at the time of testing, which must be within two hours of driving.

Pennsylvania's three-tiered approach is as follows: 1) General impairment: 0.08% to 0.099%; 2) High BAC: 0.10% to 0.159%; and 3) Highest BAC: 0.16% and up [75 Pa.C.S.A. §3802(a)(b)(c)]. Further, this DUI law provides the following BAC limitation levels for: 1) commercial drivers, a BAC of .04%; 2) school bus drivers, a BAC of .02%; and 3) minors, a BAC of .02%. The lowest tier "general impaired" also includes circumstances where the offender's alcohol concentration is not known but the offender has imbibed a sufficient quantity of alcohol so as to be rendered incapable of safe driving. An individual who has either a controlled substance in his blood or who refuses to provide a blood or breath sample faces the same penalty as a third tier "highest BAC" [75 Pa.C.S.A. §3804(c)].

Penalties range from incarceration to probation and house arrest. In addition, a person convicted of DUI might be required to attend a highway safety school program, and pay fines and court costs. The severity of the penalties increases the higher the BAC level, and with the overall number of

Table 2.4 Pennsylvania's Statutory BAC Classifications

General Impairment	0.08% to 0.099%
High BAC	0.10% to 0.159%
Highest BAC	0.16% and up; drugs or refusal of drug/alcohol testing
Commercial Drivers	BAC limit of 0.04%
School Bus Drivers	BAC limit of 0.02%
Minors	BAC limit of 0.02%

total DUI convictions for that individual. For example, a first offense general impairment DUI carries the possibility of six months of probation with a $300 fine. A fourth or subsequent DUI conviction can result in a term of imprisonment of one to five years and a fine ranging from $1,500 to $10,000. A conviction for DUI can also adversely affect an individual's life in other ways. The defendant may suffer the loss of employment, the disqualification from certain jobs, higher insurance rates, driver's license suspension, and having a criminal record.

Drug Offenses

The Controlled Substance, Drug, Device and Cosmetic Act defines prohibited conduct involving the possession or delivery of controlled substances. It also provides criminal penalties for committing drug offenses (35 P.S. §§ 780-101–780-144). The basic definitions that are used throughout Title 35 are provided in Section 780-102. Some of the relevant definitions include the following:

Contraband means any controlled substance, other drug, device or cosmetic possessed by a person not allowed to possess such item.

Controlled substance means a drug, substance, or item included in Schedules I through V of this act.

Deliver or **delivery** means the actual, constructive, or attempted transfer from one person to another of a controlled substance.

Distribute means to deliver other than by administering or dispensing a controlled substance.

Drug means: (i) substances recognized in various official pharmacy books; (ii) substances used in the diagnosis, cure, treatment of disease

Table 2.5 Pennsylvania's Schedule of Drugs

Schedule	Description	Examples
Schedule I	No accepted medical use; highest potential for abuse and addiction	Heroin, marijuana
Schedule II	Limited acceptable medical use; high potential for abuse and addiction	Cocaine, methamphetamines
Schedule III	Accepted medical use; less potential for abuse and addiction; requires a prescription	Anabolic steroids, lysergic acid
Schedule IV	Accepted medical use; low potential for abuse and addiction; requires a prescription	Valium, Xanax
Schedule V	Accepted medical use; lowest potential for abuse and addiction; available without a prescription	Cough suppressants with codeine

in man or animals; and (iii) substances intended to affect the structure or any function of the human body.

Drug paraphernalia means all equipment, products, and materials of any kind which are used or designed for planting, cultivating, growing, manufacturing, preparing, packaging, concealing, injecting, ingesting, or inhaling a controlled substance in violation of this act.

Pennsylvania categorizes controlled substances by schedules, much like the federal government does. The Controlled Substance, Drug, Device and Cosmetic Act arranges drugs in different schedules based on how addictive the controlled substance is and whether it has a medical use. The least serious drugs that have the lightest penalties are in the lowest category (Schedule V), while the most serious drugs with the heaviest penalties are in the highest schedule (Schedule I). The drug categories are delineated in 35 P.S. § 780-104(1)-(5).

Actual, Constructive, and Joint Constructive Possession

Possession of a controlled substance can be established through: (1) actual possession, (2) constructive possession, or (3) joint constructive possession (*Commonwealth v. Gladden*, 1995). Actual possession occurs where an individual actually has the controlled substance or drug on his person, such as in his pocket or in a bag that he is carrying. When contraband is not found on the defendant's person, the Commonwealth must establish constructive possession (*Commonwealth v. Haskins*, 1996).

Constructive possession is a legal fiction, a pragmatic construct to deal with the realities of criminal law enforcement. Constructive possession is an inference arising from a set of facts that possession of the contraband by the actor was more likely than not (*Commonwealth v. Mudrick*, 1986). The purpose of the "constructive possession" doctrine "is to expand the scope of possession statutes to encompass those cases where actual possession at the time of arrest cannot be shown but where the inference that there has been actual possession is strong" (Whitebread and Stevens, 1972). Constructive possession is found where the individual does not have actual possession over the illegal item but has conscious dominion over it (*Commonwealth v. Carroll*, 1986). To prove "conscious dominion," the Commonwealth must present evidence to show that the defendant had both the power to control the contraband and the intent to exercise such control (*Commonwealth v. Gladden*, 1995).

Joint constructive possession occurs where two or more people have joint control and equal access and thus all may constructively possess the contraband. Constructive and joint constructive possession can be inferred from the totality of the circumstances (*Commonwealth v. Gilchrist*, 1978). However, mere presence at the scene is insufficient to prove either constructive possession or joint constructive possession of contraband (*Commonwealth v. Valette*, 1992).

Drug Offenses and Penalties

The Pennsylvania Controlled Substance, Drug, Device, and Cosmetic Act defines illegal acts associated with drugs and their related penalties (35 Pa.C.S.A. §§780-101–780-144).

Pennsylvania law also provides increased terms of incarceration and increased fines for subsequent drug offenses. An offense is considered a second or subsequent offense, if, prior to the commission of the second offense, the offender had at any time been convicted of violating The Controlled Substance, Drug, Device and Cosmetic Act or of a similar offense under any statute of the United States or of any state relating to controlled substances (35 P.S. §780-115(f)(30).

Table 2.6 Common Drug Offenses and Penalties in Pennsylvania

Crime	Mens Rea	Actus Reus	Penalty
Possession of a controlled substance	Intentional or knowing	Active or constructive possession	Misdemeanor 1 year
Possession of a small amount of marijuana (30 grams or less)	Intentional or knowing	Active or constructive possession	Up to 30 days in jail; automatic six month suspension of driver's license
Possession of more than 30 grams of marijuana	Intentional or knowing	Active or constructive possession	Up to one year in jail; automatic six month suspension of driver's license
Possession of drug paraphernalia	Intentional or knowing	Actual or constructive possession	Up to one year in prison
Possession with intent to deliver	Intentional or knowing	Actual delivery or possession with intent to deliver	Schedule I, II or III = up to five years in prison
Possession with intent to deliver	Intentional or knowing	Actual delivery or possession with intent to deliver	Schedule IV = up to three years in prison
Possession with intent to deliver	Intentional or knowing	Actual delivery or possession with intent to deliver	Schedule V = up to one year in prison
Possession with intent to deliver (1,000 lbs. of methamphetamine, cocaine or marijuana)	Intentional or knowing	Actual delivery or possession with intent to deliver	Up to ten years in prison
Possession with intent to deliver (Schedule I or II narcotic drugs)	Intentional or knowing	Actual delivery or possession with intent to deliver	Up to fifteen years in prison

Defenses to Criminal Prosecution

Pennsylvania provides numerous defenses to criminal prosecution. State statutes define the elements of acceptable defenses and establish standards of proof and applications for each.

In the assertion of many defenses, the accused claims that the facts alleged are untrue or incorrect. It is the goal of the defense to convince the trier of fact that the prosecution has not proven the elements of the crime beyond a reasonable doubt. But there are also "affirmative defenses." An affirmative defense is one that excuses or justifies the crime but does not negate an element of the criminal offense charged (*Patterson v. New York*, 1977). Under these circumstances, the defendant does not dispute the factual allegations, but argues that the alleged criminal behavior should be excused under the law. These affirmative defenses commonly require the defendant to produce evidence in support of the argument. For instance, the burden of proving entrapment lies with the defendant. He must prove by a preponderance of evidence that he was "entrapped" by the police in order to prevail at trial. The affirmative defenses include: alibi, duress, entrapment, impossibility, intoxication, insanity, justification, self-defense, and claims that the charges were filed in violation of the statute of limitations.

Time Limitations

Pennsylvania law provides certain time limits commonly referred to as statutes of limitations that prescribe when a prosecution must be commenced (42 Pa.C.S.A. §5552). The purpose of the statute of limitations is to limit an individual's exposure to criminal prosecution on charges made "stale" by the passage of time (*Commonwealth v. Russell*, 2007).

Two separate and distinct statutes of limitations exist. The first statute of limitations provides a time limit as to when criminal charges can be instituted. For serious offenses, prosecution must begin within five years of the commission of the crime. For lesser offenses, prosecution must begin within two years of the commission of the crime [42 Pa.C.S.A. §5552(a)]. An exception has been created for those cases where the perpetrator is later identified through the discovery of human DNA (deoxyribonucleic acid) evidence. Under such circumstances, charges may be filed either within the statute of limitations or within one year after the identity of the individual is ascertained, whichever is later [Pa. C.S.A. §5552(c.1)]. Defendants who persuade the court that the charges have not been filed within the statutorily prescribed time period will have those charges dismissed.

The second type of statute of limitations concerns the time in which the prosecution may bring a case to trial after the accused has been arrested. This is commonly known as the defendant's "speedy trial" right. The right is found in the Sixth Amendment to the United States Constitution and in Article I, Section 9 of the Pennsylvania Constitution. The right was and is considered an important one to protect defendants (who are presumed innocent) from being subjected to long periods of incarceration prior to trial.

For purposes of implementation, the term "speedy" is more particularly defined in the Pennsylvania Rules of Criminal Procedure (Pa.R.Crim.P. 600). That Rule provides that defendants must be brought to trial within 365 days of the filing of charges. Defendants who are in jail awaiting trial are entitled to release on nominal bail after 180 days [Pa.R.Crim.P. 600 (E)]. Calculation of the "speedy trial run date" (the date by which the defendant must be brought to trial) will exclude any time delays caused by the defendant. For instance, if a defendant is granted a request for a two-week continuance, those two weeks will not be counted in the calculation of the run date. Most importantly, failure to bring a defendant to trial within the prescribed time period will result in dismissal of the charges.

Ignorance or Mistake

Ignorance or mistake as to a matter of fact, for which there is reasonable explanation or excuse, is a defense if, 1) the ignorance or mistake negates one of the requisite *mens rea* which is an element of the offense, or 2) the law provides that the state of mind established by such ignorance or mistake constitutes a defense (18 Pa.C.S.A. §304).

Minimum Age

The common law rule provided a rebuttable presumption that children between the ages of 7 and 14 years were incapable of committing a crime (*Commonwealth v. Kocher*, 1992). However, Pennsylvania law changed this common law concept, and now holds that children aged 10 years and older have the capacity to commit delinquent acts (42 Pa.C.S.A. §6302). Therefore, a person can be held criminally delinquent for committing a crime at the age of 10. In Pennsylvania, no minimum age exists for someone to be charged as an adult for criminal homicide. For example, in 2009, an 11-year-old boy was charged with two counts of homicide for murdering his father's fiancée, who was 8 months pregnant (Chen, 2010).

Mental Capacity (Competence, Guilty but Mentally Ill or Legally Insane)

A distinction should be made among the legal notions of competence, guilty but mentally ill, and not guilty by reason of insanity. In Pennsylvania, as in other states, an individual must be deemed to be legally competent before being permitted to testify, or before being permitted to go to trial as a defendant. Competency measures the individual's mental capacity at the time of the hearing. While competency is generally presumed, it may be challenged by the prosecution or by the defense. For instance, the defense attorney may assert that the defendant is not competent to stand trial. Because competency is generally presumed, it is the defense attorney's burden to prove by a preponderance of the evidence that the defendant is incompetent. To make this determination, the Court will want to know if the defendant is capable of understanding the charges against him and of assisting in the preparation of a defense. A defendant deemed competent by the court will proceed to trial. If the defendant is deemed incompetent, the trial will be continued until such time as the defendant, with treatment, becomes competent. If there is no reasonable expectation that the defendant will become competent with treatment and medication, the charges will be dismissed, and the fate of the defendant will be left to the state's mental health system (225 Pa. Code Rule 601).

By contrast, the legal notions of "guilty but mentally ill" and "not guilty by reason of insanity" address the defendant's mental capacity at the time of the crime. For an accused to be found guilty but mentally ill, he must either lack the capacity to appreciate the wrongfulness of his conduct or be unable to conform his conduct to the requirements of the law [18 Pa.C.S.A. §314(c)(1)]. A defendant found to be guilty but mentally ill may be sentenced to any lawful sentence to which a defendant found guilty of the same crime would be subject. Under these circumstances, however, the sentencing judge may tailor the defendant's sentence to include treatment as well as punishment.

Pennsylvania's insanity law, known as the M'Naghten rule, is set forth in Pa. C.S.A. Section 315. It was derived from the 1843 case of Regina v. M'Naghten. The M'Naghten rule sets forth two separate and distinct aspects of the insanity defense: 1) cognitive incapacity, and 2) moral incapacity. The concept of cognitive incapacity addresses the question of whether an accused knew what he was doing. The second concept, moral incapacity, addresses whether an accused understands that what he was doing was wrong (*Commonwealth v. Andre*, 2011).

The defense of insanity is an affirmative defense. That is, the defendant does not contest the facts alleged by the prosecution, but challenges his legal responsibility for his acts because of his mental state at the time of the crime. It is the defendant's burden to prove by a preponderance of the evidence that he was legally insane (as defined by the M'Naghten standard) at the time of the crime. Ultimately, four possible verdicts exist when the defense of legal insanity is offered: 1) not guilty, 2) guilty, 3) not guilty by reason of insanity and 4) guilty but mentally ill. A defendant found not guilty by reason of insanity cannot be held criminally responsible for his acts.

Involuntary or Voluntary Intoxication

Pennsylvania law specifically allows the defense of voluntary intoxication only when offered to reduce the specific intent under first degree murder to a lower degree of murder (18 Pa.C.S.A. § 308). But voluntary intoxication cannot be used as a complete defense that would exonerate or excuse the crime of murder, or any other crime (*Commonwealth v. Gordon*, 1980).

Pennsylvania law is more ambiguous about involuntary intoxication as a defense to crime. State law does not specify whether an involuntary intoxication defense is available (18 Pa.C.S.A. § 308). It is unclear whether such a defense is viable, but an implication exists that involuntary intoxication could be a defense to a crime. To date, however, no Pennsylvania case has ever held that the defense of involuntary intoxication is a viable one (*Commonwealth v. Todaro*, 1982; *Commonwealth v. Smith*, 2003).

Military Order

The Commonwealth recognizes a justification defense based upon military authority, arising from the issuance of a lawful military order by a superior officer (18 Pa.C.S.A. § 310). This defense is available when an accused is following a military order, and he commits an act that he does not know and cannot reasonably be expected to know is unlawful.

Duress

The Commonwealth provides a defense of duress when an accused engages in criminal conduct because he was coerced to do so by the threat of unlawful force or the use of unlawful force against himself or another. The threat or use of unlawful force must be such that a person of reasonable firmness in his situation would have been unable to resist.

> The elements which must be shown to establish a duress defense are: (1) an immediate or imminent threat of death or serious bodily injury; (2) a well-grounded or reasonable fear that the threat will be carried out; (3) no reasonable opportunity to escape the threatened harm except by committing the criminal act (*Commonwealth v. Morningwake, 1991*).

This defense is inapplicable in situations where the accused either recklessly or negligently places himself in a situation where it was probable that he would be subjected to duress (18 Pa.C.S.A. § 309).

Consent

Pennsylvania law provides that consent to potentially criminal conduct is a defense where it 1) negates an element of an offense, or 2) precludes the infliction of the harm or evil sought to be prevented by the law defining the offense (18 Pa.C.S.A. §311). Where lack of consent is an element of the crime, the defendant does not bear the burden of proving consent; rather the Commonwealth bears the burden of proving lack of consent, beyond a reasonable doubt.

De Minimis Infractions

Pennsylvania has a statute which provides that a court shall dismiss prosecutions of "*de minimus*" infractions (18 Pa.C.S.A. §312). A de minimis infraction is an infraction that is so insignificant that a court may overlook it in deciding an issue or case (Garner, 2009). The purpose of the statute is to remove petty infractions from the category of criminal conduct. It applies to circumstances in which no harm occurred to a victim or to society.

Entrapment

Entrapment is a defense if a law enforcement official or a person acting cooperatively with a law enforcement officer induces or encourages an accused to commit criminal conduct by either, 1) making false representations designed to induce the belief that the conduct is not criminal, or 2) persuading an accused to commit an offense where the accused lacked the intent to commit the crime. Entrapment is no defense where a police officer did nothing more than to offer an accused the opportunity to a commit crime, such as an undercover officer asking an accused to sell him drugs. To constitute entrapment, the inducement must be such that it persuades a person not predisposed to commit the crime to commit the crime. It is the defendant's burden to prove that he was "entrapped" by a preponderance of the evidence (Pa. C.S.A §313).

Justified Conduct

The Commonwealth provides an accused a justification for alleged criminal behavior under several circumstances. They include: 1) when the conduct is necessary to avoid a greater harm than the harm sought to be prevented by the statute; 2) when the conduct is authorized or required by any law concerning the performance of governmental duties; 3) when the use of force is necessary in defending oneself or another, or defending the protection of property; 4) when the use of force is necessary to make a lawful arrest; 5) when the use of force is by a parent for the purpose of safeguarding the welfare of his minor child; 6) when the use of force is necessary for maintaining discipline, safeguarding others, administrating treatment or maintaining reasonable discipline by teachers, guardians, doctors, and wardens (18 Pa. C.S.A. §§ 502–510).

Self-Defense and the Castle Doctrine

Pennsylvania law permits citizens to use reasonable force in self-defense or in the defense of other persons. Recently (in 2011), the Commonwealth joined twenty-one other states and adopted a variation of the "stand your ground" laws (National Conference of State Legislatures). These laws are based on the "Castle Doctrine." The Castle Doctrine states that a man's home is his castle, and provides a legal defense for armed response to intruders. The Doctrine allows him, in certain circumstances, to use force up to and including deadly force to defend against an intruder. Under Pennsylvania law, a "castle" includes one's residence, porch, deck, patio, or occupied vehicle.

Generally, the use of deadly force is not justifiable if the actor knows that he can avoid the necessity of using such force with complete safety by retreating [18 Pa.C.S.A. §505(b)(2)(ii)]. However, an actor is not required to retreat from his dwelling, place of work or his vehicle, and he may use deadly force if he lawfully possesses a firearm or other deadly weapon. For this doctrine to apply: 1) an intruder must be making or have made an attempt to unlawfully or forcibly enter an occupied residence or vehicle; 2) an intruder must be acting unlawfully; 3) the occupant(s) of the home or vehicle must reasonably believe that deadly force is immediately necessary to protect himself against death, serious bodily injury, kidnapping, or sexual intercourse; and 4) the occupant(s) of the home or vehicle must not have provoked or instigated an intrusion; or, provoked/instigated an intruder's threat or use of deadly force.

Defense of Property

A property owner may be permitted to use reasonable, non-lethal force in the protection of his property (*Commonwealth v. Birch*, 1994). The non-lethal force is justifiable when the actor believes that such force is immediately necessary to prevent or terminate an unlawful entry upon land or a trespass against or the unlawful carrying away of tangible property [18 Pa.C.S.A. §507(a)(1)]. Before using force, the actor must first request the person against whom such force is used to desist from his interference with the property, unless this request would be useless [18 Pa.C.S.A. §507(c)].

Alibi

A defendant may provide an alibi defense for any crime. Pennsylvania law defines alibi as the presentation of evidence which places him at a different location than that of the crime scene at the time of the crime, making it impossible for him to be guilty (*Commonwealth v. Repaci*, 1992). It is not necessary for an alibi defense to be corroborated by any other witnesses. Thus, the defendant's lone testimony is sufficient to establish an alibi (*Commonwealth v. Saunders*, 1991).

Conclusion

As citizens, we elect our representatives to enact laws designed to keep us safe. But a balance must be struck between our need for public safety and the protection of our civil liberties. To ensure that balance, laws are enacted proscribing and punishing certain conduct, and additional laws are enacted to protect the rights of the accused. Those protections include the presumption of innocence, allocation of the burden of proof to the prosecution, rules to determine who can be held criminally responsible for criminal behavior, and the delineation of statutory defenses to criminal conduct.

Legislatures frequently enact new laws and the judiciary is continuously interpreting and reinterpreting those laws. With each new law, and each new judicial opinion, the means permitted to enforce those laws may change. In this manner, criminal law and procedure are constantly changing. These aspects of law must evolve as society evolves, as new challenges to peace and order emerge and as scientific knowledge grows. The ultimate goal remains, however, to maintain a peaceful and orderly society that also respects the rights of our citizens.

Key Terms and Definitions

Accomplice liability: A legal theory that permits co-conspirators to be held responsible for a crime even if they are not direct actors.

Affirmative defense: Defenses to criminal conduct that include admission of the factual allegations, but which attempt to excuse the defendant's conduct (alibi, duress, entrapment, impossibility, intoxication, insanity, justification, self-defense, statute of limitation).

Aggravated assault: The infliction or attempt to inflict serious bodily injury, assault with a deadly weapon, or assaults against certain public officials or employees.

Beyond a reasonable doubt: The level of proof required for a criminal conviction; a doubt that would cause a reasonable person to be restrained or to hesitate before acting upon a matter of importance in his personal affairs.

Burglary: Unlawful entry into a place for the purpose of committing a crime therein.

Civil law: Statutes that proscribe particular conduct and permit an aggrieved person to institute a legal action for monetary damages or to seek an action or restraint against a person or other legal entity.

Competence: A state of mind sufficient that a defendant has the capacity to understand the charges against him and to assist in his defense.

Criminal law: Statutes that proscribe particular conduct and permit the government to institute legal action seeing punishment.

Felony: A serious crime punishable by maximum sentences of 7 years (felony of the third degree), 10 years (felony of the second degree), or 20 years (felony of the first degree).

Inchoate crimes: Incomplete crimes or crimes that are preparatory to a crime (criminal attempt, criminal conspiracy, and criminal solicitation).

Insanity: A legal status conferred by a trier of fact on the defendant such that the defendant cannot be held responsible for his criminal behavior due to a mental disease or defect as defined by the M'Naghten standard.

M'Naghten: The standard for measuring legal insanity derived from the 1843 acquittal of a defendant charged with murder; the standard requires the trier of fact to determine whether, at the time of the commission of the offense, the actor was laboring under such a defect of reason, from disease of the mind, as not to know the nature and quality of the act he was doing or, if the actor did know the quality of the act, that he did not know that what he was doing was wrong.

Misdemeanor: A crime for which the maximum penalty is five years (misdemeanor of the first degree); two years (misdemeanor of the second degree); or one year (misdemeanor of the third degree).

Murder: The unjustifiable, malicious and intentional taking of the life of another.

Preponderance of evidence: The level of proof required to be met in most pretrial criminal proceedings; more likely so than not.

Presumption of innocence: A rebuttable presumption that those accused of a crime are innocent until proven guilty beyond a reasonable doubt in a court of law.

Purdon's Pennsylvania Statutes: A compendium of Pennsylvania civil and criminal statutes.

Rape: sexual intercourse by force or threat of force, or with a person who is unconscious or otherwise incapable of giving consent to the act.

Robbery: Attempted theft of theft from a person by force or threat of force.

Substantial capacity test: A defendant may be found "guilty but mentally ill" if at the time of the act, he lacked the substantial capacity (as a result of mental disease or defect) either to appreciate the wrongfulness of his conduct or to control his conduct.

Summary offense: A lesser offense for which the maximum term of imprisonment is 90 days.

Theft: The unlawful taking of the property of another.

Websites

Legislative Reference Bureau of Pennsylvania: http://www.palrb.net/.
Pennsylvania General Assembly: http://government.westlaw.com/linkedslice/
    default.asp?SP=pac-1000.
The Pennsylvania Capitol Making Law Pennsylvania: http://www.legis.state.pa.us/
    WU01/VC/visitor_info/pdfs/makingLaw.pdf.

Review Questions

1. What are the differences between civil and criminal law?
2. What are the distinctions between moral wrongdoings and criminal wrongdoings?
3. Identify and explain the distinctions between the crimes of burglary and robbery.
4. Identify and explain the differences among the various degrees of murder, voluntary manslaughter, and involuntary manslaughter.
5. How are affirmative defenses different from other defenses? What are some of the affirmative defenses in Pennsylvania?

Critical Thinking Questions

1.	The decision by legislatures to criminalize particular human behavior varies from country to country and even from jurisdiction to jurisdiction within the United States. Identify and discuss the various cultural, sociological, and political considerations that result in differing legal approaches regarding such crimes as marijuana use and prostitution.

2.	The recent death of Trayvon Martin has resulted in much publicity and debate of new state and federal self-defense laws, and of the Castle Doctrine in particular. Should individuals have a duty to retreat, if they can do so safely, before resorting to deadly force and taking a life?

3.	The legal precept of "accomplice liability" makes co-conspirators equally guilty, even when their contributions to the criminal outcome may not be equal at all. Discuss the reasons for making accomplices similarly accountable. What are some ways that the law could better assign criminal liability based upon an individual defendant's unique role in the conspiracy?

4.	The legal concepts of "competence" and "insanity" are quite distinct, although often confused by students of criminal law. Although counterintuitive, it is accurate to say that "a defendant must be competent in order to be insane." Discuss the legal concepts of "competence" and "insanity" to fully explain why a defendant must be found to be "competent" before being found to be "insane."

References

Appeal of DaPra, 227 A.2d 491 (Pa. 1967)

Ashworth, A. & Horder, J. (2013). *Principles of Criminal Law (7th edition)*. New York: Oxford University Press.

Chen, Stephanie. *Boy, 12, faces grown up murder charges*. March 15, 2010. CNNJustice. Retrieved from: http://www.cnn.com/2010/CRIME/02/10/pennsylvania.young.murder.defendant/index.html.

Commonwealth v. Andre, 17 A.3d 951 (Pa. Super. 2011)

Commonwealth v. Birch, 644 A.2d 759 (Pa. Super. 1994).

Commonwealth v. Carroll, 507 A.2d 819 (Pa. 1986)

Commonwealth v. Evans, 494 A.2d 383 (1985)

Commonwealth v. Gilchrist, 386 A.2d 603 (Pa. Super. 1978)

Commonwealth v. Gladden, 665 A.2d 1201 (Pa. Super. 1995)

Commonwealth v. Gordon, 416 A.2d 87 (Pa. 1980)

Commonwealth v. Haskins, 677 A.2d 328, 330 (Pa. Super. 1996)

Commonwealth v. Kocher, 602 A.2d 1308 (Pa. 1992)

Commonwealth v. Morningwake, 595 A.2d 158 (Pa. Super. 1991)

Commonwealth v. Mudrick, 507 A.2d 1212, 1213 (Pa. 1986)

Commonwealth v. Repaci, 615 A.2d 796, 798 (Pa. Super. 1992)

Commonwealth v. Russell, 938 A.2d 1082 (Pa. Super. 2007)

Commonwealth v. Saunders, 602 A.2d 816 (Pa. 1991)

Commonwealth v. Smith, 831 A.2d 636, 639 (Pa. Super. 2003)

Commonwealth v. Todaro, 446 A.2d 1305 (Pa. Super. 1982)

Commonwealth v. Valette, 613 A.2d 548, 551 (Pa. 1992)

Garner, Brian A. (2009). *Black's Law Dictionary Standard Ninth Edition*. St. Paul, MN: West.

Harris v. State Board of Optometrical Examiners, 135 A. 237 (Pa. 1926)

Kendrick v. District Attorney of Philadelphia County, 916 A.2d 529 (Pa. 2007)

Knowles, David. *Vermont becomes 17th state to decriminalize marijuana, making possession of less than an ounce of pot punishable by fine.* June 6, 2013. New York Daily News Retrieved from: http://www.nydailynews.com/news/national/vermont-decriminalizes-possession-small-amounts-pot-article-1.1365354.

Legislative Reference Bureau of Pennsylvania. Retrieved from: http://www.palrb.net/.

National Conference of State Legislatures. Retrieved from: http://www.ncsl.org/issues-research/justice/self-defense-and-stand-your-ground.aspx.

Nevada Revised Statutes, Chapter 244.345 (2011).

Patterson v. New York, 432 U.S. 197 (1977).

Pennsylvania General Assembly Home. Retrieved from: http://government.westlaw.com/linkedslice/default.asp?SP=pac-1000.

Pennsylvania Juvenile Act, 42 Pa. C. S. A. §6301 (2008).

Regina v. M'Naghten, 8 Eng. Rep. 718 (1843)

The Pennsylvania Capitol. Making Law Pennsylvania. Retrieved from: http://www.legis.state.pa.us/WU01/VC/visitor_info/pdfs/makingLaw.pdf.

United States v. Cordoba-Hincapie, 825 F. Supp. 485, 489 (E.D.N.Y.1993)

Whitebread and Stevens, *To Have and To Have Not*, 58 U.Va.L.Rev. 751, 755 (1972).

Appendix A
Pennsylvania Crimes Code
18 Pa.C.S.A.

Part I	Chapter	Title
	1	General Provisions
	3	Culpability
	5	General Principles of Justification
	9	Inchoate Crimes
	11	Authorized Disposition of Offenders
Part II	25	Criminal Homicide
	26	Crimes Against Unborn Child
	27	Assault
	29	Kidnapping
	30	Trafficking of Persons
	31	Sexual Offenses
	32	Abortion
	33	Arson, Criminal Mischief and Other Property Destruction
	35	Burglary and Other Criminal Intrusion
	37	Robbery
	39	Theft and Related Offenses
	41	Forgery and Fraudulent Practices
	43	Offenses Against the Family
	47	Bribery and Corrupt Influence
	49	Falsification and Intimidation
	51	Obstructing Governmental Operations
	53	Abuse of Office
	55	Riot, Disorderly Conduct and Related Offenses
	57	Wiretapping and Electronic Surveillance
	59	Public Indecency
	61	Firearms and Other Dangerous Articles

	63	Minors
	65	Nuisances
	75	Other Offenses
	76	Computer Offenses
	77	Vehicle Chop Shop and Illegally Obtained and Altered Property
Part III	91	Criminal History Record Information
	94	Crime Victims

Chapter 3

The Criminal Justice Process in Pennsylvania

James C. Roberts and Jenny P. Roberts

Learning Objectives

After reading this chapter, students should be able to:

- Explain the major steps in the criminal justice process in Pennsylvania.
- Explain the arrest process in Pennsylvania, including probable cause for arrest warrants.
- Explain search and seizure in Pennsylvania, including probable cause for search warrants.
- Explain basic rights afforded to suspected offenders in Pennsylvania and elsewhere, such as those specified by the Supreme Court in the now famous case of *Miranda v. Arizona* (1966).
- Describe the pretrial process in Pennsylvania, including the preliminary arraignment, the preliminary hearing, the formal arraignment, plea agreements, and the filing of pretrial motions.
- Describe the trial process in Pennsylvania, including jury selection, the presentation of evidence, and jury deliberations.
- Explain the sentencing process and punishment options available to judges in Pennsylvania.

Key Terms

Arrest Warrant   Burden of Proof
Booking   Challenges for Cause

Criminal Information
Discovery
Formal Arraignment
Gideon v. Wainwright (1963)
Indicting Grand Jury
Indictment
Investigating Grand Jury
Jurisdiction
Jury Deliberations
Jury Instructions
Miranda Rights
Miranda v. Arizona (1966)

Nolo Contendere
Peremptory Challenges
Plea Agreements
Preliminary Arraignment
Pretrial Motions
Prima Facie case
Probable cause
Search Warrant
Sentencing Guidelines
Voir Dire
4th Amendment
5th Amendment

Introduction

The criminal justice process in the Commonwealth of Pennsylvania entails numerous steps or stages that take suspected offenders through each of the major components of Pennsylvania's criminal justice system (i.e., police, courts, and corrections). While some individuals suspected of criminal wrongdoing will pass through all stages of this process, others may have their cases dismissed early on due to insufficient evidence or be diverted out of the criminal justice system and into drug or mental health treatment programs. The stages of the criminal justice process in Pennsylvania, which are not dissimilar to those in other states across the country, generally occur in a specific order: crime reported, crime investigated, suspect booked, initial hearing (preliminary arraignment), preliminary hearing, formal arraignment, criminal trial, sentencing, and handing over to corrections.

The criminal justice process typically begins when a crime is reported to law enforcement by victims or witnesses. Once a crime is reported, an investigation will take place to determine whether a crime has in fact been committed. If the investigation yields a viable suspect, this individual may be arrested and booked into a detention facility. If an arrest is made, the suspect will then be taken to court for an initial appearance, known in Pennsylvania as the preliminary arraignment, so that a judge may give the accused a copy of the criminal complaint and make a determination of bail. Next, for murder, felony, and misdemeanor offenses, a preliminary hearing may be conducted, at which time the prosecuting attorney must establish a *prima facie* case. If the charges are held or waived to court, the case then proceeds to the formal arraignment where the suspect will have the opportunity to respond to the allegations against him or her. If the suspect pleads not guilty, the case will proceed to trial. If the suspect enters a guilty plea or is found guilty at trial, a sentence is imposed. It is important to note that the criminal justice process in certain cities and counties throughout Pennsylvania may deviate slightly from the process described in this chapter. The major aim here is to provide a general overview of the criminal justice process in most jurisdictions throughout the state.

General Terminology

Jurisdiction and Venue

In Pennsylvania, as in other states, the crime and location in which it is committed determines which law enforcement agencies will investigate and which courts will handle the various hearings pertaining to the crime(s) in question. Jurisdiction in Pennsylvania for the state to exercise authority over individuals accused of criminal wrongdoing is defined in 18 Pa.C.S.A. § 102. According to this statute, in the state of Pennsylvania a person may be convicted of an offense committed by his or her own conduct or the conduct of another for which he or she is legally accountable if:

- the conduct which is an element of the offense or the result which is such an element occurs within this Commonwealth;
- conduct occurring outside this Commonwealth is sufficient under the law of this Commonwealth to constitute an attempt to commit an offense within this Commonwealth;
- conduct occurring outside this Commonwealth is sufficient under the law of this Commonwealth to constitute a conspiracy to commit an offense within this Commonwealth and an overt act in furtherance of such conspiracy occurs within this Commonwealth;
- conduct occurring within this Commonwealth establishes complicity in the commission of, or an attempt, solicitation or conspiracy to commit, an offense in another jurisdiction which also is an offense under the law of this Commonwealth;
- the offense consists of the omission to perform a legal duty imposed by the law of this Commonwealth with respect to domicile, residence or a relationship to a person, thing or transaction in this Commonwealth; or
- the offense is based on a statute of this Commonwealth which expressly prohibits conduct outside this Commonwealth when the conduct bears

a reasonable relation to a legitimate interest of this Commonwealth and the actor knows or should know that his conduct is likely to affect that interest (18 Pa.C.S.A. §102(a)(1-6)).

Furthermore, the Commonwealth may exercise legal authority over conduct when an element of the crime or the result of the crime occurs within the state. For example, "When the offense is homicide or homicide of an unborn child, either the death of the victim, including an unborn child, or the bodily impact causing death constitutes a 'result' within the meaning of paragraph (a)(1) of this section, and if the body of a homicide victim, including an unborn child, is found within this Commonwealth, it is presumed that such result occurred within this Commonwealth" (18 Pa.C.S.A. §102(c)).

Pa.R.Crim.P. Rule 130 provides guidelines for venue. As in other states, where the crime was committed will determine the venue (i.e., the location where the trial will take place). One exception to this rule is when "the particular place within the judicial district in which the offense is alleged to have occurred is unknown" (Pa.R.Crim.P. Rule 130(A)(1)). When this happens, criminal proceedings may take place before any issuing authority of any magisterial district.

As in other states, law enforcement in Pennsylvania exists on the federal, state, and local levels. State and local law enforcement at the county and municipal levels have the authority to enforce state laws that occur within their jurisdictions, while federal law enforcement provides statewide enforcement of federal laws. Individuals found guilty of violating state laws may be supervised by county or state correctional agencies located throughout Pennsylvania, while those found guilty of violating federal laws may be supervised by correctional agencies in the federal system, not necessarily within the Commonwealth of Pennsylvania.

Limitations on Prosecution

In Pennsylvania, as in other states, there are limitations for beginning prosecution for certain crimes, but not for others. According to 42 Pa.C.S.A. §5551, prosecution for murder, voluntary manslaughter, or conspiracy to commit murder or solicitation to commit murder (if a murder results from the conspiracy or solicitation) may begin at any time. The same is true for:

- any felony alleged to have been perpetrated in connection with a murder of the first or second degree, as set forth in 18 Pa.C.S. §2502(a) or (b) and (d) (relating to murder);
- a violation of 75 Pa.C.S. §3742 (relating to accidents involving death or personal injury) or 3732 (relating to homicide by vehicle) if the accused

was the driver of a vehicle involved in an accident resulting in the death of any person; or

- a violation of 18 Pa.C.S. § 2702(a)(1), (2), (4) or (7) (relating to aggravated assault) if the accused knew the victim was a law enforcement officer and the law enforcement officer was acting within the scope of the officer's duties (42 Pa.C.S.A. § 5551(4-6)).

42 Pa.C.S.A. § 5552 addresses "other offenses" and states that, as a general rule, prosecution of an offense must occur within two years after it is committed (42 Pa.C.S.A. § 5552(a)). However, this rule does not apply to major offenses, major sexual offenses, and other exceptions identified in 42 Pa.C.S.A. § 5552. According to 42 Pa.C.S.A. § 5552(b), for major offenses, such as attempts to commit murder where no murder occurs, solicitation to commit murder where no murder occurs, and conspiracy to commit murder where no murder occurs, prosecution must begin within five years after it is committed. For major sexual offenses, such as rape, sexual assault, involuntary deviate sexual intercourse, incest, and sexual abuse of children, prosecution must begin within 12 years after it is committed (42 Pa.C.S.A. § 5552(b.1)). One exception to the rule governing how much time may expire before prosecution of a crime must commence is for "any sexual offense committed against a minor who is less than 18 years of age any time up to the later of the period of limitation provided by law after the minor has reached 18 years of age or the date the minor reaches 50 years of age" (42 Pa.C.S.A. § 5552(c)(3)).

42 Pa.C.S.A. § 5552 offers additional guidelines for dealing with genetic identification of evidence implicating offenders. 42 Pa.C.S.A. § 5552(c.1) states: "Notwithstanding any provision of law to the contrary, if evidence of a misdemeanor sexual offense set forth in subsection (c)(3) or a felony offense is obtained containing human deoxyribonucleic acid (DNA) which is subsequently used to identify an otherwise unidentified individual as the perpetrator of the offense, the prosecution of the offense may be commenced within the period of limitations provided for the offense or one year after the identity of the individual is determined, whichever is later."

Probable Cause

The 4th Amendment of the United States Constitution reads: "The right of the people to be secure in their persons, houses, papers, and effects, against unreasonable searches and seizures, shall not be violated; and no Warrants shall issue but upon probable cause, supported by oath or affirmation, and particularly describing the place to be searched, and the persons or things to be seized." As such, and with few exceptions, the 4th Amendment protects citizens and their property from unlawful searches and seizures. In Pennsylvania, as in other states, probable cause as it applies to searches and seizures is determined by the issuing court at the time of the application for the warrant. However, the probable cause can be challenged by the defendant prior to trial. It should be noted that the 4th Amendment protection against unlawful searches and seizures was not extended to the states until 1949 with the case of *Wolf v. Colorado*. Until this time, the limitations on law enforcement described in the 4th Amendment bound only federal law enforcement entities and courts in the United States.

Report and Investigation of the Crime

As mentioned, the criminal justice process typically begins when a crime is reported to law enforcement. Crimes may also come to the attention of police while on duty and on patrol. Crimes committed in the presence of the police may result in an immediate arrest, while for those crimes reported to law enforcement by victims or witnesses, and for which there is no immediately identifiable suspect, an arrest may not occur for days, weeks, months, or even years, if at all. When a suspect is not immediately apprehended, detectives or investigators are often brought in to assist with the investigation. Investigation techniques utilized by police officers and detectives include interviewing victims and witnesses, running background checks and gathering personal information on suspected offenders, and obtaining physical evidence (i.e., fingerprints, DNA, etc.).

Searches and Search Warrants

During a criminal investigation, police may seek to search the property and personal effects of victims, suspects, and witnesses. As mentioned, all U.S. citizens are protected against unreasonable searches and seizures by state or federal law enforcement entities. Pa.R.Crim.P. Rule 200 states: "A search warrant may be issued by any issuing authority within the judicial district wherein is located either the person or place to be searched." A warrant may be issued for the search and seizure of: "(1) contraband, the fruits of a crime, or things otherwise criminally possessed; or (2) property that is or has been used as the means of committing a criminal offense; or (3) property that constitutes evidence of the commission of a criminal offense" (Pa.R.Crim.P. Rule 201). According to Pa.R.Crim.P. Rule 203(B), "No search warrant shall issue but upon probable cause supported by one or more affidavits sworn to before the issuing authority in person or using advanced communication technology." In Pennsylvania, judicial authorities will not authorize a search to be executed between the hours of 10:00 PM and 7:00 AM unless the affidavit shows "reasonable cause" for a nighttime search. The actual warrant must identify the property to be seized and name or describe the person or place to be searched. As in other states, search warrants issued throughout the Commonwealth of Pennsylvania are limited in time and may expire. Pa.R.Crim.P. Rule 205(4) directs that the search be executed either "(a) within a specified period of time, not to exceed 2 days from the time of issuance, or; (b) when the warrant is issued for a prospective event, only after the specified event has occurred."

In accordance with the so-called knock-and-announce rule, when executing a search warrant, law enforcement officers "shall, before entry, give, or make reasonable effort to give, notice of the officer's identity, authority, and purpose to any occupant of the premises specified in the warrant, unless exigent circumstances require the officer's immediate forcible entry" (Pa.R.Crim.P. Rule 207(A)). Officers are also expected to wait for a response "for a reasonable period of time" after this announcement before entering the premises unless exigent circumstances require immediate forcible entry. Exigent circumstances include any indication that the person to be arrested is fleeing or attempting to destroy evidence. Following a search, Pa.R.Crim.P. Rule 208(A) states that law enforcement officers must leave a copy of the warrant, affidavit(s), and a receipt for the property seized with the person from whom or from whose premises the property was taken. If nobody is home at the time of the search, officers should leave these documents "at a conspicuous location in the said premises" (Pa.R.Crim.P. Rule 208(B)). Finally, law enforcement officers must make an inventory of seized items. According to Pa.R.Crim.P. Rule 209(A), "The inventory shall be made in the presence of the person from whose possession or premises the property was taken, when feasible, or otherwise in the presence of at least one witness." Officers are then required to sign a statement on the inventory that it is a "true and correct listing of all items seized" (Pa.R.Crim.P. Rule 209(A)). Items seized are then logged into evidence.

Arrests and Arrest Warrants

An arrest is the act of seizing a person or taking them into custody. An arrest warrant is a court-issued document authorizing police to make an arrest. A law enforcement officer is permitted to make an arrest without a warrant if a person commits a murder, felony, misdemeanor, or certain summary offenses (e.g., public drunkenness, disorderly conduct, etc.) in their presence. Officers are also permitted to make an arrest without a warrant for certain misdemeanors (e.g., simple assaults related to a domestic dispute) and for any felonies committed outside their presence. For crimes and circumstances that do not allow for a warrantless arrest, officers must obtain an arrest warrant. In Pennsylvania, law enforcement officers are not authorized to process arrest warrants on their own. Instead, they must complete an affidavit and submit it to the court that has jurisdiction over the case. Unlike some states, Pennsylvania has no individual form for affidavits used by all law enforcement agencies. However, the Pennsylvania State Police (PSP) use a common form within their organization and most municipal police departments throughout the state use a common form because they use the same computer program for creating affidavits.

In accordance with the 4th Amendment of the U.S. Constitution, Pa.R.Crim.P. Rule 513(B) states: "No arrest warrant shall issue but upon probable cause supported by one or more affidavits sworn to before the issuing authority in person or using advanced communication technology." Once the affidavit is submitted, a judge with jurisdiction over the case will determine whether or not probable cause exists to support the issuance of an arrest warrant. In making this determination, Pa.R.Crim.P. Rule 513(B) states that the issuing authority "may not consider any evidence outside the affidavits." Pa.R.Crim.P. Rule 515 states that an arrest may take place anywhere within the Commonwealth of Pennsylvania and that it must be executed by a police officer. Furthermore, unlike search warrants that do expire, arrest warrants in Pennsylvania are valid until the individual named in the warrant is apprehended.

In the case *Miranda v. Arizona* (1966), the Supreme Court ruled that prior to any questioning in the context of a custodial interrogation (i.e., questioning of a person when they are not free to leave), law enforcement officers must advise suspects of their rights under the Constitution, particularly their Fifth Amendment privilege against self-incrimination and right to counsel. While police are not required to read the so-called Miranda Rights until a suspect in custody is being interrogated, many law enforcement agencies in Pennsylvania and elsewhere require that their officers read the Miranda Rights during non-custodial interviews (e.g., at the suspect's residence) and at the time of arrest.

Booking

If authorities intend to detain a suspected offender prior to court proceedings, booking will take place before the preliminary arraignment (i.e., first appearance before a judge). The booking process entails fingerprinting the suspected offender (as required by state law), taking their photograph, determining their prior record, confiscating their personal items, and sometimes conducting a full body search before placing them in a holding cell. At this time, the arresting authority will also ascertain the identity of the suspected offender and make a record of personal information such as their current address and employer. While booking may take place at police headquarters or county jails, some counties throughout the state of Pennsylvania have developed Central Booking Centers that handle the entire booking process. Staff members at these centers provide copies of photographs, fingerprints, and prior records to police, prosecutors, and judges assigned to the case. Preliminary arraignments may take place from a Central Booking Center via two-way simultaneous audio-visual communication devices connecting the center to judges handling the arraignments.

Pretrial Procedures

Pretrial procedures include hearings and activities that take place between an arrest and an actual criminal trial. The first step in this stage of the criminal justice process involves bringing the arrested person before a judicial officer. In Pennsylvania, this is known as the preliminary arraignment.

Preliminary Arraignment

In Pennsylvania, arrested persons, regardless of whether the arrest occurred with or without an arrest warrant, must be brought before a judicial official "without unnecessary delay" (Pa.R.Crim.P. Rule 516(A)). As mentioned, in the Commonwealth of Pennsylvania, preliminary arraignments may take place at sites with advanced communication technology (i.e., two-way simultaneous audio-visual communication devices), such as Central Booking Centers. At the preliminary arraignment, a copy of the complaint is given to the accused. If the defendant was arrested with a warrant, a copy of the warrant and supporting affidavits is also given to the defendant. In the event that copies of the arrest warrant and supporting affidavits are not ready at the time of the preliminary arraignment, copies shall be provided to the defendant no later than the first business day after the preliminary arraignment. If the defendant is arrested and brought to the preliminary arraignment without a warrant, he or she may not be detained unless the judge handling the hearing determines that there was probable cause for the arrest (Pa.R.Crim.P. Rule 540(E)). In addition to reading them the criminal complaint, the judge will inform the defendant:

- of the right to secure counsel of choice and the right to assigned counsel in accordance with Rule 122;
- of the right to have a preliminary hearing, except in cases being presented to an indicting grand jury pursuant to Rule 566.2; and
- if the offense is bailable, the type of release on bail, as provided by Chapter 5 Part C of these rules, and the conditions of the bail bond (Pa.R.Crim.P. Rule 540(F)(1-3)).

Determining whether or not the defendant can afford private counsel is an important part of the pretrial procedures, as the Supreme Court cases of *Gideon v. Wainwright* (1963) and *Argersinger v. Hamlin* (1972) require that all indigent defendants be provided with assistance of an attorney in all critical stages of the criminal justice process. In regards to bail before a verdict, the judge handling the preliminary arraignment will set a bail amount with conditions unless the defendant has committed a capital offense or offense for which the maximum sentence is life imprisonment. Article I, § 14 of the Pennsylvania Constitution also states that a person may be denied bail if "no condition or combination of conditions other than imprisonment will reasonably assure the safety of any person and the community when the proof is evident or presumption great." For bailable offenses, the money posted by defendants is used to guarantee that they will appear for subsequent court appearances, including the preliminary hearing, and that they follow all conditions imposed by the bail authority. Unless the preliminary hearing is waived by the defendant or the attorney for the Commonwealth is presenting the case to a grand jury, the judge will "fix a day and hour for a preliminary hearing which shall not be later than 14 days after the preliminary arraignment if the defendant is in custody and no later than 21 days if not in custody" (Pa.R.Crim.P. Rule 540(G)(1)).

It is important to note that not all offenders are arrested, booked, and subjected to a preliminary arraignment prior to the preliminary hearing. For lower grade offenses, such as misdemeanors of the first, second, or third degree, suspected offenders are issued a summons by mail. Pa.R.Crim.P. Rule 510(A) states that "Every summons in a court case shall command the defendant to appear before the issuing authority for a preliminary hearing at the place and on the date and at the time stated on the summons. The date set for the preliminary hearing shall be not less than 20 days from the date of mailing the summons unless the issuing authority fixes an earlier date upon the request of the defendant or the defendant's attorney with the consent of the affiant." Furthermore, the summons will give notice to the defendant of their right to secure counsel, as well as their right to assigned counsel, that bail will be set at the preliminary hearing, and that failure to appear for the preliminary hearing will result in a bench warrant. Along with the summons, the court will send the offender a copy of the complaint against them.

Preliminary Hearing

The purpose of the preliminary hearing, which is only for murder, felonies, and misdemeanors, is to determine whether the Commonwealth has established a *prima facie* case for offenses for which the defendant is charged. As defined by the Pennsylvania Superior Court in *Commonwealth v. Hendricks*, 927 A.2d 289 (Pa. Super. 2007), "A *prima facie* case consists of evidence, read in the light of the most favorable to the Commonwealth, that sufficiently establishes both the commission of a crime and that the accused is probably the perpetrator of that crime." According to Pa.R.Crim.P. Rule 543(B), "If the issuing authority finds that the Commonwealth has established a *prima facie* case that an offense has been committed and the defendant has committed it, the issuing authority shall hold the defendant for court on the offense(s) on which the Commonwealth established a *prima facie* case. If there is no offense for which a *prima facie* case has been established, the issuing authority shall discharge the defendant." During the preliminary hearing, both the prosecution and defense may present evidence. However, it is the burden of the Commonwealth to present enough evidence to convince the judge to "bind the defendant over" for trial. At the conclusion of the hearing, the judge will publically announce his or her decision. For those who have been held over for court/bound for trial, the issuing authority will "(1) set bail as permitted by law if the defendant did not receive a preliminary arraignment; or (2) continue the existing bail order, unless the issuing authority modifies the order as permitted by Rule 529(A)" (Pa.R.Crim.P. Rule 543(C)). Furthermore, individuals who have not yet gone through the booking process must do so at this time. For persons who have been granted bail, submitting to administrative processing will be a condition of their release.

Criminal Information

After the defendant has been held to court, the prosecution will prepare and file the criminal information (i.e., the formal charging document) with the court of common pleas. The information provides defendants with a list of charges the Commonwealth will seek to prove at trial. The information should contain, among other things, the date and time of the alleged offense, the county where the offense is alleged to have been committed, and "a plain and concise statement of the essential elements of the offense substantially the same as or cognate to the offense alleged in the complaint" (Pa.R.Crim.P. Rule 560(B)(5)). Before the information is filed, the prosecutor may withdraw one or more of the charges by filing a "notice of withdrawal" with the clerk of courts. Any charges not included in the information at the time of filing are to be considered withdrawn by the Commonwealth. In Pennsylvania, prosecutors may electronically prepare, sign, and transmit the information for filing.

Grand Jury Indictment

There are two types of grand juries in Pennsylvania: investigating grand juries and indicting grand juries. According to 42 Pa.C.S.A. §4543, an attorney for the Commonwealth may file an application to the president judge of the appropriate court of common pleas requesting that a county investigating grand jury be summoned. In this application, the prosecuting attorney must state that convening a county investigating grand jury is "necessary because of the existence of criminal activity within the county which can best be fully investigated using the investigative resources of the grand jury" (42 Pa.C.S.A. §4543). According to 42 Pa.C.S.A. §4548(a), "The investigating grand jury shall have the power to inquire into offenses against the criminal laws of the Commonwealth alleged to have been committed within the county or counties in which it is summoned." If the investigating grand jury issues a "presentment" indicating that the parties being investigated appear to have committed an offense against the criminal laws of the Commonwealth, the attorney for the Commonwealth may proceed on the basis of this presentment. As such, "a complaint shall be filed and the defendant shall be entitled to a preliminary hearing as in other criminal proceedings" (42 Pa.C.S.A. §4551(e)).

Again, the second type of grand jury in Pennsylvania is an indicting grand jury. Pa.R.Crim.P. Rule 556 permits the use of an indicting grand jury as an alternative to a preliminary hearing "only in cases in which witness intimidation has occurred, is occurring, or is likely to occur." According to Pa.R.Crim.P Rule 556.2, in order to present evidence against a person accused of criminal wrongdoing to an indicting grand jury instead of a proceeding to a preliminary hearing, the attorney for the Commonwealth must submit a motion to the court, and in particular, the president judge or the judge's designee, that alleges that witness intimidation is an issue. "If the judge determines the allegations establish probable cause that witness intimidation has occurred, is occurring, or is likely to occur, the judge shall grant the motion, and shall notify the proper issuing authority" (Pa.R.Crim.P. Rule 556.2(A)(3)). At this point, the president judge, or the president's designee, will order that a grand jury be summoned for the purpose of issuing indictments or will order that a sitting investigating grand jury sit as the indicting grand jury (Pa.R.Crim.P. Rule 556.1(A)). According to Pa.R.Crim.P. Rule 556.3(A), indicting grand juries, like investigating grand juries in Pennsylvania, consist of no less than 15 and no more than 23 legally qualified jurors, as well as a minimum of 7 and not more than 15 qualified alternates. In Pennsylvania, an affirmative vote of 12 permanent jury members is required to indict (Pa.R.Crim.P. Rule 556.3(E)). If the grand jury decides to indict the defendant, an indictment will be prepared listing the offenses on which they have decided to indict. The jury foreperson, or, in their absence, the deputy foreperson, will then sign the indictment and deliver it to the judge presiding over the hearing. According to Pa.R.Crim.P. Rule 556.11(D), the judge will then: "(1) provide a copy of the indictment to the Commonwealth authorizing the attorney to prepare an information pursuant to Rule 560; and (2) forward the indictment to the clerk of courts, or issue an arrest warrant, if the subject of the indictment has not been arrested on the charges contained in the indictment." In terms of criminal justice procedure, a grand jury indictment is the functional equivalent of holding a defendant to court following a preliminary hearing.

Formal Arraignment

In Pennsylvania, unless otherwise provided by local court rule or postponed by the court for cause, the formal arraignment typically takes place no later than 10 days after the criminal information has been filed (Pa.R.Crim.P. Rule 571(A)). At this time, the defendant will be advised of the right to be represented by counsel, of the right to file various motions, such as a motion for pretrial discovery, and of the nature of the charges contained in the information (Pa.R.Crim.P. Rule 571(C)(1-3)). While some Pennsylvania counties do not require defendants to formally respond to the charges against them at the formal arraignment and instead push all cases forward with not guilty pleas, others do. According to Pa.R.Crim.P. Rule 590(A)(1), all pleas must be entered in open court, and the formal arraignment would be the first such opportunity for this. "A defendant may plead not guilty, guilty, or, with the consent of the judge, *nolo contendere*. If the defendant refuses to plead, the judge shall enter a plea of not guilty on the defendant's behalf" (Pa.R.Crim.P. Rule 590(A)(2)). Furthermore, "The judge may refuse to accept a plea of guilty or *nolo contendere*, and shall not accept it unless the judge determines after inquiry of the defendant that the plea is voluntarily and understandingly tendered. Such inquiry shall appear on the record" (Pa.R.Crim.P. Rule 590(A)(3)). At the discretion of the court, the formal arraignment, like the preliminary arraignment, may be conducted using two-way simultaneous audio-visual communication.

Plea Agreements

A defendant may enter into a plea agreement with the prosecutor for the Commonwealth at any stage in the criminal justice process. In exchange for the defendant's plea of guilty or *nolo contendere*, the prosecutor may offer certain concessions, such as a reduction of a charge to a lesser crime, the dropping of one or more offenses, a recommendation of a lenient sentence, or any combination of these things. Pa.R.Crim.P. Rule 590(B)(1) states, "When counsel for both sides have arrived at a plea agreement, they shall state on the record in open court, in the presence of the defendant, the terms of the agreement, unless the judge orders, for good cause shown and with the consent of the defendant, counsel for the defendant, and the attorney for the Commonwealth, that specific conditions in the agreement be placed on the record *in camera* and the record sealed." The judge will also conduct a separate inquiry to make sure the defendant understands and voluntarily accepts the terms of the plea. It should be noted that judges are not legally bound to pleas agreed upon by prosecutors, defense attorneys, and defendants, and may outright reject a plea. Murder cases have a unique set of rules when it comes to plea agreements. "In cases in which the imposition of a sentence of death is not authorized, when a defendant enters a plea of guilty or *nolo contendere* to a charge of murder generally, the degree of guilt shall be determined by a jury unless the attorney for the Commonwealth elects to have the judge, before whom the plea was entered, alone determine the degree of guilt" (Pa.R.Crim.P. Rule 590(C)).

Pretrial Motions

After the formal arraignment and before the actual trial, various pretrial motions may be presented to the court by either the prosecution or the defense. Such motions include: motions to suppress evidence, motions to dismiss charges, motions to delay the start of the trial, motions for change of venue, motions for severance of offenses, and motions for severance of defendants. One of the more important pretrial motions is that of discovery, which is often tied to motions to suppress evidence. The discovery motion is typically filed by both the prosecution and defense, and allows each side to obtain and review what the other intends to present at trial. In accordance with Pa.R.Crim.P. Rule 573(A), "Before any disclosure or discovery can be sought under these rules by either party, counsel for the parties shall make a good faith effort to resolve all questions of discovery, and to provide information required or requested under these rules as to which there is no dispute." Motions for discovery come into play when one party refuses to disclose items requested by the other party.

When this occurs, the "demanding party" may file a motion of discovery, which in Pennsylvania must occur "within 14 days after arraignment, unless the time for filing is extended by the court" (Pa.R.Crim.P. Rule 573(A)). Furthermore, within such motions, the filing party must "set forth the fact that a good faith effort to discuss the requested material has taken place and proved unsuccessful. Nothing in this provision shall delay the disclosure of any items agreed upon by the parties pending resolution of any motion for discovery" (Pa.R.Crim.P. Rule 573(A)). In Pennsylvania, as in most states, prosecutors are legally required to disclose practically everything they have pertaining to a particular crime and defendant to opposing counsel. This includes:

- any evidence favorable to the accused that is material either to guilt or to punishment, and is within the possession or control of the attorney for the Commonwealth;
- any written confession or inculpatory statement, or the substance of any oral confession or inculpatory statement, and the identity of the person to whom the confession or inculpatory statement was made that is in the possession or control of the attorney for the Commonwealth;
- the defendant's prior criminal record;
- the circumstances and results of any identification of the defendant by voice, photograph, or in-person identification;
- any results or reports of scientific tests, expert opinions, and written or recorded reports of polygraph examinations or other physical or mental examinations of the defendant that are within the possession or control of the attorney for the Commonwealth;
- any tangible objects, including documents, photographs, fingerprints, or other tangible evidence; and
- the transcripts and recordings of any electronic surveillance, and the authority by which the said transcripts and recordings were obtained (Pa.R.Crim.P. Rule 573(B)(1)(a-g)).

The court may also, upon the request of the defense, ask the prosecution to hand over the names and addresses of eyewitnesses, all written or recorded statements of eyewitnesses, and all written or recorded statements made by co-defendants, co-conspirators, or accomplices. Conversely, the defense is legally required to hand over to the prosecution relatively few things, including "results or reports of physical or mental examinations, and of scientific tests or experiments made in connection with the particular case, or copies thereof, within the possession or control of the defendant, that the defendant intends to introduce as evidence in chief, or were prepared by a witness whom the defendant intends to call at the trial, when results or reports relate to the testimony of that witness, provided the defendant has requested and received discovery under paragraph (B)(1)(e)" (Pa.R.Crim.P. Rule 573(C)(1)(a)). Upon the request of the prosecution, the defense is also required to hand over "the names and addresses of eyewitnesses whom the defendant intends to call in its case-in-chief, provided that the defendant has previously requested and received discovery under paragraph (B)(2)(a)(i)" (Pa.R.Crim.P. Rule 573(C)(1)(b)). Finally, if any of the expert witnesses for either the prosecution or defense have yet to prepare a report of their findings or test results, the court, through a motion filed by either side, may order an expert to prepare a report stating exactly what they plan to testify to at trial.

Criminal Trial

If no plea agreement has been reached and the defendant has pleaded not guilty, the stage is set for the criminal trial. The first step in the trial process typically involves impaneling a jury. A defendant has a right to a jury trial if he or she is charged with an offense that carries a possible punishment of more than six months of incarceration. However, defendants in all cases may waive a jury trial and elect instead to have a judge try the case without a jury. In bench trials, as such proceedings are known, "the trial judge shall determine all questions of law and fact and render a verdict which shall have the same force and effect as a verdict of a jury" (Pa.R.Crim.P. Rule 621(A)).

Jury Selection

While some counties throughout the Commonwealth of Pennsylvania rely on driver license and voter registration lists to select prospective jurors for criminal trials, others utilize a statewide, master list compiled by the Administrative Office of Pennsylvania Courts. This master list, which is compiled at least once a year, is more inclusive than those generated using only driver license and voter registration information, as in addition to persons found on driver license and voter registration lists, it may include persons listed in various telephone directories, persons participating in any state, county, or local program authorized by law, persons on school census lists, and any person whose name does not appear on the master list and who meets the qualifications for jurors in Pennsylvania and who submits an application to be listed as a prospective juror (42 Pa. Cons. Stat. §4521(a)(3)(i-iv)). County master lists of prospective jurors, which are extracted from the statewide master list and shared with requesting county jury commission boards, may also include residents of the Commonwealth who receive cash assistance or food stamps, as well as anyone who files a return of payment for taxes ((42 Pa. Cons. Stat. §4521.1(a)(1)(3)). Regardless of whether counties utilize the statewide master list or rely on their own system to generate a list of prospective jurors, all individuals randomly selected for jury duty must complete a jury qualification form. Persons deemed qualified to serve as jurors in their respective districts, based, among other things, on age and residency requirements, will receive a summons to appear in court for the *voir dire* process.

During *voir dire*, potential jurors who have been summoned to court for jury duty are questioned by both the prosecution and defense. If they have not already done so, jurors must complete a standard, confidential juror information questionnaire, which include questions such as, "Do you have any religious, moral, or ethical beliefs that would prevent you from sitting in judgment in a criminal case and rendering a fair verdict?," "Have you or anyone close to you ever been the victim of a crime?," etc. After reviewing juror responses to these questionnaires, attorneys for the prosecution and defense may use two types of challenges to dismiss prospective jurors who they deem unfit to serve. Challenges for cause, which are unlimited in number, refer to requests to dismiss potential jurors who attorneys for the prosecution or defense do not feel can fairly or impartially render a verdict in the case. Peremptory challenges, which are limited in number, refer to requests to dismiss potential jurors without identifying a specific reason. Pa.R.Crim.P. Rule 634(A)(1-3) states that for trials involving only one defendant, each side is entitled to 5 peremptory challenges for misdemeanor cases, 7 for non-capital felony cases, and 20 for capital felony cases. Once the prosecution and defense have examined potential jurors and exercised all challenges for cause, "peremptory challenges shall then be exercised by passing the list between prosecution and defense, with the prosecution first striking the name of a prospective juror, followed by the defense, and alternating thereafter until all peremptory challenges have been exhausted. If either party fails to exhaust all peremptory challenges, the jurors last listed shall be stricken" (Pa.R.Crim.P. Rule 631(E)(2)(f)). Examination of jurors continues until all peremptory challenges are exhausted or until 12 jurors and 2 alternates are accepted.

Presentation of Evidence

After a jury has been selected and sworn in, the prosecution begins the trial with an opening statement. After the prosecution has given their opening statement to the jury, the defense may make their opening statement or may choose to delay their opening statement until after the prosecution has presented its case. Regardless of when the defense chooses to give their opening statement, the prosecution will be the first to present its evidence. There are two types of evidence: physical evidence and testimonial evidence. Physical evidence may include such things as knives, bullets, clothing, drugs, fingerprints, and blood. Rebuttal evidence, which may be presented by either the prosecution or defense and which applies to either physical evidence or testimonial evidence, is offered to oppose or disprove evidence presented by opposing counsel. The defense may challenge evidence presented by the prosecution and cross-examine any witnesses called by the prosecution who are testifying about the crime and the defendant's role in it. Once the prosecution has presented all of its evidence against the defendant, they will rest their case.

Next, the defense will have the opportunity to present its case. However, because the burden of proof (i.e., the legal obligation to prove the charges against the accused beyond a reasonable doubt) rests with the prosecution, the defense is not obligated to present evidence of their own or even challenge evidence being presented by the prosecution. However, if they so choose, the defense will present its own case and evidence, including alibi witnesses, expert witnesses, and character witnesses. They may also present their own expert witnesses along with physical evidence to challenge the case made by the prosecution. The prosecution may challenge evidence and cross-examine witnesses presented by the defense. Once the defense has presented all of its evidence, they will rest their case.

Throughout the trial, the judge will regulate the manner in which evidence is presented. For example, in cases involving a child victim or child material witness, and in order to protect such victims and witnesses from suffering serious emotional distress that may impair their ability to reasonably communicate, "the court may order that the child victim's or child material witness's testimony be recorded for presentation in court by any method that accurately captures and preserves the visual images, oral communications and other information presented during such testimony" (42 Pa.C.S.A. §5984.1(a)). Following the conclusion of the presentation of evidence, the defense will give their closing argument to the jury, followed by the prosecution (Pa.R.Crim.P. Rule 604(B)). Again, since the burden of proof rests with the prosecution, they give their opening statement first and their closing argument last.

At either the close of the prosecution's case or at the close of all the evidence, the defense may "challenge the sufficiency of the evidence to sustain a conviction of one or more of the offenses charged" with a motion for judgment of acquittal (Pa.R.Crim.P. Rule 606(A)). If the motion is made at the conclusion of the prosecution's case and is not granted, the proceedings continue as if the motion were not made. If the motion is made at the close of all the evidence, "the court may reserve decision until after the jury returns a guilty verdict or after the jury is discharged without agreeing upon a verdict" (Pa.R.Crim.P. Rule 606(C)).

Jury Deliberations

The jury will retire to deliberate the verdict once the trial has ended. Before doing so, however, the judge will issue "instructions" to the jurors. Jury instructions entail making sure that jurors understand the law that applies to the case, any legal concepts that are relevant to the case, and the elements of each of the crimes for which the defendant is charged. Judges will also remind jurors that in Pennsylvania, as in other states across the country, the defendant is to be presumed innocent until proven guilty beyond reasonable doubt, and that the burden of proof rests with the prosecution. To assist them in their deliberations, jurors may be provided with "written copies of the portion of the judge's charge on the elements of the offenses, lesser included offenses, and any defense upon which the jury has been instructed" (Pa.R.Crim.P. Rule 646(B)). The judge will also instruct the jury about the use of the written charge and, at a minimum, instruct the jurors that "(a) the entire charge, written and oral, shall be given equal weight; and (b) the jury may submit questions regarding any portion of the charge" (Pa.R.Crim.P. Rule 646(B)(2)). According to Pa.R.Crim.P. Rule 646(C)(1-4), the jurors are not permitted to have any of the following during deliberations: transcripts of any trial testimony, copies of any written or recorded confessions by the defendant(s), copies of the information or indictment, or except as provided by Pa.R.Crim.P. Rule 646(B), written jury instructions.

Upon deliberating, the jurors will elect a foreperson who will poll the jurors regarding their verdict throughout the deliberations and who will announce the jury's verdict, which must be unanimous, in open court. If the verdict is not guilty, the judge will move to dismiss the case and release the defendant from custody. If the verdict is guilty, the next stage in the criminal justice process is sentencing. A "hung jury" is one that cannot reach a unanimous decision. In such instances, the judge will declare a mistrial and the case may be retried.

Sentencing and Corrections

In Pennsylvania, sentencing and correctional options for persons who have been found guilty of, or who have pleaded guilty or *nolo contendere* to, misdemeanors and felony offenses are largely determined by Pennsylvania statutes.

Punishments

In Pennsylvania, as in other states, the judge may order a psychiatric, psychological, or pre-sentence investigation report to assist them in selecting an appropriate sentence for persons who have been found guilty of, or who have pleaded guilty or *nolo contendere* to, misdemeanors and felony offenses. Judges in Pennsylvania also rely on legislatively created sentencing guidelines that assist them in determining an appropriate minimum sentence for offenders. These guidelines take into consideration the offender's prior record, the gravity of the offense committed, and the presence of aggravating and mitigating circumstances that may make the sentencing judge want to deviate slightly from the recommended sentence. Maximum sentences, like the sentencing guidelines that assist judges in determining an appropriate minimum sentence, are legislatively created. As highlighted in Chapter 2, 18 Pa.C.S.A. §1101-1105 provide that offenders may not be sentenced to imprisonment and/or fines exceeding the following time and amounts unless otherwise proscribed by statute:

- Murder of the first degree   Mandatory death or life imprisonment
- Murder of the second degree   Mandatory life imprisonment
- Felony of the first degree   20 years   — $25,000
- Felony of the second degree   10 years   — $25,000
- Felony of the third degree   7 years   — $15,000
- Misdemeanor of the first degree 5 years   — $10,000
- Misdemeanor of the second degree 2 years   — $5,000
- Misdemeanor of the third degree 1 year   — $2,000
- Summary Offense   90 days   — $300

In Pennsylvania, as in other states, there exists mandatory sentencing legislation pertaining to the use of firearms in the commission of criminal acts and for the commission of certain crimes, such as the murder of a law enforcement officer or unborn child. For such crimes, judges will bypass legislatively created sentencing guidelines and sentence offenders in accordance with mandatory sentencing laws.

42 Pa. Cons. Stat. §9711(a) states that for jury trials in which a person has been convicted of murder in the first degree, the court will hold a separate sentencing hearing in which the jury (and not the judge) will be asked to determine whether the defendant should be sentenced to death or life imprisonment. If the jury does not reach a unanimous decision to sentence the defendant to death, he or she will receive the sentence of life imprisonment. According to 42 Pa. Cons. Stat. §9711(b), if the defendant has waived his or her right to a jury trial and has instead pleaded guilty to murder in the first degree, a jury must be impaneled to determine the sentence unless waived by the defendant with consent of the Commonwealth, in which case the judge would determine the sentence. The only method of execution currently available in Pennsylvania is lethal injection.

Corrections

In addition to incarceration in county jails and state prisons, there are many corrections options available to judges in Pennsylvania, including, but not limited to, fines and restitution, probation, community service, electronic monitoring, house arrest, drug and alcohol treatment, and mental health treatment. These sanctions may be handed out individually or combined to meet the needs of the offender, the victim, and the state. These sanctions will be discussed in more detail in Chapter 6 of this book.

Conclusion

This chapter was designed to provide a detailed overview of the criminal justice process in Pennsylvania. It should be noted, however, that the criminal justice process described in this chapter is specific to adult offenders (not juvenile offenders) and persons accused of violating Pennsylvania state law (not federal law). As mentioned, the criminal justice process in Pennsylvania, while governed by certain rules and statutes, does vary slightly from county to county.

Key Terms

Arrest Warrant: A court-issued document authorizing law enforcement to make an arrest.

Booking: An administrative step taken after an arrest that entails recording the name of the person and the crimes for which they were arrested, and which may include fingerprinting, photographing, and the like.

Burden of Proof: The prosecution's legal obligation in criminal cases to prove the charges against the accused beyond a reasonable doubt.

Challenges for Cause: Requests to dismiss potential jurors during the *voir dire* process whom attorneys for the prosecution or defense do not feel can fairly or impartially render a verdict in the case

Criminal Information: The formal charging document that lists the accusations made by the prosecution against the accused.

Discovery: The exchange of facts and evidence between the prosecution and defense prior to the start of trial.

Formal Arraignment: The stage in the criminal justice process at which the indictment or criminal information is read in open court and the defendant is requested to respond thereto. The accused will be advised of the right to be represented by counsel, of the right to file various motions, and of the nature of the charges contained in the information. At this time, the accused will also have the opportunity to respond to the allegations against them.

Gideon v. Wainwright (1963): The Supreme Court case that made the Sixth Amendment's right to counsel applicable to state proceedings.

Indicting Grand Jury: A type of grand jury that is used as an alternative to a preliminary hearing in cases in which witness intimidation has occurred, is occurring, or is likely to occur.

Indictment: An accusation against a defendant rendered by a grand jury based on evidence constituting a *prima facie* case.

Investigating Grand Jury: A grand jury with the power to inquire into offenses against the criminal laws alleged to have been committed within the county or counties in which it is summoned.

Jurisdiction: The power granted to the state to exercise authority over individuals accused of criminal wrongdoing.

Jury Deliberations: The jury's retirement to a private room to deliberate the verdict following closing arguments and judicial instructions as to how to consider facts and evidence presented against the accused.

Jury Instructions: Statements made by the judge to jury members informing them of law that applies to the case, any legal concepts that are relevant to the case, and the elements of each of the crimes for which the defendant is charged.

Miranda Rights: Rights due to suspects by law enforcement prior to questioning in the context of a custodial interrogation, which include their Fifth Amendment privilege against self-incrimination and right to counsel.

Miranda v. Arizona (1966): The Supreme Court case that established the so-called Miranda rights and required law enforcement to inform suspects of their Fifth Amendment privilege against self-incrimination and right to counsel prior to custodial interrogations.

Nolo Contendere: A Latin phrase meaning "I will not contest it"; a *nolo contendere* plea has a similar legal effect as pleading guilty in criminal cases.

Peremptory Challenges: Requests to dismiss potential jurors during the *voir dire* process without identifying a specific reason.

Plea Agreement: An agreement made between the prosecution and defense for certain leniencies in return for a guilty or *nolo contendere* plea.

Preliminary Arraignment: The defendant's initial appearance before a judge following an arrest, at which time the judge will give them a copy of the criminal complaint and make a determination of bail.

Pretrial Motions: Motions made before trial, including motions to suppress evidence, motions to dismiss charges, motions to delay the start of the trial, motions for change of venue, motions for severance of offenses, and motions for severance of defendants.

Prima Facie **case**: A case in which there exists sufficient evidence to convict the defendant unless otherwise contradicted.

Probable cause: The evidentiary criterion needed to sustain an arrest or an arrest or search warrant; facts that would lead a reasonable person to believe that the accused committed the crime charged.

Search Warrant:A court order authorizing law enforcement to conduct a search of a person, location, or vehicle for evidence of a crime.

Sentencing Guidelines: Rules that set out uniform sentencing policy for defendants convicted of crimes that take into consideration the individual's prior record, the gravity of the offense committed, and the presence of aggravating and mitigating circumstances.

Voir Dire: The process by which attorneys for the prosecution and defense question potential jurors to select those who are acceptable.

4th Amendment: Constitutional amendment that protects citizens and their property from unlawful searches and seizures.

5th Amendment: Constitutional amendment that provides citizens with, among other things, their privilege against self-incrimination.

Websites

Constitution of the Commonwealth of Pennsylvania. (n.d.). Retrieved July 3, 2013 from http://sites.state.pa.us/PA_Constitution.html.

Title 18 Crimes and Offenses—Pennsylvania Code. (n.d.). Retrieved July 3, 2013, from http://www.legis.state.pa.us/WU01/LI/LI/CT/HTM/18/18.HTM.

Title 234 Rules of Criminal Procedure—Pennsylvania Code. (n.d.). Retrieved July 3, 2013 from http://www.pacode.com/secure/data/234/234toc.html.

Review Questions

1. How does the concept of probable cause differ in terms of its application to search warrants and arrest warrants?
2. What happens at the preliminary arraignment and what is the importance of this stage in the criminal justice process?
3. What happens at the preliminary hearing and what is the importance of this stage in the criminal justice process?
4. What happens at the stage in the criminal justice process known as discovery and how is it tied to motions to suppress evidence?
5. How are juries impaneled in the state of Pennsylvania?

Critical Thinking Questions

1. Why do you think states like Pennsylvania have moved towards the use of legislatively created sentencing guidelines? What potential problems do you think states utilizing this sentencing model are trying to avoid?
2. Why do you think states like Pennsylvania involve juries in sentencing decisions for persons convicted of murder in the first degree? Do you see this as an indictment of judges and their ability to be fair and impartial in these matters?
3. What would you say is the primary role of judges in the criminal justice process? Do you think their role is any easier or more difficult than that of prosecutors and defense attorneys?
4. Why do you think states like Pennsylvania require that prosecutors begin the prosecution of suspected offenders within a specified period of time? Are such time restrictions fair to prosecutors? Are they fair to crime victims?
5. Why do you think Pennsylvania still retains the use of grand juries while other states have moved away from grand jury systems? What would be the potential advantages or drawbacks to Pennsylvania abandoning the use of grand juries?

References

Argersinger v. Hamlin, 407 U.S. 25 (1972)
Commonwealth v. Hendricks, 927 A.2d 289 (Pa. Super. 2007)
Constitution of the Commonwealth of Pennsylvania. Article I, § 14.
Gideon v. Wainwright, 372 U.S. 335 (1963).

Miranda v. Arizona, 384 U.S. 436 (1966)
Pa.R.Crim.P. Rule 130
Pa.R.Crim.P. Rule 200
Pa.R.Crim.P. Rule 201
Pa.R.Crim.P. Rule 203
Pa.R.Crim.P. Rule 205
Pa.R.Crim.P. Rule 207
Pa.R.Crim.P. Rule 208
Pa.R.Crim.P. Rule 209
Pa.R.Crim.P. Rule 510
Pa.R.Crim.P. Rule 513
Pa.R.Crim.P. Rule 515
Pa.R.Crim.P. Rule 516
Pa.R.Crim.P. Rule 540
Pa.R.Crim.P. Rule 543
Pa.R.Crim.P. Rule 556
Pa.R.Crim.P. Rule 560
Pa.R.Crim.P. Rule 571
Pa.R.Crim.P. Rule 573
Pa.R.Crim.P. Rule 590
Pa.R.Crim.P. Rule 604
Pa.R.Crim.P. Rule 606
Pa.R.Crim.P. Rule 621
Pa.R.Crim.P. Rule 631
Pa.R.Crim.P. Rule 634
Pa.R.Crim.P. Rule 646
Wolf v. Colorado, 338 U.S. 25 (1949)
4th Amendment. (1791). United States Constitution.
18 Pa.C.S.A. § 102
18 Pa.C.S.A. § 1101-1105
42 Pa. Cons. Stat. § 4521
42 Pa. Cons. Stat. § 4521.1
42 Pa. Cons. Stat. § 9711
42 Pa.C.S.A. § 4543
42 Pa.C.S.A. § 4548
42 Pa.C.S.A. § 4551
42 Pa.C.S.A. § 5551
42 Pa.C.S.A. § 5552
42 Pa.C.S.A. § 5984

Chapter 4

Law Enforcement in Pennsylvania

Michael J. Jenkins

Learning Objectives

After reading the chapter, students will be able to:

- State the numbers of police personnel and police departments in Pennsylvania.
- Distinguish among the various levels of policing in Pennsylvania.
- List the main structural characteristics of law enforcement agencies at the state and local level.
- Describe the distinct and the similar activities of the various agencies.
- List the basic requirements for being hired as a sworn officer with municipal, county, and state law enforcement agencies.
- Situate Pennsylvania police within the larger context of Pennsylvania's criminal justice process as well as within the greater policing profession.

Key Terms

Act 120 training
Attorney general
Centralized state police department
Civilian personnel
Commissioner

Constable
Decentralized state police department
Deputy sheriffs
The Great Anthracite Strike of 1902
Jurisdiction

Limited (or special) jurisdiction
Municipal Police Officers Education
and Training Commission
Municipality
Rank structure

Statewide regulatory enforcement
boards
Sworn personnel
Taskforce

Introduction

There are numerous police agencies in Pennsylvania operating under federal, state, municipal,[1] and special jurisdictions. This chapter focuses on those 1,117 state and local agencies whose jurisdiction is limited to Pennsylvania. In line with the extremely fragmented and local nature of policing in the United States, a majority of police personnel are employed at the local level, by municipal or county police departments and with little mandated coordination among them. Other police agencies in Pennsylvania have a more limited (or "special") jurisdiction. These include university police and transit police, whose authority is limited to areas on and bordering their respective geographies. For example, the 256 law enforcement officers (Reaves, 2011) who police the Southeastern Pennsylvania Transportation Authority (SEPTA) and the Amtrak Railroad Police are limited to enforcement activities on their transportation lines; university police have jurisdiction over their campuses and the areas adjacent to them.

In 2012, there were 33,737 full-time employees in Pennsylvania's law enforcement agencies. Of those, 28,515 were full-time sworn personnel. Females made up 9.7% of police officers (*Crime in Pennsylvania*, 2012). There were 2.23 police officers per 1,000 Pennsylvanians in 2012. Notably, nearly 90% of reporting departments employed 25 or fewer full-time law enforcement officers (excluding the Pennsylvania State Police and the Pennsylvania Narcotics and Investigation and Drug Control unit in the Pennsylvania Attorney General's office) (*Crime in Pennsylvania*, 2012). In addition to their law enforcement responsibilities, these personnel spend their time investigating crimes, informally settling disputes, directing traffic, and educating the public.

Federal Law Enforcement in Pennsylvania

Law enforcement in the United States is overwhelmingly a local pursuit. There is no national police force. Federal law enforcement agencies generally

---

1. In Pennsylvania, "municipality" refers to a county, city, borough, town or township.

enforce only federal laws found in the United States Code. Federal agencies (e.g., the Drug Enforcement Administration, the Bureau of Alcohol Tobacco Firearms and Explosives, the Federal Bureau of Investigations and Immigration and Customs Enforcement) fall within one of two federal departments — the U.S. Department of Justice or the Department of Homeland Security (which was created in 2003, in response to the September 11, 2001, terrorist attacks). The agencies within these two departments have nationwide, geographic jurisdiction, and specialize in the content of the federal laws they enforce (i.e., drugs and alcohol, or immigration cases).

Federal law enforcement agencies maintain field offices throughout the United States. In 2008 there were approximately 120,000 people with police power employed by federal law enforcement agencies (Reaves, 2012). Pennsylvania was home to 3,789 of them (including officers of the courts and correctional officers, which are not counted in the state and local numbers above) (Reaves, 2012). This means there are at least 87% fewer federal law enforcement officers in Pennsylvania than there are local and state officers. The Philadelphia police department and the Pennsylvania State Police each employ more law enforcement personnel in Pennsylvania than do the federal law enforcement agencies.

Federal officers (as compared to their state and local counterparts) in Pennsylvania are more likely to be involved in criminal investigation and enforcement efforts (1,386) than in patrol or response functions (392) (Reaves, 2012). Some crimes involve national or international criminal groups, affect multiple state jurisdictions, or violate both federal and state statutes. In these instances, federal law enforcement agencies might conduct their own, independent investigations, supplement local and state police investigations, or collaborate closely with representatives from multiple levels of law enforcement. For example, a local police department attempting to curb an open-air drug market in their area might engage law enforcement officials from many agencies at both the state (e.g., the Pennsylvania Attorney General's Office and the Pennsylvania State Police) and federal levels (e.g., the BATFE, the FBI, and ICE) to assist in their efforts. Such taskforces allow for a more efficient use of limited financial, personnel, and expert resources. They also enhance necessary intelligence sharing among various law enforcement agencies.

State Policing

In 1905, Governor Samuel Pennypacker signed legislation establishing the nation's first uniformed state police agency. (Texas and Massachusetts had earlier created less formal state police departments.) Formed in response to the Great

Anthracite Strike of 1902 (Pennsylvania State Police, 2005), the Pennsylvania State Police (PSP) took on a uniquely militaristic form, recruiting only those with experience in the National Guard or Army (Roberg, Novak, Cordner & Smith, 2012).

Today, the PSP employs more than 6,200 men and women from varied backgrounds. It is the third largest state police department in the United States (Reaves, 2011). The core purpose of the PSP is "[t]o seek justice, preserve peace, and improve the quality of life for all" (PSP, 2013). They categorize their activities into public services, law enforcement services, and public safety services. Public safety services range from conducting child safety seat checks to providing lethal weapons training (commonly referred to as Act 235).

Structure

State police departments in the United States follow either a centralized model (in which one agency provides both law enforcement and traffic enforcement services) or a decentralized model (where one agency investigates crimes and a separate provides statewide highway patrol). North Carolina and Georgia exemplify the decentralized model. They each have a separate highway patrol and a state bureau of investigation. The PSP was the first modern police agency to combine the traffic enforcement and criminal investigation duties into a centralized model.

A Commissioner leads the PSP with the assistance of three deputy police commissioners (of Administration and Professional Responsibility, of Operations, and of Staff). The Governor appoints each of them; the Commissioner serves also with the advice and consent of the Pennsylvania Senate (The Commonwealth of Pennsylvania, 2011). The PSP is divided into a total of 71 bureaus, offices, divisions, and troops.

The ranks of the PSP reflect their organization's quasi-military tradition. For example, after completing the police academy, a police cadet joins the ranks of the "troopers." The military nomenclature holds up through the rank of the Commissioner, who holds the rank of Colonel. This rank structure and the centralized organization of the PSP created a model for other states to follow (e.g., state police in New Jersey and New York). The rank structure of the PSP includes:

- Colonel;
- Lieutenant Colonel;
- Major;
- Captain;

- Lieutenant;
- Sergeant;
- Corporal;
- Trooper First Class;
- Trooper; and
- State Police Cadet.

(Adapted from PSP Historical, Educational and Memorial Center. *Pennsylvania State Police Insignias*. Available online at: psp-hemc.org/insignias/index.html.)

Seventy-three State Police substations provide close to one-for-one coverage of the Commonwealth's 67 counties. Headquarters in adjoining counties make up one of sixteen, lettered troops. Each troop is headed by a commanding officer (at the rank of Captain). For example, Troop R, located in Dunmore, is responsible for the northeast section of the Commonwealth (consisting of Lackawanna, Susquehanna, Wayne, and Pike Counties). A Captain commands the Troop. Lieutenants head each of the Criminal Investigation, Patrol, and Staff Services sections (serving the troop's territory). Sergeants are responsible for a police station in each of the remaining counties of the troop.

Requirements for Becoming a Trooper

To be appointed to a cadet's position in the state police academy, an individual must be:

- Between the ages of 21 and 40;
- A resident of Pennsylvania;
- A US citizen;
- In possession of a valid Pennsylvania's driver's license; and
- In possession of a high school diploma or General Equivalency Degree plus an Associate's degree or 60 college credits.

One can waive up to half of the required credit hours with prior law enforcement or military experience or by completing Act 120 training (PAtrooper.com, 2012). During the 27-week training in 2012, cadets received a bi-weekly salary of $1,161.60.

Function

The reader will already notice the myriad responsibilities of the PSP. From providing basic police service for rural areas of Pennsylvania that do not have their own municipal police departments, to engaging in high-level criminal investigations, the PSP provide an array of law enforcement, investigative, and public service functions. In areas serviced by a local police department, the State Police limit their activities to patrolling state highways within those jurisdictions. One-third of the agency's time is spent on criminal investigations and support services. Traffic enforcement and public safety services occupy the agency's remaining time. Troopers are individually assigned to criminal investigations, support services, or patrol. They offer their services both directly to the citizens and by way of training local police and supplementing local police department capabilities. As stated in *The Pennsylvania Manual* (2011, p. 4–89), "The facilities, manpower, equipment, and expertise of the Pennsylvania State Police are available to all police departments in Pennsylvania."

Law Enforcement Services

The large size of the PSP organization and their budget allow them to offer services that many, smaller municipal police departments cannot provide on their own. The PSP provide investigative expertise to municipal police departments dealing with major cases such as a homicide or robbery and drug rings that span multiple municipal jurisdictions. For 20% of the state's population, the PSP are the sole purveyor of law enforcement services (*The Center for Rural Pennsylvania,* 2006). They do not, however, enforce municipal ordinances. They only enforce state laws. The PSP also provide the following:

- Forensic services (e.g., Automated Fingerprint Identification System, DNA, trace evidence, and serology) in six regional laboratories
- Polygraphs
- Equestrian detail
- Computer crime investigations
- Amber Alert Activations
- Collision Analysis and Reconstruction
- K-9 units
- Seven aviation patrol units
- Training and seminars for law enforcement and criminal justice personnel from state and local agencies in:
  - Legal issues
  - Lethal weapons
  - Forensic services
  - Collision reconstruction
  - Drug evaluation and classification
  - Commercial vehicle safety

Additionally, the Municipal Police Officers' Education and Training Commission, chaired by the Commissioner of the PSP, sets the curriculum for and delivers the basic police training (i.e., Act 120) in 21 schools across the commonwealth (Pennsylvania State Police, 2013a).

The PSP also serves as a clearinghouse for crime data and intelligence. Analysts for the Pennsylvania Criminal Intelligence Center (PaCIC) provide all levels of law enforcement with digestible intelligence, data, and analytical findings. The Commonwealth Law Enforcement Assistance Network (CLEAN) provides criminal justice agencies with information on driver license, motor vehicle, state criminal, and protection from abuse histories and is part of the FBI's National Crime Information Center (NCIC), the National Law Enforcement Telecommunications System (NLETS) and the International Justice and Public Safety Information Sharing Network (Pennsylvania State Police, 2013a). Also in line with FBI requirements, the PSP assists local police departments with collecting and submitting crime data through the Pennsylvania Summary Uniform Crime Reporting System. It are to these data that local media outlets refer when publishing annual changes in crime in Pennsylvania (see, for example, Davis, 2013). The PSP also collect data on all police vehicle pursuits. Police agencies submit a vehicle pursuit form any time one of their officer's engages in a pursuit.

Public Safety Services

The PSP Community Safety/Public Information Officers (CS/PIO) work with other law enforcement agencies and community groups to provide education on PSP activities and safety information. The PSP provides presentations and brochures on the following:

- School bus safety;
- Child safety seat checks;
- Changes in traffic law and enforcement statistics;
- Assistance for victims of crime;
- Camp Cadet Program for children 12–15 years old; and
- Pennsylvania College Campus Security Assessment Report (Pennsylvania State Police, 2013b).

Public Services

Finally, the PSP provides on their website links to a number of commonly requested PSP data sources and services. These include:

- Information on National Drug Take Back Day locations;
- Megan's Law Sex Offender searches;

- Firearms dealing and purchasing information;
- Crime statistics;
- Criminal history requests;
- Compliment or complaint submission; and
- Details on how to become a trooper or Liquor Control Enforcement Officer (Pennsylvania State Police, 2013c).

Other Statewide Law Enforcement Agencies

Sworn personnel from the PSP often enforce regulations governed by other, civilian boards. For example, the Bureau of Liquor Control Enforcement (part of the state police) enforces laws against selling alcohol to minors as well as violations of liquor licenses (such as smoking indoors or nuisance complaints). In these cases, an administrative law judge from the civilian Pennsylvania Liquor Control Board presides over enforcement hearings. The Pennsylvania Gaming Control Board shares a similar relationship with the state police's Bureau of Gaming Enforcement.

The Capitol Police, a Division of the Bureau of Police and Safety, is located in Harrisburg, the state's capitol. It is overseen by the Department of General Services. They have full arrest power within its jurisdiction boundaries in Harrisburg, Philadelphia, and Scranton. The overall mission of the Capitol Police is:

> to achieve a safe environment free of crime, to protect and serve employees and visitors while on state property as well as protecting property and grounds throughout the Capitol Complex and at state office buildings in Philadelphia, Pittsburgh and Scranton (Pennsylvania Dept. of General Services, 2013).

They accomplish this through the tactics of foot, bicycle, K-9 and vehicle patrols.

Rangers for the Pennsylvania Department of Conservation and Natural Resources protect the third largest system of state parks in the US and have full powers of arrest within state forests. Similarly, the 191 enforcement officers (Reaves, 2011) for the Pennsylvania Game Commission have the authority to arrest those individuals in violation of laws pertaining to game or wildlife in Pennsylvania. As the only state with two separate agencies for fishing, boating, and wildlife, Pennsylvania also has the Fish and Boat Commission whose Waterways Conservation officers enforce fishing and boating laws. Pennsylvania House Resolution 129, in 2013, proposes a merging of these two commissions to reduce costs and increase efficiency (Mayer, 2013).

Attorney General's Office

The Pennsylvania Constitution places the honor of chief legal and law enforcement officer of the commonwealth with the Attorney General. In this position, the Attorney General's office prosecutes organized crime and corruption and investigates matters of statewide importance (i.e., fraud and the illicit drug trade) (Pennsylvania Attorney General, 2010).

To this end, the Attorney General's Office has units in the following areas: organized crime; child predation; drug strike force; environmental crimes; insurance fraud; and Medicaid fraud. The largest single section within the office, the Criminal Law division organizes the investigations, prosecutions, and enforcement of behaviors that violate these laws. In addition, the Attorney General's office offers educational programs in internet safety, gun violence in communities, and teen drug abuse (Pennsylvania Attorney General, 2010a).

Local Policing

The Pennsylvania General Assembly classifies municipal governments into four types (i.e., county, city, borough, and township). Each type is made up of various classes based upon population size.[2] Philadelphia, for example, is Pennsylvania's only first class city, and Allegheny County is Pennsylvania's only county of the second class (The Commonwealth of Pennsylvania, 2011). Each municipality has the authority to create a local police department. As in other states, a majority of Pennsylvania's sworn personnel are employed at the local level, in municipal police departments. Not surprisingly, the average municipality in Pennsylvania spends one-third of its budget on policing—one of the largest expenditures for a municipal government (*Governor's Center*, 2010). In lieu of creating its own full-service police department, a municipality can contract with nearby communities to access all or part of its police services or can consolidate with surrounding departments. Approximately 11% of police departments in Pennsylvania contract for services, and less than 3% are regional (*The Center for Rural Pennsylvania*, 2006).

---

2. A city of the first class is has a population of one million or more. Those with a population of two hundred fifty thousand and under one million are considered second class cities. Those with a population of eighty thousand and under two hundred fifty thousand and which by ordinance elect to be a city of the second class A shall constitute the second class A. Third class cities have a population under two hundred fifty thousand and have not elected to become a city of the second class.

In 2003, there were 1,124 municipal police departments in Pennsylvania (*The Center for Rural Pennsylvania*, 2006). Seventy of those are countywide agencies. In fact, Pennsylvania is home to more police departments than any other state (Reaves, 2011). Police officers in these agencies enforce state laws as well as municipal ordinances. They have primary jurisdiction within their municipal territory. However, Pennsylvania statute authorizes any sworn police officer to perform the functions of their office (i.e., enforce the law) outside of their territory when they have probable cause to believe a felony has occurred, are in hot pursuit, are on official business within the Commonwealth, or have the prior authorization from the court and chief law enforcement agent in that municipality (e.g., when executing an arrest warrant).

The top 10 largest municipal police departments are:

- Philadelphia City;
- Pittsburgh City;
- Allegheny County;
- Harrisburg City;
- Allentown City;
- Erie City;
- Allegheny County Sheriff;
- Bethlehem City;
- Reading City; and
- Scranton City (*Crime in PA: Annual UCR*, 2011).

Though the general structure and function of local police departments are similar, the daily operational and cultural realities of even the 10 largest police departments can differ greatly. For example, the police departments in both Philadelphia and Scranton have a hierarchical chain of command, share similar ranks, have some of the same divisions, enforce traffic laws, investigate drug crimes, and partake in community outreach. However, differences in the size of the police departments and the communities they police beget different policing styles, activities, and concerns for each department.

The Scranton Police Department

Scranton, a 2a class city, is home to almost 75,000 residents and is located in the northeast corner of the commonwealth. In 1856, amidst the turmoil of the industrial revolution and the booming coal industry, Scranton elected a constable as its first law enforcement official (Walker, 1978). He commanded 16 assistants. By 1866, civic leaders incorporated Scranton as a city and passed an ordinance creating the Scranton Police Department with fewer than 60 employees (Walker, 1978). Today, the Scranton Police Department (SPD) has 147 police officers.

The SPD rank structure includes:

- Chief;
- Captain;
- Lieutenant;
- Sergeant;
- Corporal;
- Detective; and
- Patrol Officer.

The SPD is made up of a Patrol Division, Administrative Division, and a Criminal Investigations Division. A Canine Unit and a Highway Unit fall under the Patrol Division. The Administrative Division includes units for Crime Prevention, Records, Training and School Resource Officers. They also maintain individual Arson, Auto Theft, Child Abuse, Child Predators, Crime Scene, Criminal, Juvenile, and Special Investigations units. Specialized units include the Bomb Unit, Special Operations, and Hostage Negotiations (Scranton Police Department, 2013a).

Within these units and divisions, SPD personnel engage in regular vehicle patrols, criminal investigations, educational programs, and community outreach. They fulfill a mission similar to many other departments' stated missions:

> To protect and preserve life and property; to understand and serve the needs of the Scranton neighborhoods; and to improve the quality of life by maintaining order, recognizing and resolving community problems, and apprehending criminals (Scranton Police Department, 2013).

In line with a community-oriented policing function, personnel from the SPD act as school resource officers and sponsor the National Night Out, a Citizens Police Academy, and a Junior Police Academy. They also offer a number of educational, crime prevention, and safety resources for the community (e.g., Senior Citizen crime prevention, gun safety, and residential and commercial security surveys).

The Philadelphia Police Department

Philadelphia, one of the largest and most well-known cities in the United States, is the only first class city in Pennsylvania. It is also Pennsylvania's only city-county. The Pennsylvania Legislature passed a law in 1845 establishing the Philadelphia Police Department (PPD). By 1850, the Legislature had passed a law giving the PPD authority over the surrounding districts. Four years later, Philadelphia and its police department were consolidated into one city-county. There were 1,000 police officers in that area (The Committee of Seventy, 1998).

There are over 7,400 people (including 6,600 sworn) working for the PPD today, making it the 4th largest police department in the United States (Philadelphia Police Department, 2013). The PPD provides primary law enforcement services to the 1.5 million residents of the Philadelphia city-county. Their organizational chart encompasses comparable units and divisions as the smaller, SPD. It also includes many more offices and bureaus (e.g., the Office of Field Intelligence and Analysis, the Homeland Security Bureau, and the Office of Strategic Intelligence and Information Sharing). The PPD rank structure reflects the more complex nature of the organization and the responsibilities they fulfill, compared to smaller police departments such as the one in Scranton. Ranks include:

- Commissioner;
- Deputy Commissioner;
- Chief Inspector;
- Inspector;
- Staff Inspector;
- Captain;
- Lieutenant;
- Sergeant;
- Corporal;
- Detective; and
- Police Officer.

Analogous to the SPD's 1) Administrative, 2) Criminal Investigations, and 3) Patrol Divisions are the PPD's 1) Organizational Services, 2) Specialized Investigations and Homeland Security, and 3) Patrol Operations (respectively). Geographically, the PPD is divided into two major sections (North and South). A Chief Inspector within Patrol Operations leads each section. The sections further break down into six geographic divisions, each headed by a Divisional Inspector. These are further divided into 22 districts. A captain leads each of these.

The mission statement of the PPD reads similarly to that of the SPD. It states:

> Our mission is to be the model of excellence in policing by working in partnership with the community and others to:
> - Fight crime and the fear of crime, including terrorism;

- Enforce laws while safeguarding the constitutional rights of all people;
- Provide quality service to all our residents and visitors; and
- Create a work environment in which we recruit, train and develop an exceptional team of employees (Philadelphia Police Department, 2013a).

Worth noting in the mission statement of Pennsylvania's largest municipal police department is their inclusion of fighting terrorism and the section devoted to developing police personnel. Like those of the SPD listed above, the PPD is involved in a variety of community-oriented, educational, and service activities that go beyond the commonly-associated police activity of enforcing the law.

The Municipal Police Officers' Education and Training Commission

Though each municipality has the authority to create its own police department, the state does require minimum entry-level and on-going training of all sworn law enforcement officers (*Governor's Center*, 2010). In 1974, Act 120 created the Municipal Police Officers' Education and Training Commission (MPOETC), setting minimum requirements for all police officers in Pennsylvania (e.g., campus police, municipal police, transit police) (The Commonwealth of Pennsylvania, 2011). Potential recruits can enter the police academy and pay for their own tuition prior to signing on with a police agency. If they prefer to wait until they are hired by a police agency, the agency will pay for the newly hired police officer to go through the academy. To be a police officer in Pennsylvania one must:

- Be at least 18 years old;
- Possess a GED or high school diploma;
- Be a US citizen;
- Score at least a 9th grade reading level on the Nelson-Denny reading test;
- Meet certain physical requirements, to include: being free from addiction, being of a physical ability consistent with the requirements of the job, and having the necessary hearing and sight ability;
- Pass a psychological exam;
- Successfully complete a basic police training course; and
- Pass a background investigation (The Municipal Police Officers' Education and Training Commission, 2013a).

Individual municipalities may have additional or more stringent requirements than those mandated by the state. For example, the Philadelphia Police Department requires its recruits to be residents of Philadelphia for at least one year prior to being hired.

Table 4.1 Functions and Tasks of a Patrol Officer in Pennsylvania

Function	Task
Respond to and initially investigate various crimes and events	Secure crime scene; protect evidence
Protect crime scene and collect evidence and Information	Collect and package evidence; determine need for special investigators
Arrest and detain persons	Advise them of their Miranda rights
Conduct search and seizure	Fully search arrested persons
Provide emergency services	Apply basic first aid
Respond to and investigate motor vehicle accidents	Inspect vehicles to assess damage; search for physical evidence
Enforce DUI and other motor vehicle laws	Administer field sobriety test; explain local traffic ordinance to the violator
Operate emergency vehicle	Engage in high-speed pursuits
Stop motor vehicles and investigate occupants	Investigate suspicious vehicle; identify unusual or suspicious actions
Use physical force and exertion to perform duties	Break up fights; carry immobile child or adult; climb over a fence
Develop positive community relationships	Talk with people on the beat; behave in a positive and fair manner
Read and write reports and documents	Prepare criminal complaints and affidavits
Present evidence and testimony	Work with the prosecutor to prepare testimony; present testimony and evidence in court
Intervene in and control human conflicts	Offer alternatives to resolve conflicts between disputants
Use deadly force	Discharge firearm at person
Perform general patrol duties	Issue citations for non-traffic offenses.

Adapted from: Municipal Police Officers' Education and Training Commission. (2013). *Essential Functions and Tasks.*

Table 4.1 lists 16 essential functions of a municipal police department's patrol officer in Pennsylvania (and a sample of the many tasks they must perform to fulfill them). This list demonstrates the varied physical, intellectual, mental, and emotional abilities expected of local police aspirants.

County Police Agencies

Counties in Pennsylvania encompass multiple townships, cities, and boroughs. All five iterations of Pennsylvania's constitutions dating back to 1776 authorize counties to establish their own sheriff's offices (Clark, 1997). All 67 counties have done so. Three additional countywide departments serve a supplementary investigative and public safety function. Two of the additional departments are separate countywide detective agencies (the Armstrong County Detective Bureau and the Beaver County Detective Bureau). The other is a supplemental reserve agency in Allegheny County.

Whereas the mayor, city administrator, or other governing body appoints the chief law enforcement officers of city, town, and borough police departments, citizens elect sheriffs to serve as head of the sheriff's department. As such, the sheriff is the chief law enforcement officer of the county. The sheriff appoints deputy sheriffs to fulfill the mandate of the sheriff's department. There are approximately 1,900 deputy sheriffs in Pennsylvania (County of Berks, 2013). Their typical day consists of court- and prison-related duties. Specifically, these include transporting prisoners, guarding courthouses, issuing and maintaining firearm permits, patrolling county parks and properties, and conducting sales of foreclosed property. Counties often provide jails and coordinate services (such as 9-1-1 dispatch or DUI processing) for the other municipalities within their territories.

Common law and case law regarding sheriffs' departments' function are somewhat contradictory. Generally, though, deputy sheriffs who are certified under Act 120 have the same authority as police officers to enforce commonwealth laws (*Commonwealth v. Leet*, 537 Pa. 89, 641 A.2d 299, 1994). The Municipal Police Officers' Education and Training Commission (MPOETC) and the Deputy Sheriffs' Education and Training Advisory Board stipulate the deputy sheriffs' training requirements that allow deputy sheriffs to enforce Pennsylvania's motor vehicle and criminal statutes (Clark, M. 1997). Like the MPOETC, the deputy sheriffs' advisory board was also created by an act of the Pennsylvania legislature (Pennsylvania Commission on Crime and Delinquency, 2013). In practice, nearly all sheriffs' deputies fulfill only those non-law enforcement functions discussed in the section below. The example of the Montgomery County Sheriff's Department will highlight some of these features of county policing in Pennsylvania.

The Montgomery County Sheriff's Department

Pennsylvania's third largest county, Montgomery County, is located in southeastern Pennsylvania, just outside of Philadelphia. It elected its first sheriff in

1789. In addition to the Sheriff and chief deputy, there are 124 deputy sheriffs, administrative personnel, and clerical staff (Montgomery County, 2013). The current sheriff, Eileen Whalon Behr, is a former police chief for the Whitemarsh Police Department. Among the 17 bullet points of the Montgomery County Sheriff's Department mission are:

- Protect and serve the citizens in the areas of law enforcement and public safety;
- Quell civil unrest;
- Provide Bomb and Hazardous Device Disposal Unit, Emergency Response Teams and Patrol Units to all municipalities throughout the county;
- Serve bench warrants, protection from abuse orders and civil papers;
- Transport detainees from their respective institutions to the courthouse;
- Assist local, state and federal law enforcement with five DUI processing centers and DUI checkpoints;
- Process applications for license to carry a concealed firearm;
- Conduct sheriff's sales;
- Provide community services such as D.A.R.E. and the Senior Citizens Aid in Education programs;
- Ensure a safe and secure environment in and around the courthouse; and
- Provide services as requested by the president judge and commissioners of Montgomery County (Montgomery County, 2013a).

The sheriff's department does much more than just enforce the law. The county sheriffs have primary responsibility for transporting detainees, protecting county property (i.e., courthouses), and processing gun permits. Like the other levels of policing that this chapter has covered, sheriff's deputies engage and serve the community in many ways. Similar to the Pennsylvania State Police, sheriff's departments also supplement the activities of local police departments by offering space, resources, and expertise that are otherwise not available to smaller departments.

Police Constables

Constables served as the first form of law enforcement in the colonial United States. In Pennsylvania, they were selected from among landowning males and were compelled to serve, executing warrants and keeping the peace (Penn Constable Police, 2012). By the 1830s, the establishment of municipal police departments in the larger towns and cities weakened the constable's position (Penn Constable Police, 2012). After finding a home in the judiciary, as enforcer for the local justice of the peace, the constable's role in the criminal justice system again came into question in the 1970s.

Today, the office of the constable falls under the umbrella of the Pennsylvania Commission on Crime and Delinquency. Pennsylvania State Constables are elected to six-year terms and can appoint deputies to serve under them. The judiciary uses constables on an as-needed basis. They are compensated following a fee-based structure (Miller, 2013). With the proper state certification and training, constables in Pennsylvania serve as the judiciary's law enforcement arm. They serve primarily the district court and sometimes the court of common pleas at the request of the sheriff (Penn Constable Police, 2012). The Constables' Education and Training Board advises the Pennsylvania Commission on Crime and Delinquency regarding the requirements for state constables.

Conclusion

The many women and men who swear to protect and serve the citizens of Pennsylvania come from a multitude of backgrounds and work for a variety of police agencies. This chapter reveals the fragmented nature of policing in Pennsylvania. With more police departments than any other state, it is important that citizens and police personnel understand the structure and function of all police in the Commonwealth, and that the rules and laws that govern police practice clearly delineate the expectations that the policed have of the police.

Key Terms and Definitions

Act 120 training: The statutorily mandated minimum training for all sworn police personal in Pennsylvania, giving them the authority to enforce state laws.

Attorney general: The chief legal and law enforcement official of Pennsylvania.

Centralized state police department: A structure of enforcing state criminal and motor vehicle laws in which one department provides both law enforcement and traffic enforcement services.

Civilian personnel: Employees of a police department who do not have the authority to enforce state laws, but might perform a variety of other functions in support of law enforcement efforts.

Commissioner: Head of the Pennsylvania state police, upon appointment by the governor and approval of the legislature.

Constable: The earliest form of policing in Pennsylvania.

Decentralized state police department: A structure of enforcing state criminal and motor vehicle laws in which one department investigates crimes and a separate department provides a statewide highway patrol with primary authority over the state's roads.

Deputy sheriffs: Appointed by the sheriffs to help fulfill the mandate of the (county) sheriff's department.

The Great Anthracite Strike of 1902: A dispute between coal miners and the coalmine operators over working conditions and wages. It sparked violence between those striking and those who refused to strike. This prompted intervention from local police, the National Guard and US President Theodore Roosevelt. This event factored into Governor Samuel Pennypacker's decision to create the Pennsylvania State Police to help respond to such unrest.

Jurisdiction: Both the geographic and content areas in which a police department has the authority to legally enforce the state's laws.

Limited (or special) jurisdiction: Occurs when a police department's authority to enforce the law pertains to a specific geographic or content area.

Municipal Police Officers Education and Training Commission: A group of community leaders, law enforcement personnel and educators responsible for creating training and educational standards for Pennsylvania police.

Municipality: A geographic area within the state that has the authority to create a local police department (e.g., county, city, town).

Rank structure: The titles held by employees of a police department that denote one's position, responsibilities, authority, subordinates and supervisors within the department.

Statewide regulatory enforcement boards: Enforcement agencies with statewide geographic jurisdiction and specific content jurisdiction (e.g., The Pennsylvania Liquor Control Board and the Pennsylvania Gaming Control Board). These groups work alongside state police personnel to enforce the regulatory laws in their areas.

Sworn personnel: Employees of a police department who are authorized by state statute to enforce violations of state criminal laws and motor vehicle statutes.

Taskforce: A group of representatives from various levels and types of law enforcement agencies that meet regularly to coordinate information, intelligence, data and efforts to solve a shared crime problem.

Websites

Constitution of the Commonwealth of Pennsylvania: http://www.pahouse.com/
pa_const.htm.

The Constitution of the United States: http://www.archives.gov/exhibits/charters/
constitution_transcript.html.

Crime Statistics in Pennsylvania: http://ucr.psp.state.pa.us/UCR/Reporting/
RptMain.asp.

The Census of State and Local Law Enforcement Agencies: http://www.bjs.gov/
index.cfm?ty=dcdetail&iid=249.

Municipal Police Officers' Education and Training Commission: http://www.
mpoetc.state.pa.us/portal/server.pt/community/mpoetc/7545.

Review Questions

1. How do the jurisdictions of police agencies at the state and local level differ? How are they similar?
2. What's the difference between a sheriff's department and a city police department?
3. How are the various levels of police agencies organized in Pennsylvania?
4. What are the similarities and differences of the police function at the state level compared to their function at the local level?
5. How do special police (e.g., transit police, university police) differ from municipal and state police agencies? How are they similar?
6. What acts, commissions and boards govern the basic requirements for being hired as a sworn police officer in Pennsylvania? What are some of those requirements?
7. How do police in Pennsylvania compare to other states? How has policing in Pennsylvania influenced other states' police departments?

Critical Thinking Questions

1. Create an emergency scenario in which the Pennsylvania State Police, a city police department, a university or transit police department and a county sheriffs' office are required to work together to respond to the emergency. What other police or governmental agencies might also need to respond?

2. What inefficiencies do you see in the current organization of policing in Pennsylvania? What suggestions do you have for making policing more efficient?

3. Imagine you are a member of the Municipal Police Officers' Education and Training Commission. Given the varied responsibilities of police in Pennsylvania, what else do you think police departments should require of their recruits?

4. What responsibilities do police have that you think they should not have? Are there any responsibilities that you would add to the police function?

References

Clark, M. (1997). *The Sheriff's Office in History.* Sheriffs' Association of the Commonwealth of Pennsylvania. Available online at: http://www.pasheriffs. org/about-us/sheriff-history/.

County of Berks (2013). *What is a sheriff?* Available online at: http://www.co. berks.pa.us/dept/sheriff/pages/whatisasheriff.aspx.

Commonwealth v. Leet, 537 Pa. 89, 641 A.2d 299, (1994). Available online at: http://www.leagle.com/decision/1994626537Pa89_1615.

Crime in Pennsylvania: Annual Uniform Crime Report, 2012. Available online at: http://www.paucrs.pa.gov/UCR/Reporting/Annual/AnnualFrames.asp? year=2012.

Davis, C. (27 January 2013). A spate of violence plagues young Black men in Norristown, *Philadelphia Inquirer.* Available online at: http://articles.philly. com/2013-01-27/news/36565846_1_norristown-police-ryan-ladson-singleton-young-black-men.

Governor's Center for Local Government Services (November 2010). *Administering Police Services in Small Communities: A Manual for Local Government Officials,* 6th edition.

Mayer, F. (2013). Pa house mulls merger of game and fish and boating commission, *The River Reporter.* Available online at: http://www.riverreporter.com/news/ 4302/2013/06/05/pa-house-mulls-merger-game-and-fish-and-boat-commission.

Miller, M. (2013). Pa supreme court tightens reins on state's constables. *The Patriot News.* Available online at: http://www.pennlive.com/midstate/index. ssf/2013/05/supreme_court_tightens_reins_o.html.

Montgomery County. (2013). *About the Department.* Available online at: www. montcopa.org/index.aspx?NID=428.

Montgomery County. (2013a). *Mission of the Sheriff's Department*. Available online at: www.montcopa.org/index.aspx?NID=435.

Municipal Police Officers' Education and Training Commission. (2013). *Essential Functions and Tasks*. Available online at: http://www.mpoetc.state.pa.us/portal/server.pt/community/mpoetc/7545/essential_functions_and_tasks/747573.

Municipal Police Officers' Education and Training Commission. (2013a). *Officer Certification: Rules and Regulations*. Available online at: http://www.portal.state.pa.us/portal/server.pt/community/mpoetc/7545/certification/590508.

Patrooper.com (2012). *Requirements*. Available online at: www.patrooper.com/requirements.html.

Penn Constable Police. (2012). *History of the office of constable*. Available online at: pscpolice.org/history.html.

Pennsylvania Attorney General. (2010). *Mission statement*. Available online at: http://www.attorneygeneral.gov/theoffice.aspx?id=168.

Pennsylvania Attorney General. (2010a). *Protecting Pennsylvania against crime*. Available online at: http://www.attorneygeneral.gov/drugs.aspx?id=175.

Pennsylvania Commission on Crime and Delinquency (2013). *Deputy Sheriffs' Education and Training Program*. Available online at: http://www.portal.state.pa.us/portal/server.pt/community/deputy_sheriffs%27_education_and_training/5387.

Pennsylvania Department of General Services. *Police and Safety*. Available online at: www.portal.state.pa.us/portal/server.pt/community/police_and_safety/1251.

Pennsylvania State Police. (May 2005). Pennsylvania State Police Turns 100, *Law and Order*, p. 112.

Pennsylvania State Police (2013). Available online at: http://www.portal.state.pa.us/portal/server.pt?open=512&objID=4451&&PageID=485150&mode=2.

Pennsylvania State Police (2013a). *Law Enforcement Services*. Available online at: http://www.portal.state.pa.us/portal/server.pt/community/psp/4451/law_enforcement_services/452782.

Pennsylvania State Police (2013b). *Safety Education*. Available online at: http://www.portal.state.pa.us/portal/server.pt/community/psp/4451/public_safety/760900.

Pennsylvania State Police (2013c). *Services and General Information*. Available online at: http://www.portal.state.pa.us/portal/server.pt/community/psp/4451/public_services/452780.

Pennsylvania State Police Historical, Educational and Memorial Center. *Pennsylvania State Police Insignias*. Available online at: psphemc.org/insignias/index.html.

Philadelphia Police Department (2013). *About the Department*. Available online at: http://www.phillypolice.com/about.

Philadelphia Police Department (2013a). *Mission Statement*. Available online at: http://www.phillypolice.com/about/mission-statement/.

Reaves, B.A. (June 2012). Federal law enforcement officers, 2008. Bureau of Justice Statistics. Available online at: http://www.bjs.gov/content/pub/pdf/fleo08.pdf.

Reaves, B.A. (July 2011). Census of state and local law enforcement agencies. Bureau of Justice Statistics. Available online at: http://www.bjs.gov/index.cfm?ty=pbdetail&iid=2216.

Roberg, R., Novak, K., Cordner, G. & Smith, B. (2012). *Police and Society*, 5th edition. New York: Oxford.

Scranton Police Department (2013). *Chief of Police*. Available online at: www.scrantonpa.gov/scrantonpd/Administrative.asp.

Scranton Police Department (2013a). *Supervisors*. Available online at: www.scrantonpa.gov/scrantonpd/supervisors.asp.

The Center for Rural Pennsylvania. (March 2006). *Survey of small town police departments*.

The Committee of Seventy. (1998). *Philadelphia police department governance study*. Philadelphia, PA.

The Commonwealth of Pennsylvania (2011). *The Pennsylvania Manual*, v. 120.

Walker, S. (1978). The police and the community: Scranton, Pennsylvania, 1866–1884 a test case. *American Studies*, 19, 1, pp. 79–90.

Chapter 5

Pennsylvania Courts

Jana Nestlerode and Jerry Morano

Learning Objectives

After reading the chapter, students will be able to:

- Describe the judicial hierarchy of the Commonwealth of Pennsylvania.
- Explain the duties and responsibilities of the Pennsylvania Attorney General, the county District Attorneys, and Public Defenders.
- Explain how judges are selected and retained in Pennsylvania.
- Distinguish competitive elections from retention elections in Pennsylvania.
- Explain the differences between the arbiter of law and the trier of fact in criminal cases.
- Explain the value of specialty courts.

Key Terms

Administrative Office of Pennsylvania Courts
Attorney General of the Commonwealth of Pennsylvania
Court Administrator
Courts of Common Pleas
Declaration of Rights
District Attorneys
Magisterial District Courts

Municipal Courts
Pennsylvania Constitution
Pennsylvania Commonwealth Court
Pennsylvania Superior Court
Pennsylvania Supreme Court
Public Defenders
Retention Elections
United States Constitution

Introduction

The United States is composed of fifty individual states, but actually has fifty-two "jurisdictions" each with its own separate laws and governing bodies. Created by the United States Constitution of 1789, the federal government is comprised of three branches: the legislative, the executive and the judicial. In general, the legislative branch is charged with creating the laws; the executive branch is charged with enforcing the laws; the judicial branch is charged with interpreting the laws. These three federal branches have authority throughout all fifty states. Each state, however, has its own Constitution, and its own system of government. The legislative, executive, and judicial branches of each state have authority ("jurisdiction") only within that state. The fifty-second "jurisdiction" is the District of Columbia which has its own governing body and court system.

Article III, Section 1 of the United States Constitution vests judicial power in a Supreme Court. The Article also empowers Congress to create lesser national courts as needed. To date, the United States Congress has created ninety-four United States District Courts and thirteen United States Courts of Appeals. The United States Congress has also created specialty courts. Of greatest interest to students of criminal justice is the FISA court. The FISA court hears special law enforcement warrant applications that involve national security issues or that require the use of classified information.

Under the leadership of Benjamin Franklin, Pennsylvania adopted its first Constitution in 1776, many years before the first United States Constitution was adopted in 1789. In fact, the Pennsylvania Constitution provided a template for our national Constitution.

In this founding document, a tricameral system of government was created. The purpose of the tricameral system of government was to divide power among the branches, preventing any one from becoming too powerful. Each branch provided a "check and balance" on the others. Article II provided for the establishment of the legislative branch. This branch was empowered to create the laws of the Commonwealth. Article IV provided for the establishment of the executive branch. The responsibilities of the executive included the enforcement of the laws. Article V provided for the establishment of a "unified judicial system." The responsibilities of this judicial system included the interpretation of the laws.

Pennsylvania has had a total of five Constitutions in its history, all keeping the tricameral system of government. The original Constitution of 1776 was rewritten in 1790 in order to streamline the original document and remove unworkable provisions. The Constitution of 1838 kept the original framework, but provided important amendments. The fourth Constitution was adopted in 1874 and addressed primarily legislative issues. The most recent state Constitution was adopted in 1968. In this document a "unified judicial system" was created, along with a new intermediate appellate court, the Commonwealth Court. Administrative authority over all state courts was given to the Pennsylvania Supreme Court. In addition, a Judicial Inquiry and Review Board was established to address judicial discipline (Pennsylvania's Constitution: A Brief History, 2013).

Pennsylvania is founded on a deep respect for individual rights. The federal protection of civil rights is lodged primarily in the Bill of Rights, a document created and ratified separately, four years after the adoption of the United States Constitution. By contrast, the Pennsylvania Constitution includes a "Declaration of Rights" as a first order of business in Article I. Section 6 of that Article states:

> Trial by jury shall be as heretofore, and the right there of remain inviolate. The General Assembly may provide, however, by law, that a verdict may be rendered by not less than five-sixths of the jury in any civil case. Furthermore, in criminal cases, the Commonwealth shall have the same right to trial by jury as does the accused.

Section 9 of Article I states, inter alia:

> In all criminal prosecutions the accused hath a right to.... a speedy public trial by an impartial jury of the vicinage.

Section 11 states:

> All courts shall be open; and every man for an injury done him in his lands, goods, person or reputation shall have remedy by due course of the law, and right and justice administered without sale, denial or delay. Suits may be brought against the Commonwealth in such manner, in such courts and in such cases as the Legislature may by law direct.

Further protections for citizens can be found in Section 15, prohibiting special criminal tribunals:

> No commission shall issue creating special temporary criminal tribunals to try particular individuals or particular classes of cases.

Courts, whether federal or state, can be generally divided into two categories. Courts of original jurisdiction resolve issues of both fact and law. If a judge is presiding over a jury or non-jury trial, that judge is generally presiding over a court of original jurisdiction. Courts of appellate jurisdiction resolve only issues of law. If a judge is presiding over post-trial motions or hearing arguments on appeal, that judge is presiding over a court of appellate jurisdiction. These courts do not revisit the factual findings, but review cases for legal errors.

Federal Courts in Pennsylvania

Overview

The federal court system is comprised of ninety-four United States District Courts. Federal district court judges preside over both jury and non-jury trials involving violations of federal criminal and civil laws. There are approximately 677 federal judges serving in these 94 United States District Courts. The number of judges serving in each United States District Court is determined by federal statute and set forth in Title 28 of the United States Code, Section 133.

These ninety-four judicial districts are divided into twelve regional circuits. Each of these regional circuits is presided over by a United States Court of Appeals. An appeal from the United States District Court would be taken to the United States Court of Appeals for that region. The ruling of that particular United States Court of Appeals is binding on the United States District Courts within its region, but not on other United States Courts of Appeals. In addition, there is a Court of Appeals for the Federal Circuit which enjoys nationwide jurisdiction to hear appeals from specialized federal courts. The number of judges in each Circuit is determined by law and delineated in Title of the 28 U.S. Code Section 44. The smallest Circuit (the First Circuit) has only six judges. The largest Circuit (the Ninth Circuit) has 28 judges. In total, approximately 179 federal judges serve on the United States Courts of Appeals. Appeals from rulings of the United States Courts of Appeals may be taken to the United States Supreme Court (United States Courts, Understanding the Federal Courts, Courts of Appeals, 2013).

The United States Supreme Court is comprised of a Chief Justice and eight Associate Justices. Unlike the lower federal courts, the United States Supreme Court may refuse to hear an appeal. Each year, over 10,000 appeals (petitions) are made to this High Court. These appeals may originate as a result of rulings from either state or federal courts. However, in only about one hundred cases does the Court grant "certiorari," or review (Supreme Court of the United States, The Justices' Caseload, 2013). At least four of the sitting Justices must vote to grant certiorari or the petition to hear the case is denied. Under these circumstances, the lower court's ruling is undisturbed. The rulings of the United States Supreme Court are final. There is no higher court to which to appeal (Supreme Court of the United States, A Brief Overview of the Supreme Court, 2013).

There are times, however, when the United States Supreme Court will reverse itself on an issue it has previously decided. In the 1942 case of *Betts v. Brady*, the United States Supreme Court held that indigents in state criminal courts had no right to a free defense attorney in most cases. They held that the right

Figure 5.1 Geographic Boundaries of the United States Circuit Courts of
Appeals and United States District Courts

to an attorney was not essential to due process (fundamental fairness). Twenty-one years later, the Court changed its mind. In the now famous 1963 case of *Gideon v. Wainwright*, the United States Supreme Court ruled that indigents in state criminal courts did indeed have the right to free counsel.

All federal judges are nominated by the President of the United States. These nominees then appear before the United States Senate Judiciary Committee for hearings on their qualifications for this high office. The United States Senate Judiciary Committee will then make its recommendations to the full United States Senate. A nominee must receive at least 51 votes from the 100 Senators to be confirmed to the bench (Supreme Court of the United States, A Brief Overview of the Supreme Court 2013).

According to Article III of the United States Constitution, federal judges "shall hold their Offices during, good Behaviour." Judges who fail to meet that standard may be impeached. Impeachment is a process by which the United States House of Representatives institutes proceedings to determine if there is sufficient evidence of wrongdoing or misconduct that a judge should be removed from the bench. If the United States House of Representatives determines that there is sufficient evidence, the United States Senate then conducts a trial. A vote of two-thirds of the Senate is required to convict. Fifteen federal judges have been impeached by the United States House of Representatives, but only eight have been convicted by the United States Senate (United States Senate, 2013).

United States District Courts

The United States District Court for the Eastern District of Pennsylvania is historically significant as it is one of the original 13 federal judiciary districts created by the Judiciary Act of 1789. The District was divided into Eastern and Western Districts in 1818. The two Districts were again divided into Eastern, Middle and Western Districts in 1901. These courts hear criminal and civil cases involving violations of federal law that have occurred within their geographical boundaries (United States District Court, Eastern District of Pennsylvania, 2013).

The United States District Court for the Eastern District of Pennsylvania serves nine of Pennsylvania's sixty-seven counties, and hears cases at locations in Philadelphia, Allentown and Reading (United States District Court, Eastern District of Pennsylvania, 2013). There are twenty-two judgeships on this Court, and they address over 40,000 filings each year (United States Courts, Federal Courts Management Statistics, 2010).

The United States District Court for the Middle District of Pennsylvania serves 33 Pennsylvania counties, and hears cases in Harrisburg, Scranton, Williamsport and Wilkes-Barre (United States District Court, Middle District of Pennsylvania, 2013). There are six judgeships on this court, and they address approximately 3,000 filings each year (United States Courts, Federal Courts Management Statistics, 2010).

The United States District Court for the Western District of Pennsylvania hears cases in Pittsburgh, Erie and Johnstown (United States District Court, Western District of Pennsylvania, 2013). There are ten judgeships on this court, and they address approximately 3,000 filings each year (United States Courts, Federal Courts Management Statistics, 2010).

United States Court of Appeals (Third Circuit)

The United States Court of Appeals for the Third Circuit was established in 1891 (Federal Judicial Center, History of the Federal Judiciary, 2013). Its jurisdiction extends to civil and criminal appeals from the United States District Courts in Pennsylvania, Delaware, New Jersey and the Virgin Islands. The court is physically located in Philadelphia. As originally constituted, the court employed only two federal judges. Since then it has grown to its present size of fourteen federal judges (United States Court of Appeals, Third Circuit,

Figure 5.2 Federal Judicial Districts: Pennsylvania

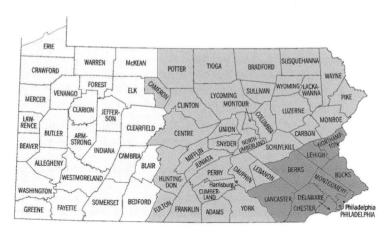

Source: http://www.fedstats.gov/mapstats/fjd.img/42.png.

2013). This court hears approximately four thousand appeals annually. Fewer than half of these appeals are generated by criminal or prisoner issues; the others are civil or administrative appeals (United States Courts, Federal Courts Management Statistics, 2010).

Attorneys in Federal Courts

In criminal cases, United States Attorneys serve as prosecutors in the United States District Courts. A United States Attorney is appointed by the President and confirmed by the United States Senate for each judicial district. Serving under the United States Attorney are scores of Assistant United States Attorneys. The primary responsibility of the United States Attorney and his Assistant United States Attorneys is the prosecution of criminal cases involving violations of federal law. These include firearms violations, narcotics violations, public corruption, crimes against children, internet crimes, and crimes related to national security. The United States Attorney also bears responsibility for the defense of civil matters where the United States is a party, and the collection of debts owed to the federal government when those debts cannot be collected by administrative measures (Federal Judicial Center, History of the Federal Judiciary, 2013).

United States Attorneys work closely with local, state and federal law enforcement authorities. Federal law enforcement authorities include the Federal Bureau of Investigation; The Bureau of Alcohol, Tobacco, Firearms and Explosives; the Drug Enforcement Administration; the U.S. Immigration and Customs Enforcement (ICE); the Office of Homeland Security Investigations (HSI); the U.S. Secret Service; IRS-Criminal Investigation Division (IRS-CI); the U.S. Postal Inspection Service; and the U.S. Marshals Service (Federal Judicial Center, History of the Federal Judiciary, 2013).

Persons accused of criminal wrongdoing in federal courts are guaranteed the right to representation in the United States Constitution, Amendment VI:

> In all criminal prosecutions, the accused shall ... have the assistance
> of counsel for his defence.

In most federal prosecutions, the defendant is represented by privately retained defense counsel. The United States Supreme Court has held that when a defendant cannot afford counsel in a federal court, one must be provided for him (Johnson v. Zerbst, 1938).

The Federal Public Defender in each District is appointed to a four-year term by the United States Court of Appeals for that District. The Federal Public Defender then appoints Assistant Federal Public Defenders as approved by the United States Court of Appeals for that District. Other personnel may be appointed as approved by the Director of Administrative Office of the U.S. Courts (National Legal Aid & Defender Association, 2013).

Pennsylvania Courts

Overview

Article V of the Pennsylvania Constitution addresses the creation and functions of the various state courts. Section 1 establishes a "unified judicial system." Further statutory authority for the Pennsylvania Court system and its administration is provided in Title 42 of Purdon's Pennsylvania Statutes. The Pennsylvania court system is multi-layered and hierarchical. This judicial system consists of the Supreme Court, the Superior Court, the Commonwealth Court, Courts of Common Pleas, specialty courts, municipal courts, and magisterial district courts (42 Pa.C.S.A. § 301). This unified judicial system is overseen and managed by the Administrative Office of Pennsylvania Courts (42 Pa.C.S.A. § 1902). A Court Administrator, appointed by the Pennsylvania Supreme Court oversees this Office and is responsible for the prompt and efficient administration of the matters before the various courts (42 Pa. C.S.A. § 1901) (The Unified Judicial System of Pennsylvania, Judicial Administration, 2013).

Pennsylvania Supreme Court

Originally established in 1722, the Pennsylvania Supreme Court is the oldest appellate court in the nation (The Unified Judicial System of Pennsylvania: The Pennsylvania Supreme Court). It was further authorized under Article V, Section 2 of the Pennsylvania Constitution. It was statutorily authorized in Title 42 of Purdon's Pennsylvania Statutes, Sections 501–504. Its jurisdiction is further detailed in Sections 721–727 of that same Title. It is the highest court in the Commonwealth, and is the Court of "last resort" in the state. It is the final word on the interpretation of the state constitution and state laws. With few exceptions, this Court has the authority to grant or deny allocatur (review). (The most notable exception is death penalty cases. In Pennsylvania, death sentences are automatically appealed to the Pennsylvania Supreme court.) The positive vote of at least two Justices is required for allocator to be granted. A refusal of allocatur has the effect of letting the lower court's ruling stand. However, if the issues brought by the parties are of federal constitutional dimension, the case can be appealed by the parties to the federal courts, even if the Pennsylvania Supreme Court has refused to hear the case (The Unified Judicial System of Pennsylvania, Supreme Court of Pennsylvania, 2013).

There are seven Pennsylvania Supreme Court justices, including a Chief Justice. The Chief Justice is generally chosen on the basis of seniority (longest continuous service). Justices to the Pennsylvania Supreme Court are elected by the voters of the Commonwealth for ten-year terms. At the end of the term, the Justice may choose to run for another term in what is called a "retention" election. Retention elections require the voters to simply approve or disapprove the Justice for another term. The Justice does not run against an opponent as in a traditional election. If a majority of the voters elect to retain the Justice, he or she will serve another ten-year term. If the Justice does not receive majority approval, the seat will be vacated. To fill a vacancy, the governor of the state will appoint a replacement, who must be confirmed by a two-thirds vote of the Pennsylvania Senate (The Unified Judicial System of Pennsylvania, Judicial Elections and Retention, 2012).

The Court holds eight judicial sessions per year. These sessions are held in Philadelphia (winter, spring, and fall), Harrisburg (spring) and Pittsburgh (spring and fall). The Court receives approximately 3000 appeals per year (The Unified Judicial System of Pennsylvania, Supreme Court of Pennsylvania, 2013).

The administration of the Pennsylvania Courts is detailed in Article V, Section 10 of the Pennsylvania Constitution. It states that:

> The Supreme Court shall exercise general supervisory and administrative authority overall the courts and justices of the peace ...

It states, in addition, that:

> The Supreme Court shall appoint a court administrator and may appoint such subordinate administrators and staff as may be necessary and proper for the prompt and proper disposition of the business of all courts and justices of the peace.

By this authority, the Pennsylvania Supreme Court oversees and supervises all of the courts in the Commonwealth of Pennsylvania. To assist in this endeavor, the Administrative Office of the Pennsylvania Courts (AOPC) was created. The purpose of this Office is to ensure the prompt and appropriate conduct of the Pennsylvania courts. The Pennsylvania Supreme Court appoints the Court Administrator to head this Office. The Pennsylvania Rules of Judicial Administration (Rules 501–506) list the responsibilities of this Office. They include:

- Ensuring safety and accessibility of our courts;
- Providing reliable information about the court system to citizens and the media;
- Reviewing the conduct of the courts, operations and processes;
- Providing guidance on policy;
- Assisting the 67 President Judges of the Courts of Common Pleas and the hundreds of Magisterial District Justices and administrators in court management;
- Developing and maintaining information technology to effectively manage case, financial and administrative systems of the courts; and
- Conducting continuing education programs for judges and judicial staff (The Unified Judicial System of Pennsylvania, Judicial Administration, 2013).

Pennsylvania Superior Court

The Pennsylvania Superior Court is authorized by the Pennsylvania Constitution, Article V, Section 3. It was originally created by law in 1895; the state Constitutional Convention of 1968 gave it constitutional authority. It is further authorized in 42 Pa. C.S.A. §§ 541–544. It is an intermediate appellate court with statewide jurisdiction. Defendants in the state's criminal trial courts have an automatic right to appeal to the Pennsylvania Superior Court.

Fifteen judges serve on the Pennsylvania Superior Court. These judges are elected by popular vote of the citizens of the state for a term of ten years. From among the fifteen, a President Judge is elected by a majority of the judges. The President Judge is elected to that position for a five-year term. Like the Pennsylvania Supreme Court Justices, members of the Pennsylvania Superior Court must run for retention elections at the end of the ten-year term. If a Pennsylvania Superior Court judge fails to win approval by a majority of the votes cast, the seat is vacated. The vacated seat will be filled by gubernatorial appointment and the approval of two-thirds of the state Senate.

Unlike the Pennsylvania Supreme Court, the Pennsylvania Superior Court does not have a predetermined number of sessions each year. The number of sessions is generally established by the number of appeals which must be heard. The Pennsylvania Superior Court commonly sits as three-judge panels, the composition of which may change quite frequently. Approximately three to six times per year the Court will hold "en banc" (the entire court) sessions. These sessions may be held in Harrisburg, Philadelphia, or Pittsburgh. The Court may also hold special sessions in other cities upon request of the judges of the Court of Common Pleas and the county bar association.

The Pennsylvania Superior Court generally hears appeals from decisions of the Courts of Common Pleas. On appeal, the Court will determine whether a reversible error of law occurred at the lower court. If so, the Pennsylvania Superior Court will overturn the lower court's ruling. This Court also has authority to rule on wiretap and electronic surveillance applications.

This Court hears approximately 8,000 cases per year and is among the busiest appellate courts in the country. The National Center for State Courts has recognized the Pennsylvania Superior Court as one of the most productive appellate courts in the nation (Unified Judicial System of Pennsylvania, The Superior Court of Pennsylvania, 2013).

Pennsylvania Commonwealth Court

The Pennsylvania Commonwealth Court is authorized by Article V, Section 4 of the Pennsylvania Constitution, and was created by the Constitutional Convention of 1968. It is further authorized in Title 42 of Purdon's Pennsylvania Statutes, Sections 561–564. It is a statewide court consisting of nine judges elected by the citizens of the state for a ten-year term. The judges of the Commonwealth Court elect a President Judge to serve for a term of five years. As with the members of the Pennsylvania Supreme and Pennsylvania Superior Courts, the judges may run in a retention election at the end of the ten-year terms. If a majority of the voters approve, the judge is returned to the bench for another ten-year term. If a majority of the voters do not approve, the governor, with the approval of two-thirds of the state senate, may appoint a replacement. The Pennsylvania Supreme Court also selects six senior judges to sit with the Commonwealth Court.

The Court holds nine monthly sessions per year. It does not sit in January, July, or August. The sessions are held in Harrisburg, Philadelphia, and Pittsburgh. In addition, the Court may choose to hold special sessions in any other judicial district in the state when needed.

The Commonwealth Court hears appeals and sometimes original cases in which the state or local government is involved. The cases cover a wide range of subject matters including taxation; land use; labor law; election law; and insurance, banking, utility and environmental regulations. The Commonwealth Court has unique jurisdiction over appeals from orders of state agencies such as the Environmental Hearing Board, the Public Utility Commission, and the Unemployment Compensation Board of Review. It also hears appeals from arbitrations involving the Commonwealth and state employees. The Commonwealth Court has original jurisdiction over civil actions by or against the state and election matters involving statewide offices (The Unified Judicial System of Pennsylvania, Commonwealth Court of Pennsylvania, 2013).

Pennsylvania Courts of Common Pleas

The Pennsylvania Courts of Common Pleas are authorized by Section 5 of Article V of the Pennsylvania Constitution and Title 42 of Purdon's Pennsylvania Statutes, §§ 901–962. The Pennsylvania Courts of Common Pleas are organized into sixty judicial districts. Fifty-three of Pennsylvania's sixty-seven counties have a dedicated Court of Common Pleas. The remaining fourteen counties share seven Courts of Common Pleas. The number of judges serving in each judicial district varies from only one judge to more than one hundred judges. When a Court has eight or more judges, the President Judge is elected by the sitting judges for a five-year term. When a Court has fewer than eight judges, the judge with the longest continuous service serves as the President Judge.

The Pennsylvania Courts of Common Pleas are the primary trial courts of the state. Generally, the Pennsylvania Courts of Common Pleas have unlimited original jurisdiction in both civil and criminal matters. Here, jury and non-jury trials are held. The criminal divisions handle non-violent crimes such as theft, to the most serious violent crimes such as murder. The civil divisions handle cases involving personal injury, contract disputes, and estate settlements. This Court also handles family matters such as divorce, custody, adoption, and support. In addition, the Court will handle child abuse cases and issue Protection From Abuse orders. The jurisdiction of the Court of Common Pleas includes appeals taken from the Magisterial District courts, and appeals from various state agency decisions (relating to such things as motor vehicle violations, liquor code violations, rulings by state offices on inheritance and estate taxes, public employee disputes, and other occupational matters). Judges of the Court of Common Pleas may also hear petitions for reviews of awards by arbitrators in controversies between local government agencies and their employees (The Unified Judicial System of Pennsylvania, Pennsylvania Courts of Common Pleas, 2013).

All Courts of Common Pleas have a Trial Division. Larger courts have additional divisions to handle categories of cases. Judges are assigned to serve in a particular division for various lengths of time. An administrative judge presides over each division and assists the President Judge.

The Philadelphia Court of Common Pleas has a Trial Division which handles both criminal and civil cases. It also has an Orphans' Court Division. This Court protects the rights of persons who may not be capable of handling their own affairs. In this context, the word "orphan" denotes one lacking protection. This includes certain matters concerning minors, incapacitated persons, and decedents' estates. It also includes matters concerning nonprofit corporations and trusts (The Philadelphia Courts, Orphans' Division, 2013).

The Family Court Division is divided into two branches: Juvenile Court and Domestic Relations. The Juvenile branch includes juvenile court, juvenile probation, and Children and Youth Services (which address the needs of dependent or ungovernable children). The Domestic Relations branch handles cases involving divorce, custody, paternity, support, and visitation (The Philadelphia Courts, Family Division, 2013).

The Court of Common Pleas of Allegheny County has four divisions. The Civil Division handles civil matters such as contract disputes, personal injury trials, and miscellaneous tort litigations. The Criminal Division handles criminal matters including pretrial motions, jury and non-jury trials, post-trial motions, and sentencings. The Orphan's Court and Family Courts handle similar matters as the corresponding courts in Philadelphia (Fifth Judicial District of Pennsylvania, County of Allegheny, 2013).

Generally, litigants who do not prevail at the Court of Common Pleas may appeal the decisions. Such appeals may be taken to the Pennsylvania Superior Court or to the Pennsylvania Commonwealth Court, depending on the subject matter.

Magisterial District Courts

Magisterial District Courts are commonly called the "peoples' courts." These courts are authorized in Title 42 of Purdon's Pennsylvania Statutes, Sections 1511–1523. The Pennsylvania legislature (General Assembly) establishes each magisterial district based on population. Changes to the number and/or boundaries of judicial districts can be made by the General Assembly, but only with the advice and consent of the Pennsylvania Supreme Court (Pa. Constitution Article V, Section 11).

There are approximately 550 Magisterial District Courts in the Commonwealth of Pennsylvania. The President Judge of the Court of Common Pleas has supervisory and administrative authority over all of the Magisterial District Courts in the judicial district (The Unified Judicial System of Pennsylvania, Learn, 2013).

Presiding over these Courts are Magisterial District Judges who are elected by the voters of the jurisdiction to six-year terms and are employees of the Commonwealth of Pennsylvania. Magisterial District Judges must be citizens of the United States, residents of the district in which they hold office, and at least twenty-one years of age. They need not have law degrees to qualify for the position. Article V, Section 12 of the Pennsylvania Constitution requires that those without law degrees, however, attend and pass a four-week course administered by the Minor Judiciary Education Board (MJEB) at the Pennsylvania Judicial Center in Harrisburg. The Board is responsible for the creation of the curriculum, qualifying instructors, reviewing examinations and issuing final certificates to successful attendees. Magisterial District Judges are the only elected officials in Pennsylvania who have to pass an exam before taking office. The course includes criminal law, criminal procedure, civil procedure, ethics, vehicle laws, fishing and boating laws, game commission regulations, dog laws, and the Pennsylvania Rules of Judicial Conduct. In addition to this training, all newly elected magisterial district judges, including lawyers, must take a one-week course before assuming office. Magisterial District Judges must also attend 32 hours of continuing education each year in order to retain office (The Unified Judicial System of Pennsylvania, Minor Judiciary Education Board, 2013).

Magisterial District Courts conduct non-jury hearings involving civil cases in which the amount in controversy does not exceed $12,000. They also hear landlord-tenant disputes. In the criminal arena, these courts conduct non-jury hearings involving summary offenses and traffic offenses, and hold preliminary hearings in more serious criminal cases. In addition, Magisterial District Judges review and approve arrest and search warrants, hold informal arraignments at which bail is set, provide emergency relief under the Older Adult Protective Services Act and Protection From Abuse Act and perform marriage ceremonies. Defendants have no right to a jury trial in Magisterial District Courts, but can appeal a conviction or judgment to the Court of Common Pleas. Defendants may avail themselves of their right to a jury trial in the Court of Common Pleas in non-summary criminal offenses and most civil matters (The Unified Judicial System of Pennsylvania, Minor Courts, 2013).

Philadelphia is the only Pennsylvania county that does not have a Magisterial District Court System. Until recently, it had two minor courts: the Philadelphia Municipal Court and the Philadelphia Traffic Court. Judges in the Philadelphia Municipal Court must be lawyers. The Philadelphia Municipal Court handles matters similar to the other Magisterial District Courts in Pennsylvania.

The Philadelphia Traffic Court had suffered multiple scandals over the past decade. In the spring of 2013, federal authorities arrested nine judges of the court for crimes including ticket-fixing. On June 12, 2013, the Pennsylvania Senate passed a bill disbanding the Philadelphia Traffic Court and reassigning the duties of that court to a division of the Philadelphia Municipal Court (Worden, 2013). Governor Tom Corbett signed the bill on June 19, 2013 (Associated Press, 2013). Because the Philadelphia Traffic Court was established in the Pennsylvania Constitution, the state legislature has approved legislation to change the document. If subsequently approved by the voters, the state Constitution will be amended to remove language authorizing the Philadelphia Traffic Court.

The Pittsburgh Municipal Court replaced the Pittsburgh Magistrate Courts by Order of the Pennsylvania Supreme Court of November 29, 2004. Housing, Criminal, and Traffic Courts are subdivisions of the Pittsburgh Municipal Court. The Pittsburgh Municipal Court handles similar matters as the Magisterial District Courts throughout the Commonwealth.

These courts, collectively, are sometimes referred to as the "minor judiciary" in Pennsylvania. Thus the "minor judiciary" would include the Magisterial District Courts, the Philadelphia Municipal Court, and the Pittsburgh Municipal Court. These courts are among the busiest courts in the nation, hearing more than two million cases per year (The Judicial Branch: Pennsylvania's Unified Judicial System, 2013).

Juvenile Courts

As described later in Chapter 8, Pennsylvania has a separate criminal court system for children. Individuals from the age of ten to the age of seventeen who are charged with a crime enter the juvenile justice system, not the adult

Figure 5.3 Pennsylvania Courts

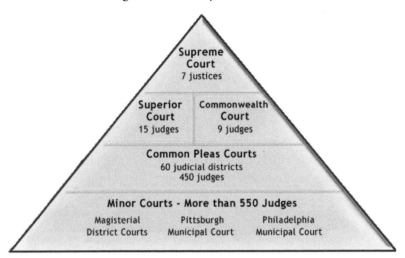

Adapted from: http://www.libraries.psu.edu/psul/researchguides/socialsciences/pacourts.html

criminal justice system. There are occasions when a child within that age group has committed a very serious crime. Under those circumstances, the child may be charged as an adult and processed in the adult criminal justice system; alternatively, the juvenile court judge may hold a hearing to determine whether the case should be transferred to adult criminal court. For more about juvenile courts see Chapter 8.

Specialty Courts

Some jurisdictions in Pennsylvania have created specialty courts, also called problem-solving courts, to address particular issues. The first such court in Pennsylvania was an adult drug court begun in 1997 in Philadelphia. Shortly thereafter, similar courts were initiated in Chester, York, and Lycoming Counties. Eighteen counties now have adult drug courts; six counties have juvenile drug courts; two counties have family drug courts. The goals of these courts are to more effectively rehabilitate individuals who are suffering from addiction to drugs and/or alcohol. Candidates for these courts are carefully screened in advance. Instead of sentences of incarceration, defendants are provided treatment, counseling, education and needed healthcare. Each case is carefully monitored by the judge to determine the success of the prescribed treatments and the progress being made by the defendant (Problem-Solving Courts, 2012).

Other specialty courts have been created to address other issues. Seven counties now have mental health courts; eight counties have DUI (driving under the influence) or underage drinking courts; six counties have veterans' courts. These courts are given leeway to experiment with various kinds of sentences and treatment modalities with the goals of successful rehabilitation of offenders and a reduction in recidivism.

These specialty courts contribute to the advancement and quality of the criminal justice system in several ways. First, these alternative treatments reduce the population of the state's correctional facilities, thereby reducing prison overcrowding. Second, they have been shown to reduce the rate of recidivism for targeted populations of offenders. In addition, these courts permit individualized attention to defendants who are motivated to turn away from criminal and addictive behavior. Lives are changed for the better by these non-traditional and individualized approaches (Problem-Solving Courts, 2012).

Attorneys in Pennsylvania Courts

Pennsylvania Attorney General

The Pennsylvania Attorney General is the chief law enforcement officer of the state, and charged with ensuring the safety of the citizens of the Commonwealth. The Pennsylvania Attorney General was originally an appointed position, the governor having the authority to select the state Attorney General. A 1980 amendment to the state Constitution authorized the election of the state Attorney General. Since then, the Pennsylvania Attorney General has been elected by the voters of the Commonwealth (Pennsylvania Constitution, Article IV, Section 4). To minimally qualify for the office, the candidate must be at least thirty years of age, an inhabitant of the Commonwealth for at least seven years, and a member of the bar of the Supreme Court of Pennsylvania. Should an Attorney General fail to complete his or her four-year term, the Governor nominates a replacement to complete the remainder of the term. The nominee must be approved by two-thirds of the Pennsylvania Senate (Pennsylvania Attorney General, 2013).

The Commonwealth Attorneys Act lists the primary responsibilities of the Pennsylvania Attorney General. Those duties and responsibilities include:

- The investigation and prosecution of organized crime, public corruption, fraud and other crimes against the citizens of the Commonwealth of Pennsylvania;
- The collection of debts and taxes owed to the Commonwealth;

- The representation in court of the Commonwealth and its agencies in legal matters brought against them;
- The administration of consumer protection laws;
- The review of the legality of proposed rules and regulations promulgated by Commonwealth agencies, as well as deeds, leases, and other state-related contracts.

The Criminal Law Division is the largest section within the Office of the Attorney General. This Division investigates and prosecutes a wide variety of crimes. These include public corruption, organized crime, Internet child pornography and related crimes, drug trafficking, gun violence, environmental crimes, tax crimes, insurance fraud, and Medicaid fraud. In addition, this Division often handles cases referred by county District Attorneys.

The Office also emphasizes crime prevention and offers educational programs to citizens of the state. "Operation Safe Surf" is an internet safety program for schools, parents, and children. "Think Again" is an educational program that informs citizen of the dangers of gun violence and the effects of straw purchasers. "Truth & Choices" is a drug and alcohol abuse education program designed for teenagers.

To fulfill the Attorney General's charge to protect consumers, several divisions have been created. The Bureau of Consumer Protection accepts complaints regarding a variety of consumer-related issues such as substandard construction work, violations of Pennsylvania's Do Not Call law, and fraudulent advertising. The Bureau receives more than 50,000 consumer complaints each year. Other divisions include the Health Care Section which protects consumers from unfair health care practices, the Antitrust Section which addresses unfair business practices, the Charitable Trusts & Organizations Section which ensures that charitable donations are not misused or misappropriated, the Tobacco Enforcement Section which ensures that tobacco companies are complying with the law, and the Civil Rights Enforcement Section which investigates alleged civil rights violations. In addition, the Office of Consumer Advocate acts an independent division addressing consumer interests in matters involving public utilities (Pennsylvania Attorney General, 2013).

District Attorneys

Each of Pennsylvania's sixty-seven counties has a District Attorney's Office. These Offices are charged with the prosecution of crimes that have occurred within their respective counties. The District Attorney is elected by the voters of the county to a four-year term, and hires Assistant District Attorneys to carry the prosecutorial caseload. Common divisions within this Office include: pretrial unit, trial unit, and the appeals unit. These prosecutors are sworn to uphold the state and federal constitutions and to seek justice. They must seek not only to provide justice to victims of crime, but to prevent wrongful convictions of innocent defendants. In doing so, prosecutors rely on an attendant investigative unit whose detectives work for the District Attorney. These detectives have county-wide jurisdiction, and investigate misdemeanors, felonies, and murders that have taken place within that jurisdiction. Many offices also have a Victim Services unit that addresses issues unique to those who have been hurt by crime. These include special services to victims of domestic violence, information about victims' compensation funds and education about Pennsylvania's Victims' Bill of Rights.

Public Defenders

The right to counsel in criminal proceedings is fundamental to both the Pennsylvania constitution and to the United States Constitution. Article I Section 9 of the Pennsylvania Constitution provides:

> In all criminal prosecutions, the accused hath a right to be heard by himself and his counsel....

Amendment VI of the United States constitution provides that:

> In all criminal prosecutions, the accused shall ... have the right to the assistance of counsel for his defence.

This essential right was interpreted by the United States Supreme Court in the 1932 case of *Powell v. Alabama* to mean that indigents had the right to free counsel in capital cases. In 1938 the High Court held, in *Johnson v. Zerbst*, that indigents in federal criminal courts enjoyed the right to free counsel. Finally, in 1963 the United States Supreme Court extended the right to free counsel for indigent defendants to state courts as well. A unanimous court in the now famous case of *Gideon v. Wainwright* held that:

> ... lawyers in criminal courts are necessities, not luxuries. The right of one charged with crime to counsel may not be deemed fundamental and essential to fair trials in some countries, but it is in ours (at 344).

Largely as a result of that single United States Supreme Court case, state public defenders' offices were born.

In Pennsylvania specifically, the legislature responded by enacting the Public Defender Act in 1968. This act required all counties in Pennsylvania (with the exception of Philadelphia) to create and fund the office of Public Defender. It also specified the duties of the office. The Public Defender's primary responsibility is to provide legal representation to indigent individuals accused of a crime in Pennsylvania whenever that person's liberty is at risk. This includes the representation of both adults and juveniles accused of capital crimes, misdemeanor and felony offenses, and summary offenses that carry a mandatory sentence of incarceration, and those subject to commitment proceedings under the Mental Health Procedures Act.

The Public Defender Act requires that the Public Defender and Assistant Public Defenders be attorneys admitted to practice before the Supreme Court of Pennsylvania. The Public Defender is appointed by the County Commissioners and the Office is funded by the County Commissioners.

The Defender Association of Philadelphia was created as an independent non-profit corporation in 1934, significantly predating the United States Supreme Court's decision in Gideon. A Board of Directors governs the Association. This Board is composed of representatives of city government, the bar association and the community. The Board appoints both the Chief Defender and the First Assistant, and determines policies and procedures for the Association. While the Board is an independent one, most of the funding for the Association is derived through a contract with the City of Philadelphia to provide legal representation to indigents in criminal proceedings (Defender Association of Philadelphia, 2013).

Judges in Pennsylvania

In the Commonwealth of Pennsylvania, judges of the Pennsylvania Supreme Court, the Pennsylvania Superior Court, the Pennsylvania Commonwealth Court, and the sixty Courts of Common Pleas are elected by the citizens. Elections occur in odd-numbered years. Candidates for judgeships are normally endorsed by the Democratic or Republican Party in the state and run in primary elections to win a spot on the final ballot. After winning the position in the general election, judges serve a ten-year term.

At the end of that ten-year term, judges may seek another term by virtue of a "retention election." These judges do not run in the spring primary elections, but run only in the November general election. In a retention election, the jurist is not affiliated with a particular political party. In fact, no party affiliation is indicated on the ballot. Voters merely indicate approval or non-approval of the jurist seeking to retain his or her position on the bench. If a majority of the voters "approve," the jurist wins another ten-year term.

Pennsylvanians have chosen retention elections of jurists to reduce partisanship in this most important endeavor. Judges are not required to campaign against an opponent, nor are they forced to engage in political fundraising. As neutral arbiters of law, judges are supposed to be nonpartisan and objective. Therefore, this retention election process is a means by which to hold judges accountable to the citizens of the state. The Judicial Evaluation Commission of the Pennsylvania Bar Association will review the jurist's qualifications, performance, and temperament and make a public statement that the jurist is either "recommended" or "not recommended" for retention. Some county bar associations will also provide guidance to voters on jurists running for retention in the Court of Common Pleas in their jurisdictions. There is no limit to the number of terms to which a jurist may be elected. However, Pennsylvania has a mandatory retirement age of 70 for its judges. After the age of 70, judges may be asked to serve as "senior judges" for a limited time.

Judges of the Philadelphia Municipal Court are elected to six-year terms by the voters of the jurisdiction. At the end of their six-year terms, judges of these courts who seek another term must run in a "retention election" similar to the judges of the higher courts in the state. Magisterial district judges are also elected to six-year terms by the voters of their jurisdictions. However, at the end of their six-year terms, they must run for re-election in the November general election, perhaps against an opposing candidate (The Unified Judicial System of Pennsylvania, Judicial Elections and Retention, 2012).

According to Article VI, Section 3 of the Pennsylvania Constitution, upon election or appointment to the judiciary and before taking office, judges must take the following oath or affirmation:

> I do solemnly swear (or affirm) that I will support, obey and defend the Constitution of the United States and the Constitution of this Commonwealth and that I will discharge the duties of my office with fidelity.

This is similar to the oath of office taken by members of the federal judiciary.

Judges in Pennsylvania are held to high standards of conduct. The Pennsylvania Code of Judicial Conduct in the Pennsylvania Rules of Court (applicable to appellate and trial judges) is modeled after the American Bar Association 1972 Model Code of Judicial Conduct. The Rules of Conduct, Office of Standards, and Civil Procedures for Magisterial District Judges delineate the rules and standards of behavior for those judges serving in the minor judiciary.

Investigations of alleged misconduct by judges in Pennsylvania are conducted by the Judicial Conduct Board. The Board is composed of twelve Pennsylvania citizens: three judges, three attorneys and six non-attorneys. Six members of the Board are chosen by the Governor; six are chosen by the Pennsylvania Supreme Court. Members are appointed to four-year terms and serve without remuneration. The Board members are tasked to accept, review, and investigate allegations of judicial misconduct. The Board will generally accept complaints about misconduct that is alleged to have occurred within the prior four years. Complainants may be anonymous, although that anonymity makes the Board's investigation more difficult. Complaints alleging legal error in a judge's decision will not be accepted. The kinds of complaints the Board will accept for review include allegations of physical or mental disability that render the judge incapable of performing the duties of the position and allegations of ethical misconduct. Ethical misconduct can include a wide variety of unprofessional or improper behavior, including criminal activity. Examples include: negligence or failure to perform the duties of the office; accepting a bribe or item of value in return for a particular ruling; extreme delay in deciding a case; engaging in profane, vulgar, or disrespectful behavior on the bench; sexual harassment; or intoxication in court (Judicial Conduct Board of Pennsylvania, 2013).

The Board's decision to dismiss a complaint is final and cannot be appealed. If the Board determines by clear and convincing evidence that the complaint has merit, the matter is referred to the Court of Judicial Discipline. This Court is composed of four judges, two lawyers, and two non-lawyers. Half of the members are chosen by the Governor, the other half by the Pennsylvania Supreme Court.

The Court of Judicial Discipline then holds a hearing on the allegations. These hearings are open to the public. If the Court finds that the allegations have been proven by "clear and convincing evidence," it may impose sanctions on that judge. Judges who are found to be in breach of ethical standards may be reprimanded, suspended for a period of time with or without pay, or permanently removed from the bench. A judge found to be in violation of the state's codes of conduct may appeal the Court's decision to the Pennsylvania Supreme Court. The Pennsylvania Supreme Court may review only legal rulings on the matter, and may not revisit the factual findings of the Court of Judicial Discipline. If the jurist disciplined is a member of the Pennsylvania Supreme Court, the jurist's appeal is heard by a special tribunal of seven judges of the Pennsylvania Superior Court and the Pennsylvania Commonwealth Court (Judicial Conduct Board of Pennsylvania, 2013).

This process is not to be confused with impeachment. Article VI of the Pennsylvania Constitution provides that state civil officers (including judges) may be impeached "for any misbehavior in office." The Pennsylvania House of

Representatives has the sole power of impeachment. (Impeachment merely means the bringing of charges against a civil officer.) The Pennsylvania Senate then conducts a trial on the articles of impeachment. Two-thirds of the members of the Senate must vote to convict. If that occurs, the judge is then removed from office and rendered ineligible to hold an office of trust or profit in the Commonwealth.

Even so, Pennsylvania was recently rocked by a terrible scandal involving two judges of the Court of Common Pleas of Luzerne County. On February 18, 2011, Judge Michael Ciavarella was convicted by a federal jury of twelve counts of federal criminal activity, including racketeering. The jury found that he had illegally taken payments of nearly one million dollars from a private builder of a local juvenile detention facility. In turn, the judge had improperly sentenced scores of juveniles to the facility for minor offenses. This scheme, dubbed "cash for kids," devastated the lives of many children. He was sentenced to twenty-eight years in prison. Judge Michael Conahan pled guilty in federal court to racketeering and conspiracy in connection with this scheme. He was sentenced to seventeen and one-half years in federal prison (Associated Press, 2011).

Investigation into the scandal was initiated by the Pennsylvania Juvenile Law Center. Founded in 1975, the Center boasts that it is the "oldest non-profit public interest law firm for children in the United States." It is a nationwide advocate for the rights of children who come into contact with the juvenile justice system or child welfare agencies. The Center filed federal class action lawsuits on behalf of the children and parents who suffered physical, psychological, and/or financial injuries as a result of this corruption. The suits seek monetary damages from the former judges, the former owners of the facilities, the developer, and the facilities themselves (Juvenile Law Center, Luzerne Kids-for-Cash Scandal, 2013). An agreement by the builder of one of the private juvenile detention facilities to pay seventeen million, seven hundred and fifty thousand dollars in settlement of the suit against him was approved by United States District Judge for the Middle District of Pennsylvania, A. Richard Caputo, in December of 2012 (Needles, 2012). In October of 2012, the book *Kids for Cash: Two Judges, Thousands of Children, and a $2.8 Million Kickback Scheme* by William Ecenbarger was published documenting these events.

Juries in Pennsylvania

In early England, the accused was tried by a jury of witnesses. Individuals who allegedly observed the crime testified against the defendant. Those same witnesses then determined the verdict. With the Magna Carta of 1215, the system evolved to require impartial jurors. That document provided that:

> no free man shall be taken or imprisoned or outlawed or exiled or in anywise destroyed, save by the lawful judgment of his peers.

Juries have responsibilities that are distinct from those of the judge. In our judicial system, the judge is the "arbiter of law." The primary responsibilities of the arbiter of law include determining what law applies in the case, interpreting that law, and determining the admissibility of evidence. The jury is the "trier of fact" in a jury trial. The primary responsibilities of the trier of fact are to determine the credibility of witnesses, to determine the weight of the evidence, and to render the verdict in a criminal case, or the judgment in a civil case. In a non-jury trial (also referred to as a bench trial), the judge is both the arbiter of law and the trier of fact.

Defendants in Pennsylvania have the right to a jury trial when charged with any offense that may lead to incarceration, including a summary offense. Originally, the defendant had the sole right to decide to be tried by a jury or a judge. But in 1998, the state Constitution was amended to provide the Commonwealth with the right to a jury trial as well. Generally, however, the defendant may choose the size of the jury. He or she may choose as few as six jurors or as many as twelve jurors. Regardless of the size of the jury in criminal trials, the verdict, whether "guilty" or "not guilty," must be unanimous. That is, all of the jurors must vote to convict or to acquit.

Conclusion

Pennsylvania has a rich historical record of the protection of citizens' fundamental rights. The state's first constitution was adopted in September of 1776 and included a Declaration of Rights that not only established strong protections for citizens from an oppressive government, but provided a template for the writing of the United States Constitution in 1787 and the ensuing Bill of Rights of 1791. This Declaration of Rights has been re-established in each of the four ensuing major revisions of the state constitution.

The protections ensured to the people include access to the court system, to public trials where the public and the press can judge the fairness of the proceedings for themselves and the right to counsel (and later to free counsel for indigents) for those accused of crime. To reduce political partisanship and promote neutrality and objectivity, Pennsylvania judges are elected by the citizens and then held accountable to the voters through periodic retention elections. Pennsylvania was one of the first states to adopt specialty courts to address specific issues of classes of defendants and has used innovative and creative treatment modalities to reduce prison populations, reduce recidivism and help troubled defendants lead law-abiding lives. Pennsylvania's history, its contributions to both the federal and sister state constitutions, and its evolution as a contemporary and innovative justice system are sources of great pride for its citizens.

Key Terms and Definitions

Administrative Office of Pennsylvania Courts: Led by the Court Administrator, this office bears responsibility for the supervision and management of all of Pennsylvania's courts.

Attorney General of the Commonwealth of Pennsylvania: The chief law enforcement officer of the Commonwealth of Pennsylvania elected by the voters and charged with the investigation and prosecution of organized crime and public corruption and other crimes.

Court Administrator: Appointed by the Pennsylvania Supreme Court, the Court Administrator is responsible for the efficient and proper handling of the business of all Pennsylvania Courts and leads the Administrative Office of the Pennsylvania Courts.

Courts of Common Pleas: The primary trial courts located in each county.

Declaration of Rights: Article I of the Pennsylvania Constitution which delineates the fundamental rights retained by the people.

District Attorneys: Prosecuting attorneys who handle criminal cases in the Court of Common Pleas.

Magisterial District Courts: Minor courts in Pennsylvania that hear summary criminal offenses, preliminary hearings, bail hearings, informal arraignments, and some civil matters.

Municipal Courts: Philadelphia and Pittsburgh minor courts.

Pennsylvania Commonwealth Court: An intermediate appellate court that hears appeals from rulings of state agencies and regulatory board as well as disputes between agencies.

Pennsylvania Constitution: The state's founding legal document and the supreme law of the state; all state laws must comport with the Pennsylvania Constitution, initially adopted in 1776.

Pennsylvania Superior Court: The state's intermediate appellate court.

Public Defenders: Criminal defense attorneys who are paid by the county supervisors to represent indigent defendants.

Pennsylvania Supreme Court: The highest court in the state; considered a court of last resort, and the final arbiter of the interpretation of the Pennsylvania Constitution and state statutes.

Retention elections: Elections where judges are simply approved or disapproved; these judges do not run against an opponent, nor are they affiliated with a political party.

United States Constitution: The founding document of the United States and the supreme law of the nation. No state of federal law may contravene the provisions of the United States Constitution.

United States Supreme Court: The highest court in the United States. It is a court of last resort, from which there is no appeal.

Websites

Constitution of the Commonwealth of Pennsylvania of 1874, as amended. Retrieved from: http://www.pahouse.com/pa_const.htm.
Pennsylvania Attorney General. (2013). Retrieved from: http://www.attorney general.gov/.
Problem-Solving Courts. (2012). Retrieved from: http://www.pacourts.us/assets/files/setting-2236/file-1748.pdf?cb=be888a.
The Judicial Branch: Pennsylvania's Unified Judicial System (2013). Retrieved from: http://www.palawhelp.org/resource/the-judicial-branch-pennyslvanias-unified-jud.
The Unified Judicial System of Pennsylvania. Commonwealth Court of Pennsylvania. (2013). Retrieved from: http://www.pacourts.us/courts/common wealth-court/.

Review Questions

1. What is the "unified judicial system" of Pennsylvania? When was it established and how is it organized?
2. What are the various responsibilities of the county District Attorneys and the Pennsylvania Attorney General? How are the responsibilities of the county District Attorneys different from the responsibilities of the Pennsylvania Attorney General in terms of geographical and subject matter authority?

3. How are courts of original jurisdiction different from courts of appellate jurisdiction? Which federal courts are courts of original jurisdiction? Which federal courts are courts of appellate jurisdiction? Which state courts are courts of original jurisdiction? Which state courts are courts of appellate jurisdiction?
4. What are "specialty courts"? How do they address specific problems in the criminal justice system?

Critical Thinking Questions

1. In some states judges are appointed; in others, judges are elected. Discuss the strengths and weakness of having judges appointed to their positions. Discuss the strengths and weakness of having judges elected to their positions.
2. In Pennsylvania, judges preserve their positions through "retention elections." Discuss the value of retention elections as a means to ensure judicial integrity. What are the weaknesses of the "retention election" system?
3. Pennsylvania has recently suffered embarrassing judicial scandals in the Court of Common Pleas in Luzerne County and in the Philadelphia Traffic Court. How were the Luzerne County judges able to get away with their criminal conduct for so long? Why did the Pennsylvania disciplinary system fail? Why was the Philadelphia Traffic Court particularly susceptible to corruption? How will the elimination of the Philadelphia Traffic Court and the transfer of its responsibilities to the Philadelphia Municipal Court reduce the changes of future corruption?
4. In some states, the state Attorney General is appointed by the Governor. In Pennsylvania, the state Attorney General is elected separately by the voters. What are the advantages and disadvantages of having an independent state Attorney General?

References

Associated Press. (September 24, 2011). Crooked judge gets 17.5 yrs. Retrieved from: http://articles.philly.com/2011-09-24/news/30198318_1_ciavarella-conahan-william-d-elia.

Associated Press. (June 12, 2013). Pa. Senate votes to abolish Philadelphia Traffic Court. Retrieved from: http://abclocal.go.com/wpvi/story?section=news/local&id=9135908.

Commonwealth Attorney's Act, 71 Pa. C.S.A. §732-101 (2009).

Constitution of the Commonwealth of Pennsylvania of 1776. Pennsylvania Historical & Museum Commission. Retrieved from: http://www.portal.state.pa.us/portal/server.pt/community/documents_from_1776_-_1865/20424/pa_constitution_of_1776/998585.

Constitution of the Commonwealth of Pennsylvania of 1874, as amended. Retrieved from: http://www.pahouse.com/pa_const.htm.

Criminal Justice Act of 1964, 18 U.S.C. §3006A.

Defender Association of Philadelphia. (2013). Retrieved from: http://www.philadefender.org/.

Ecenbarger, William (2012) *Kids for Cash: Two Judges, Thousands of Children, and a $2.8 Million Kickback Scheme,* New York: The New Press.

Fifth Judicial District of Pennsylvania, County of Allegheny. (2013). Retrieved from: http://www.alleghenycourts.us/Home/Default.aspx.

Gideon v. Wainwright, 372 U.S. 335 (1963)

Johnson v. Zerbst, 304 U.S. 458 (1938)

Judicial Conduct Board of Pennsylvania. Rules Governing Standards of Conduct of Magisterial District Judges. (2013). Retrieved from: http://judicialconductboardofpa.org/legislation/rules-governing-standards-of-conduct-of-magisterial-district-jud/.

Judiciary Act of 1789, U.S.C.A. Const. Art. III, §1.

Judiciary and Judicial Procedure, 42 Pa.C.S.A. §§101–1523 (1976).

Juvenile Law Center. Luzerne Kids-for-Cash Scandal. (2013). Retrieved from: http://www.jlc.org/current-initiatives/promoting-fairness-courts/luzerne-kids-cash scandal.

Needles, Zach (2012, December 26). "Fed. Judge Approves $17.75 Mil 'Kids for Cash' Settlement" *Legal Intelligencer.* Retrieved from: http://www.law.com/jsp/pa/PubArticlePA.jsp?id=1202428035822&slreturn=20130505231411.

Pennsylvania Attorney General. (2013). Retrieved from: http://www.attorneygeneral.gov/.

Pennsylvania Code of Judicial Conduct, 42 Pa.C.S.A. §3301 (2005).

Pennsylvania's Constitution: A Brief History. Pennsylvania Bar Association, Constitutional Review Commission. Retrieved from: http://www.pabarcrc.org/history.asp.

Pennsylvania Crime and Victims Act, 18 Pa. C.S.A. §11.101 (2009).

Pennsylvania General Assembly. Pennsylvania Constitution. (2013). Retrieved from: http://www.legis.state.pa.us/wu01/vc/visitor_info/creating/constitution.cfm.

Powell v. Alabama, 287 U.S. 45 (1932)

Problem-Solving Courts. (2012). Retrieved from: http://www.pacourts.us/assets/files/setting-2236/file-1748.pdf?cb=be888a.

Public Defender Act, 16 Pa.C.S.A. § 9960 (1968).

The Judicial Branch: Pennsylvania's Unified Judicial System (2013). Retrieved from: http://www.palawhelp.org/resource/the-judicial-branch-pennyslvanias-unified-jud.

The Magna Carta of Edward 1 (1297), 25 Edw. 1.

The Philadelphia Courts. Family Division. (2013). Retrieved from: http://www.courts.phila.gov/common-pleas/family/.

The Philadelphia Courts. Orphans' Division. (2013). Retrieved from: http://courts.phila.gov/common-pleas/orphans/.

The Unified Judicial System of Pennsylvania. Commonwealth Court of Pennsylvania. (2013). Retrieved from: http://www.pacourts.us/courts/commonwealth-court/.

The Unified Judicial System of Pennsylvania. History. (2013). Retrieved from: http://www.pacourts.us/learn/history.

The Unified Judicial System of Pennsylvania. Judicial Administration. (2013). Retrieved from: http://www.pacourts.us/judicial-administration/.

The Unified Judicial System of Pennsylvania. Judicial Elections and Retention. (2012). Retrieved from: http://www.pacourts.us/assets/files/setting-2236/file-1750.pdf?cb=828fcf.

The Unified Judicial System of Pennsylvania. Learn. (2013). Retrieved from: http://www.pacourts.us/learn?q=supreme.

The Unified Judicial System of Pennsylvania. Learn. How Judges are Elected. (2013). Retrieved from: http://www.pacourts.us/learn/how-judges-are-elected.

The Unified Judicial System of Pennsylvania. Minor Courts. (2013). Retrieved from: http://www.pacourts.us/courts/minor-courts/.

The Unified Judicial System of Pennsylvania. Minor Judiciary Education Board. (2013). Retrieved from: http://www.pacourts.us/courts/supreme-court/committees/supreme-court-boards/minor-judiciary-education-board.

The Unified Judicial System of Pennsylvania. Pennsylvania Courts of Common Pleas. (2013). Retrieved from: http://www.pacourts.us/courts/courts-of-common-pleas/.

The Unified Judicial System of Pennsylvania. The Superior Court of Pennsylvania. (2013). Retrieved from: http://www.pacourts.us/courts/superior-court/.

The Unified Judicial System of Pennsylvania. Supreme Court of Pennsylvania. (2013). Retrieved from: http://www.pacourts.us/courts/supreme-court/.

Worden, Amy. (2013, June 12). Senate votes to abolish Phila. Traffic Court. *Philadelphia Inquirer*. Retrieved from: http://articles.philly.com/2013-06-12/news/39927841_1_philadelphia-traffic-court-municipal-court-president-judge.

Chapter 6

The Corrections System in Pennsylvania

John T. Conlon and Harry R. Dammer

Learning Objectives

After reading this chapter, students will be able to:

- Define the various components of the federal correctional system in Pennsylvania.
- Describe the role that Pennsylvania had in the development of corrections in America.
- Summarize the current size and scope of the Pennsylvania state correctional system.
- Explain the classification process for criminal offenders in Pennsylvania.
- Describe the role of county jails in Pennsylvania.
- Explain the most prominent kinds of community-based correctional programs utilized in Pennsylvania.
- Summarize the recent correctional programs developed to reduce system crowding and recidivism in Pennsylvania.

Key Terms

Augustus, John

Boot Camp

Classification

Community-based corrections

Community corrections centers

County parole

Determinate sentence
Electronic monitoring
Federal Bureau of Prisons
Good time
Indeterminate sentence
Intermediate punishments (sanctions)
Jail
Maximum sentence
Minimum sentence
New generation jails
New York (Auburn) system
Parole
Penitentiary
Pennsylvania system of prison management (also called the Separate system)
Prison
Probation
Recidivism Risk Reduction Incentive (RRRI)
Special conditions of probation/parole
Standard conditions of probation/parole
State parole
Supervised release
Walnut Street Jail

Introduction

As in the areas of police and courts, corrections exists on the federal, state, and local levels. At each of these levels, there are three main components of corrections—prisons, jails, and community-based corrections. Jails generally are facilities authorized to hold pretrial detainees, those awaiting transfer to other institutions, and offenders serving sentences for misdemeanors. In recent years, especially in state systems where prison crowding is a major problem, jails have begun to house more serious felons, such as drug offenders. Prisons are institutions that house offenders convicted of serious crimes, generally felons and those sentenced to serve more than one year of incarceration. Community corrections, also called community-based corrections, can be defined as non-incarcerative programs for offenders who remain within the community while serving their sentences usually under some form of supervision. Over two-thirds of all local, state, and federal offenders are supervised in the community rather than in jail or prison. This chapter will discuss each of these three main components of corrections as they relate to the Commonwealth of Pennsylvania. First, we will discuss the role that the federal correctional system plays within the state boundaries of Pennsylvania.

Federal Corrections

The Federal Bureau of Prisons

The Federal Bureau of Prisons (BOP) was established in 1930 to provide for the care and custody of offenders who committed federal offenses. The crimes over which the federal criminal law has formal jurisdiction are limited to those involving interstate commerce, serious felonies involving federal employees, crimes committed across state lines, and crimes perpetrated on federal property. Most typically, federal prisons house offenders who have committed bank robbery, white collar crimes, and drug offenses. In fact, drug offenders make up over 50% of all federal inmates (Federal Bureau of Prisons, 2013).

Within the facilities operated by the BOP, there are five classifications or security levels: high, medium, low, minimum, and administrative. Security levels are based on such characteristics as the presence of external patrols, towers, security barriers, detection devices, type of housing within the institution, internal security features, and the staff-to-inmate ratios. Most federal offenders are placed in low to minimum security settings. The BOP operates three main types of facilities: penitentiaries, correctional institutions, and prison camps. Penitentiaries are high security institutions with very secure perimeters and generally single or double cells. Federal Correctional Institutions (FCIs) make up the majority of the federal corrections system and they house the majority of inmates. FCIs are either low or medium security. Prison camps are always minimum security institutions with few restrictions on the freedom of inmates who live in dormitory style housing. These smaller facilities (housing 150–300 inmates) provide inmate labor to the main prison and to off-site work-programs. In addition, the BOP utilizes detention centers (FDCs) for pretrial detainees (jails) and those awaiting transfer, centers for inmates with chronic or serious medical conditions, a classification center, and institutions run by private companies.

Changes in federal antidrug policies, the abolishment of federal parole, the establishment of sentencing guidelines, and mandatory sentencing have led to a significant increase in the number of offenders in federal prisons since the 1980s. Only one BOP institution in Hazelton, WV, is responsible for the secure confinement of women.

The BOP currently (as of November 2013) includes 119 institutions and is responsible for housing approximately 219,005 inmates. Approximately 81 percent of these inmates are confined in Bureau-operated facilities, while the rest (29,700 +/−) are confined in the fifteen privately managed facilities or local jails. Included among those inmates in private institutions are nearly 100 juveniles.

Table 6.1 Federal Facilities that House Inmates in Pennsylvania

Facility	Type	Security Level	Population*
Allenwood	USP (U.S. Penitentiary)	High	1072
Allenwood	FCI (Federal Correctional Institution)	Low	1290
Allenwood	FCI	Medium	1345
Canaan	USP	High	1307
Lewisburg	USP	High	1199
Loretto	FCI	Low	1310
McKean	FCI	Medium	1168
Moshannon Valley	FCI (Private)	Low	1738
Schuylkill	FCI	Medium	1237
Philadelphia	FDC (Federal Detention Center)	High	1041

Source: Bureau of Prisons: Weekly Population Report, Northeast Region, 2013. Retrieved August 24, 2013 from www.bop.gov.
    * Excludes offenders in prison camps.

In total, those incarcerated in federal prisons number less than eleven percent of all persons locked up in the United States (Federal Bureau of Prisons, 2013).

Federal Correctional Facilities in Pennsylvania

In the state of Pennsylvania, the BOP operates ten different correctional facilities including one privately managed institution (CI Moshannon Valley). These facilities house approximately 11,000 inmates in three penitentiaries, six FCIs, and one federal detention center — each with between 1,000 and 1,500 inmates (see Table 6.1) (Federal Bureau of Prisons, 2013).

Federal Supervision in the Community

Probation, parole, and supervised release are three types of community-based supervision at the federal level. Probation, on both the state and federal levels, is generally defined as both an agency that supervises people in the community who are convicted but not sentenced to jail or prison, and a court-ordered sentence that allows an offender to remain in the community while on supervision with certain conditions including refraining from committing new crimes. If an offender violates the terms of supervision, the respective court has the authority to revoke probation and impose a period of incarceration. Parole, again on both the state and federal levels, is the conditional release of an offender from incarceration under supervision in the community after part of the prison sentence has been served. Parole and supervised release are different within the federal system of corrections as compared to the states.

Until 1984, the federal government utilized indeterminate sentencing whereby an inmate could obtain an early release via parole and it was determined and controlled by the Parole Commission. For decades, the decision to provide conditional release was made by a federal parole board. Critics were unhappy with the Parole Commission and judges wanted more control over offenders. After the Sentencing Reform Act of 1984 went into effect on November 1, 1987, the federal government abolished parole by a parole board and determinate sentences were implemented. Determinate sentences are those with a fixed period of incarceration imposed by the court. Offenders can receive 54 days of good time credit per year towards their sentence. Once released from prison or a halfway house, offenders are instructed to report within 24 hours to the District Office (probation) where they reside. They are placed on supervised release and the court has jurisdiction over them. All offenders sentenced to one year or longer in prison receive an additional sanction of supervised release. Supervised release is set by statute (U.S. Federal Criminal Code and Rules) depending upon the grade of offense. For offenders who have been sentenced to less than one year in prison, a period of supervised release is discretionary.

Supervised release on the Federal level in Pennsylvania is handled in three Federal Probation Departments located in the Eastern (Philadelphia), Middle (Scranton), and Western (Pittsburgh) parts of Pennsylvania, as well as satellite offices which are part of the Third Judicial Circuit. As is the case with correctional institutions, the number of offenders in the federal community-based system is substantially smaller than the county and state offices. At the end of 2012, a total of 4,613 federal offenders were under active post-conviction supervision in Pennsylvania (U.S. Courts, 2012).

The majority of offenders under community supervision are under one of three forms of federal supervision: 3,812 are on supervised release, 749 are on probation, and 43 are on parole. The latter low number is former inmates who committed an offense prior to 1987 when the indeterminate sentencing laws were changed. The majority of federal offenders on probation, supervised release, and parole are white, older males (median age of 39 years) who committed drug violations (Motivans, 2011).

In addition to the federal inmates who are under supervision in the community, the BOP also supports over 9,000 offenders in Residential Reentry Centers (RRCs) located across the United States. Between 300 and 400 of these offenders are in the RRCs within the Commonwealth of Pennsylvania. These centers, similar to halfway houses on the state level, provide assistance to inmates who are nearing release. RRCs provide a safe, structured, supervised environment, as well as employment counseling, job placement, financial management assistance, and other programs and services. RRCs help inmates gradually rebuild their ties to the community and facilitate supervising ex-offenders' activities during this readjustment phase. An important component of the RRC program is transitional drug abuse treatment for inmates who have completed residential drug abuse programs while confined in a BOP institution (Federal Bureau of Prisons, 2013).

United States' Corrections Today

It is well known that beginning in the late 1970s the Unites States experienced a tremendous increase in the incarceration population due to what is now referred to as the Retributive Era. Since that time, phrases, such as "the war on crime," "the war on drugs," and "get tough," became very popular especially when it appeared that rehabilitation and reintegration were ineffective in the fight against the rising crime rates of the 1970s and 1980s. The impact of the retribution era on the prison population was extraordinary. In 1980, the prison incarceration rate in the United States was 96 per 100,000 Americans. By 2008, after 35 years of steady growth, the rate ballooned to 506 per 100,000.

Today, there are almost 7 million offenders in the United States under the supervision of the adult correctional systems. Approximately 4 million offenders are on probation, 900,000 are on parole, and over 2 million are in jails and prisons. About 2.9 percent of adults in the United States (or 1 in every 34 adults) were under some form of correctional supervision at year end 2011 (Glaze & Parks, 2012). The United States corrections system now employs over seven thousand administrators, psychologists, correctional officers, and others. The federal government, the 50 states, over three thousand counties, and uncounted municipalities and townships, and public and private organizations administer corrections at an average cost of over $70 billion per year (Clear, et al., 2012). As a result, there is now a growing concern that the federal and state correctional systems have grown too much and that the cost of those systems has reached unsustainable levels. With budget deficits in most states, political leaders have become leery about investing in corrections when it appears that the return on the investment is minimal. This problem is nationwide and Pennsylvania is surely not immune to these same financial issues.

The Early History of Corrections in Pennsylvania

As has been well documented, Pennsylvania has contributed significantly to the early history of corrections not only in the United State, but around the world. In fact, the first and most important prison reform movements began in Philadelphia in the 1770s and continued for the next fifty years throughout the United States. However, the history of prisons in Pennsylvania actually began prior to the founding of the United States.

In 1682, William Penn was granted a charter by King Charles II of England which contained a tract of land in America which was to be called Pennsylvania. In the next year the laws of the local Duke of York were superseded by those adopted by Penn's first assembly. These laws, called the *Great Law* or the *Body of Laws of the province of Pennsylvania* were the first to separate the practices of the Quakers, and the Puritans in other American colonies, from those of the mother country. From that time until 1718 the Quakers of Pennsylvania developed a system of punishment that was opposed to the cruel physical punishments common at the time and eventually led to the substitution of corporal punishment for most crimes with imprisonment. In 1718, however, the Quaker laws were overridden by English (Anglican) and Puritan codes supported by the reign of George I (Barnes, 1968).

Prior to the outbreak of the Revolutionary War in 1776, a Quaker named Richard Wistar began to visit a local jail and was taken by the misery of the inmates. In 1773, a new institution called the Walnut Street Jail was opened and it soon became the main provincial jail of Philadelphia. The Walnut Street Jail was originally opened to house petty offenders and debtors and well as those awaiting trial or sentencing.

During this time period most of the severe punishment laws remained but when the American Revolution was complete in 1783, legal reformers in Philadelphia such as Benjamin Franklin, William Bradford, Benjamin Rush, and Robert Vaux helped change the ways criminals were punished. It should be noted that these reformers were also influenced by the Age of Enlightenment in Europe and the writings of philosophers like Montesquieu, Voltaire, Hume, and Jeremy Bentham. Another key figure during that time was English prison reformer John Howard whom many in Philadelphia admired for his views on prison administration. In 1790, a revision of the penal code called for substituting imprisonment for hard labor for the punishment of crimes, the separation of inmates by status and gender, and a new block of cells in the Walnut Street Jail for the solitary confinement of serious criminals.

These series of events eventually also led to the formation of the Philadelphia Society for Alleviating the Miseries of Public Prisons in 1787. Eventually the Society was responsible for convincing the Pennsylvania legislature in 1818 to build a penitentiary in Allegheny County and in 1821 to vote to build a state penitentiary in the County of Philadelphia. Each would utilize the Pennsylvania system of prison administration that called for solitary confinement with labor. Henceforth, the Pennsylvania system was also called the separate system. Pennsylvania opened Western Penitentiary in Pittsburgh in 1826, and in 1829 Eastern State Penitentiary at Cherry Hill, near Philadelphia, starting taking prisoners. The penitentiary was an institution originally intended to isolate prisoners from society and from one another in order to reflect on their crimes, repent, and undergo reformation (Clear, et al., 2012). The formation of the two penitentiaries in Pittsburgh and Philadelphia essentially began what was to be known around the world as the Pennsylvania System of prison administration. It should be noted that although many believe the term penitentiary originated in Pennsylvania, history tells us otherwise. The term "penitentiary" is credited to a Benedictine monk named Jean Mabillon who first coined the phrase in the seventeenth century.

Although well intended, the total isolation from others caused many inmates in the Pennsylvania System to go insane, suffer from other psychological problems, or commit suicide. Moreover, by design, the separate system was expensive to operate and ineffective. By the Civil War, most states, including Pennsylvania, abandoned the separate system for the New York (Auburn) system. In this new system, inmates were held in isolation at night, but worked with other prisoners during the day under the rule of total silence. Eastern State Penitentiary continued to operate until 1970. Today it is a national historic landmark and open for tours.

Pennsylvania's Correctional System

From 1953 until 1984, corrections in Pennsylvania were under the control of the Bureau of Corrections, except for a brief period (1980–1984) when the Office of General Counsel to the Governor held jurisdiction (Cohn, 2006). The state's prison system, accredited by the American Correctional Association (ACA), is currently operated by the Pennsylvania Department of Corrections (DOC), which was created in 1984 as a cabinet-level agency within the Commonwealth. The mission statement of the DOC is as follows:

> The Pennsylvania Department of Corrections operates as one team, embraces diversity, and commits to enhancing public safety. We are proud of our reputation as leaders in the corrections field. Our mission is to reduce criminal behavior by providing individualized treatment and education to offenders, resulting in successful community reintegration through accountability and positive change (Pennsylvania Department of Corrections, 2013a).

The 2013–14 fiscal year budget for the DOC was $1.94 billion, a slight increase from the '12–'13 budget of $1.87 billion and up from $1.24 billion in 2002 (Pennsylvania Office of the Budget, 2013). Over the last thirty years the Pennsylvania DOC budget grew 1,700% and is now the third largest department in the state budget. Much of the increase in the budget is tied to the drastic increase in the incarceration rate. Since 1980, the same time as the implementation of the "war on crime" that we discussed earlier, the prison population in the state has increase from 8,000 inmates to the current 51,000 inmates.

Correctional facilities differ in terms of inmate classification, operational management, size, and costs. The DOC is responsible for 26 state correctional institutions (SCI), 53 community corrections centers and private community corrections facilities, and one boot camp. The DOC employs nearly 15,000 employees and maintains custody over 51,000 inmates. The state's newest prison is the SCI Benner Township located in Bellefonte and was formally dedicated on April 1, 2013. Two other prisons, Phoenix East and West, are under construction while construction for a third in Fayette County (SCI German) was cancelled. The two facilities at Phoenix, as well as an adjacent small woman's transition facility, will eventually replace SCI Graterford which will be closed due to the costs of maintaining such a large and antiquated institution. Graterford was opened in 1929 to alleviate prison crowding at Eastern Penitentiary. Correctional facilities at Cresson and Greenburg were closed in 2012–2013. Two institutions, SCI Cambridge Springs and SCI Muncy, house female offenders.

Classification of Offenders

As in the Federal system and most states, inmates who are sentenced to incarceration undergo a process called classification. Classification is the proper assignment of inmates to specific institutions for custody and treatment based upon a review of objective criteria such as the length/type of sentence, nature of the crime, prior record in the criminal justice system, the medical (physical and mental) needs of the offender, history of violence, and past substance abuse patterns. Once completed (normally within 3–6 months), the inmate is assigned a security level (mentioned above) and is sent to an appropriate institution to start serving the sentence meted out by the court. Offenders are periodically reassessed at which point security levels can be increased or decreased depending upon their adjustment.

In Pennsylvania, once an offender is sentenced in county court to a state prison, the local Sheriff transports the individual back to the county prison to await transfer to the state correctional institution. To determine what institution would best fit the needs of the inmate, and the correctional system, inmates are soon sent to a diagnostic and classification center. For men, the facility for this purpose is SCI Camp Hill, while female prisoners are sent to SCI Muncy. Depending upon the availability of deputy sheriffs, this process may take a few days to several weeks. Upon arrival at the state correctional institution, the new commitment is placed in a special housing unit for assessment and classification that includes a battery of tests and a review of the offender's case file.

The Department of Corrections uses five levels of security for its correctional facilities, although some facilities may have multiple levels within the same institution. These levels of custody include: minimum, medium, close, maximum and a separate designation for offenders placed in community corrections. The majority of offenders in the Department of Corrections are classified in minimum or medium security levels. Inmates can move up or down the different levels of classification based on a number of factors including their age, prison behavior, programmatic needs, time served, and projected release date.

Once an inmate is incarcerated in a state facility, they have the opportunity to participate in a variety of prison programs. The most common of these programs are the different types of educational programs. Academic educational programs provide inmates who do not have a high school diploma with a GED diploma. Some institutions provided adult basic education (ABE), English as a second language (ESL), special education, and some junior college level educational classes. Vocational training is provided at some institutions including some training in technology, computers, and trade occupations. A third type of educational programs is the variety of social and life skills programs offered throughout the Commonwealth. These programs include victim awareness, multiculturalism, wellness, and parenting enhancement programs.

Pennsylvania also provides rehabilitation programs for a variety of specific populations of offenders with a wide range of issues. Such "rehab" programs include those for sex offenders, domestic violence perpetrators, special needs offenders, female offenders, parole violators, and geriatric offenders, and may include victim awareness and faith-based programs. One of the largest and most commonly utilized set of rehabilitation programs is under the auspices of the Alcohol and Other Drug Abuse Program (AOD). The AOD provides offenders with screening, assessment, detoxification, and a variety of related programs to address alcohol and drug addiction. To address the many deficits that inmates have relative to their job skills, the state has a correctional industries program in approximately fifteen prisons that tries to teach good work habits and provide the skills necessary to secure employment upon release. The correctional industries program in Pennsylvania operates under a state-use system whereby goods and services produced by inmates can only be purchased by federal, state, and local governments as well as by other non-profits. Examples of items made by correctional industries include uniforms, office furniture, and all of the Commonwealth's license plates.

Prisons and Prisoners in Pennsylvania

In most instances, offenders sentenced to state prison by the courts have committed felony offenses, violent in nature, or have been repeat violators. Sentences range from a minimum of at least two years to a maximum of life. As of October 2013 there were 50,068 state inmates in 26 Pennsylvania prisons (Pennsylvania Department of Corrections, 2013b). Further inspection of the most current data available reveals that at the end of 2011, the population was comprised of 85.6 percent sentenced offenders and 14.1 percent parole violators. A demographic breakdown of the department's inmates indicates that offender race, age, and gender have remained relatively constant over the past few years. In December 31, 2011, 38.9 percent were white, 49.4 percent were black, and 10.9 percent Hispanic. Almost half of all offenders housed by the Department of Corrections were 25–39 years of age (47 percent) with another 40 percent age 40 or over. Only 13.5 percent of the population was under 25 years of age. The average age of offenders serving time in state prison was 37 years (Lategan, O'Neill & Santore, 2011).

In 2011, almost half (46.8 percent) of inmates incarcerated in the Pennsylvania system were convicted of Part I offenses. Approximately 20 percent of the prisoners committed either murder (first, second, or third degree) or aggravated assault crimes. Thirty-eight percent of the inmates were convicted of Part II offenses, the majority being drug violations. The average minimum sentence length for Part I offenders was 9.1 years and the average maximum sentence length was 20.1 years. For Part II offenders, the average minimum and maximum sentence lengths were 4.4 years and 10.0 years, respectively. Overall, the average time served for all inmates released in 2011 serving both Part I and Part II Offenses was 47.4 months (Annual Statistical Report, 2011). The total numbers of offenders serving sentences of over 20 years or life was more than 7% with another 195 offenders on death row (Pennsylvania Department of Corrections, 2013c).

Jails in Pennsylvania

Early jails in the early years of the United States served various functions with the most common being pretrial and presentence detention. Some jails also served to house prisoners of war, political prisoners, and those who had not paid debts or taxes or fines. Because jails were run by local governments, and housed both convicted and unconvicted persons, they were more like today's jails than prisons or penitentiaries.

Jails today are still the entryway to corrections; the jail is the first institutional contact that most criminals experience. The population in county jails is very heterogeneous in nature. County jails hold those awaiting trial, those convicted of felonies and misdemeanors, those awaiting transfer to another correctional facility, and even inmates who violate federal immigration and military laws. By midyear 2012, the average daily jail population in the United States was 744,524 (Minton, 2013). In most county jurisdictions, county jails house convicted offenders sentenced to a period of confinement usually less than one year. However there are at least two exceptions to this rule. In states like California, due to prison crowding judges have forced county jails to take inmates with terms of more than one year. Also, the state of Pennsylvania is unique in that it has always accepted inmates convicted of lesser felonies in county jails for up to five years. While state prisons are administered by the executive branch of state government, county jails are confinement facilities operated by the local government. In many states, county jails are administered by sheriffs who are usually elected officials. In Pennsylvania, jails are administered by wardens who are appointed by the county executive or county commissioner.

When jails are administered by elected officials, jail policies are often dictated by politics, party patronage, and the local economy. Jail practices can also affect probation, parole, and community-based programs. For example, if the county is on strong financial footing, more probation staff and more programs for offenders are available. In the majority of instances, county facilities do not have the number and quality of programs and services as are offered in the state or federal prison system.

Jails in Pennsylvania differ in size and design, based upon funding and when the structure was built. For centuries, jails were built in a linear design with small (1–2 persons) adjacent cells that open to a long hallway or tier. The tiers were often stacked on top of each other in a radial design much like the design of the Eastern Penitentiary. The oldest remaining county jail in Pennsylvania, built in 1851, is in Schuylkill County and was renovated in 1986. In fact, most of the tier style jails in Pennsylvania have been renovated or replaced with new generation jails (NGJs). Twelve county jails have been built since 2000 and all are NGJs. These facilities have a podular unit architectural design. The podular units are triangular structures, their perimeter lined with sleeping rooms and center area left open as a dayroom and activity area. Each podular unit is a self-contained living area for a group of inmates (12–50) composed of either a dormitory style or individual cells and open areas for social interaction. The number of podular units in use at any one time varies by the number of inmates and the number of podular units available in the respective counties. New generation jails have a much different inmate management policy than the old style tier prisons. NGJs emphasize direct supervision of inmates which creates more interaction between inmates and staff and, if financially possible, the provision of better and more services to inmates.

In podular units, the correctional officer's desk and control console are located in the common area. The officer works within the living area or pod and has direct supervision and access to all inmates. This type of design creates a self-contained control area that allows for increased contact between inmates and officers, while decreasing the need to move inmates among different areas of the jail. Usually inmates are placed into these "pods" based upon security levels. Officers working within these pods are not armed, but carry radios equipped with an emergency button. In addition video cameras are placed throughout the jail to ensure all space is visible to a central command station. The central command has the ability to lock and unlock all doors throughout the jail.

There are 63 county jails in Pennsylvania operating at the local level with a total average in-house population of 37,185 in 2012 (Pennsylvania Department of Corrections, 2013b). The Curran-Fromhold Correctional Facility in Philadelphia maintains an average of over 3,000 inmates while the Union County Jail has a population of 35. The majority of county jails house a few hundred inmates. The costs of housing inmates in jail can be as low as $43.97 a day (Blair County) to a high of $136.99 (Elk County) (Pennsylvania Department of Corrections, 2013b). Offenders usually serve a sentence of less than two years in county jails. Although recent legislation allows prisoners, under limited circumstances, to serve 2–5 year sentences in county jails (with the consent of the sentencing Judge and Office of the District Attorney). The jail administrator would have to comply with this request and the jail population must be less than 110 percent of rated capacity (PCCD, 2013).

In all jails across the Commonwealth, all new inmates undergo an evaluation and diagnostic process, which includes classification, orientation, medical examination, and issuance of inmate rules/regulations, clothing, and personal care items. Depending upon the size and fiscal status of the county, inmates may be provided with a variety of educational, religious, self-help, vocational, and training programs.

Community-Based Corrections

When most Americans think of corrections they have visions of Alcatraz or Attica or maybe even their local jail or prison. However, this is actually a misconception because, in fact, over two-thirds of offenders in corrections are supervised in the community rather than housed in jails and prisons. And with the exception of the small percentage of offenders serving a life sentence, the majority of criminals will eventually be released back to society. At year end 2011, there were about 4,814,200 offenders under community supervision (probation and parole) in the United States and one in 50 adults were on some form of community supervision (Glaze & Parks, 2012). As a result of prison overcrowding and the costs of confinement, community-based programs are being used as an alternative to incarceration across the United States.

Probation began in the United States with the work of John Augustus (1784–1859) who is known as the "father of probation." He believed that imprisonment was not appropriate for all offenders and he convinced judges in the Boston courts to allow him to help offenders live in the community and avoid incarceration. The state of Massachusetts provided for paid probation services beginning in 1878 and by 1920 all states provided probation for juveniles and by 1930 the federal government and 36 states did the same. Currently, probation constitutes a sentence upon which the Court orders an offender to be placed on supervision with conditions and to refrain from committing new crimes. Probation agencies require an offender to sign a standard form usually containing a variety of rules or conditions. Conditions are generally divided into two types: standard conditions which are applicable to all probationers and special conditions, which are tailored to the criminogenic needs of the particular offender. Standard conditions may include the following:

- reporting requirements;
- compliance with all federal, state, and local laws;
- maintaining employment or school programs;
- notifying and receiving approval to change residence;
- no possession of a firearm or other dangerous weapons;
- abstain from the use of controlled substances and excessive use of alcohol;
- payment of supervision fees, court costs, and fines;
- following a treatment plan or program of supervision;

- refraining from consorting with certain types of people or frequenting certain places; and
- compliance with special conditions ordered by the court.

Special conditions of probation can be ordered directly by the court or directed by the probation contract and may include payment of restitution, performance of community service, and undergoing medical or psychiatric treatment. For example, an offender who has a compulsion to steal may be told to attend mental health counseling; not all offenders require this condition. Conditions of probation and parole are similar, if not identical, and the state does not differentiate between the terms "probation officer" and "parole officer" in Pennsylvania. If an offender violates the terms of supervision, the court has the authority to revoke probation and impose a period of incarceration or other sentencing options. Conversely, if the offender complies with all the terms and conditions during the period of supervision assigned by the court, the offender will be successfully released.

Parole was first implemented in the United States in 1876 at the Elmira Reformatory in New York. Zebulon Brockway, the superintendent at Elmira, was influenced by the work of Alexander Maconochie, who, while superintendent at Norfolk Island Prison in the South Pacific in the 1840s, first developed the "marks" and "ticket of leave" systems. These ideas became the cornerstones of indeterminate sentencing and parole (Morris, 2002). States first adopted these ideas in earnest in the mid-1920s, and by 1932, forty-four states and the federal government had put some parole mechanism in place. Today, all jurisdictions have some mechanism for releasing offenders from prison, although states differ as to the type of parole decision-making mechanism they use. Two dominant models include the use of parole boards and mandatory releases in which release dates are usually set near the completion of the inmate's prison sentence minus any good time. Good time is the reduction of a sentence based on the good behavior of an inmate or his/her participation in rehabilitation programs.

Once released on supervision, conditions of parole are very similar, if not identical, to conditions of probation. If the parolee fails to abide by these conditions, the court or parole board may revoke the parole and remand the offender back to prison. If parolees adhere to the conditions of supervision they are discharged after serving the sentence of the court. Parolees comprise the smallest number of offenders under correctional supervision.

Probation and Parole in Pennsylvania

Probation has been utilized used in different parts of Pennsylvania since the late nineteenth century. In 1909, the Pennsylvania criminal courts were given the statutory authority to suspend sentences and impose terms of probation on criminal offenders and probation became a more formalized process across the Commonwealth when it passed the 1911 Probation Act. Probation in Pennsylvania is generally a local criminal justice function rather than a state function. Almost all offenders across the Commonwealth are supervised by county probation departments. Sixty-five of the 67 counties in Pennsylvania operate county adult probation and parole departments. The Pennsylvania (State) Board of Probation and Parole provides adult probation/parole supervision in Mercer and Venango counties. There were 77,248 offenders on probation as of December 31, 2012, under the auspices of 65 county probation departments (Commonwealth of Pennsylvania Board of Probation and Parole, 2013a).

In some cases, the Pennsylvania Board of Probation and Parole is requested to supervise offenders on "special probation." According to Section 17 of the 1941 Parole Act, a special probation case is one where the county court has directed the supervision of certain offenders by the county probation department as well as the state Board of Probation and Parole. The Board has established criteria to either accept or deny requests made by the county courts for supervision. Usually, cases forwarded to the Board are for felony offenders with long periods of supervision. Many of the special probation cases occur when a person who is already on probation in one jurisdiction commits an offense and is placed on probation in a second jurisdiction. In effect, special probation is a dual supervision system. In the two counties without probation departments, the Board is obligated to accept all special probation cases. The Pennsylvania Board of Probation supervised 5,757 "Special Probation" cases at the end of April 2013 (Commonwealth of Pennsylvania Board of Probation and Parole, 2013a). Special probation is not to be confused with intensive probation supervision (ISP). ISP is used around the country and in Pennsylvania as a method of supervising those on probation with the highest risk of reoffending such as drug offenders or sex offenders. Probation officers who have ISP caseloads will have fewer offenders to supervise and are expected to be in regular contact, in some cases daily, with each probationer.

Parole first appeared in Pennsylvania as a procedure for releasing juveniles from the Philadelphia House of Refuge in 1826. Thirty-five years later, in 1861, the General Assembly of Pennsylvania passed the first "good time" laws whereby inmates could be granted "time off" for good behavior. In 1909, the first statute authorizing the release of prisoners from state penitentiaries was enacted. This statute, called the 1909 Parole Act, defined indeterminate sentences that require a minimum and maximum term and specified that an offender is not eligible for parole until he/she has served the minimum sentence imposed by the court. After serving the minimum, parole may be approved, deferred to a later date, or denied. A maximum sentence is the maximum amount of time spent imposed by the court that an inmate can be required to serve before being released from prison. Thirty years later, the 1941 Parole Act made drastic changes in Pennsylvania's parole system when it created the Pennsylvania Board of Probation and Parole as an independent parole board that was not under the control of any state agency. Under this Act, The Parole Board was created and given exclusive jurisdiction over all offenders sentenced by common pleas courts to terms of imprisonment in state prisons. The Parole Board has a total of nine members appointed by the governor and approved by the legislature. Parole board members must have at least six years of professional experience in probation, parole, social work, or related areas including one year in a supervisory or administrative capacity. A minimum of a bachelor's degree is required. Board members may not hold any other office or employment, and are not permitted to take any active part in politics. This system and its requirements for participation remain to this day (Wile, 1993).

Pennsylvania has a unique system of parole: the authority to parole is split between common pleas courts and the Parole Board. The common pleas courts of 67 counties have exclusive parole jurisdiction over all offenders serving sentences imposed by that court having a maximum term of less than two years. This is commonly referred to as "county parole." Offenders serving county parole remain under the control of a county probation/parole officer and the county court has the authority to grant or revoke parole. The Parole Board has exclusive parole jurisdiction over all offenders serving sentences imposed by the courts with maximum terms of two years or more. Most offenders and criminal justice practitioners refer to this as "state parole." At present, there are 47,783 county parolees under supervision and 30,025 offenders on state parole (Commonwealth of Pennsylvania Board of Probation and Parole, 2013a).

In addition to county and state parole, there is a third type of parole in existence in Pennsylvania that is called "Special Parole." Special parole can be requested wherein the Pennsylvania Board of Probation and Parole can supervise an offender serving a maximum sentence of two years or less if requested by a common pleas court. The Board is not required to accept all requests for "special parole" and may establish criteria for acceptance of the cases. There are 1,031 offenders being supervised on "special parole." Offenders supervised by county adult probation and parole departments represent 86.7 percent of the total number of adult offenders on supervision, while offenders supervised by the Pennsylvania Board of Probation and Parole represent the remaining 13.3 percent (Commonwealth of Pennsylvania Board of Probation and Parole, 2013b).

In September 2004 there were four acts passed into law by the state legislature of Pennsylvania. Each of the four acts (Acts 81, 82, 83, and 84) has had a significant impact on parole, jails, and prisons. Act 81 includes, among other things, changes to inmate booking centers, clarifies some parole guidelines, and modifies some rules related to when the state is required to take inmates and when the county should incarcerate. The Act also encouraged the development to the Recidivism Risk Reduction Incentive (RRRI) (see below in next section). Act 82 addressed prisoner transportation issues and their relationship with county sheriffs. Act 83 changed the parole process in the Commonwealth so that parole jurisdiction is now based on place on confinement with judges controlling parole decisions for prisoners confined within their respective county jails (county paroles) and the Pennsylvania Board of Probation and Parole (PBPP) determining parole for inmates in the Department of Corrections (state parole). The Pennsylvania Board of Probation and Parole no longer extends parole to offenders committed to county prisons. Finally, Act 84 expands the release of terminally ill patients and use of victim notification systems.

In addition to probation and parole, Pennsylvania also utilizes a variety of other community-based sanctions for offenders that are more restrictive than probation, but less severe than confinement in jail or prison. These "intermediate punishments" or "intermediate sanctions" include work release, house arrest, day reporting centers, and various forms of electronic monitoring.

Work release is a jail or prison release program in which inmates are allowed to be released into the community in order to meet job and/or educational responsibilities. Day reporting centers are locations where offenders on pre-trial release, probation, or parole are required to appear to receive supervision or participate in rehabilitation programs. House arrest, also called home confinement, is when an offender is sentenced to a term of confinement but serves that term in his or her own home. House arrest is often combined with some form of electronic monitoring.

Electronic monitoring (EM) is a form of community supervision, usually combined with house arrest, which utilizes electronic means to supervise offenders. EM is used on the state and county levels in Pennsylvania with probation and parole personnel being able to obtain up-to-the-minute information on their computers regarding the whereabouts of the people they supervise. The system alerts the agency when an issue arises that requires its attention. There have been different types of EM systems used over the last thirty or so years with the most common being continuous contact and programmed contact devices. With the continuous contact system, a signal from a transponder worn by the offender is constantly sent to a receiver. If the signal is broken, a message is sent to the monitoring computer and the authorities are alerted. Unlike the continuous contact system, the programmed contact device is a passive monitor that responds only on request. The offender may receive an automated telephone call from the probation or parole office or via the computer. Then the offender must verify his/her identity through voice activation and then a wrist device is inserted into the phone to show that they are present. Over the last decade, and now adopted by most states, is the use of supervising offenders in the community through the use of Global Positioning Systems (GPS). Criminal offenders are released from jail, probation, or parole and they are often monitored with a GPS tracking device in the form of an ankle bracelet. This device allows the criminal offender to be tracked via computer around the clock to make sure that the geographic restrictions set for the probation period are consistently followed. These devices are programmed to inform the authorities if the offender is not in the correct place at the correct time. EM and GPS are most often used for less violent criminals, those with short jail or prison terms, or even with early release inmates. Their use is also valuable with juvenile offenders who wish to remain in school or work. The Pennsylvania state Board of Probation and Parole has recently begun to train parole agents to utilize global positioning systems to track offenders. Another form of electronic surveillance utilized in Pennsylvania is the SCRAM bracelet. SCRAM, technically called secure continuous remote alcohol monitoring, is an intermediate sanction that allows an offender to remain in the community while being connected to an electronic bracelet that monitors alcohol use transdermally (i.e., through the skin).

Once placed on probation or parole, there are two ways the sentence can be removed—through termination or revocation. Termination can occur either at the end of the maximum date of probation or parole supervision set by the court, or through a petition to the court requesting to reduce the period of supervision based on good behavior and compliance of conditions. The court may choose to reduce the period of supervision or to reduce only the supervision level (e.g., less reporting, less drug testing) or the number of conditions.

The processes for revocation of probation and parole in Pennsylvania are very similar. A probation or parole revocation procedure can occur for either a new offense or for a technical violation. Technical violations occur when an offender violates his/her standard or special (also called punitive) conditions of probation or parole. In most cases the probation or parole officer initiates the violation then the following options are available:

- verbal reprimand by the officer,
- written reprimand by the officer,
- administrative hearing before a court administrator or judge, or
- imposition of additional conditions by the court. In this case a new hearing is required.

If the probation or parole officer or the court moves towards revocation, then two additional hearings are required. The Gagnon I hearing is informal and held before a neutral body and is similar to a preliminary hearing in that probable cause must be determined. In the Gagnon II hearing, which is a more formal hearing before a judge, the preponderance of evidence must be shown. Also at the Gagnon II hearing, the judge can resentence to jail, send to prison or continue on probation with new or longer conditions (e.g. intensive probation supervision). The Gagnon hearings were developed in response to the 1973 U.S. Supreme Court case *Gagnon v. Scarpelli* that ruled that probation cannot be revoked without following certain elements of due process.

In the case of parole revocation, much of the process is the same as for those who commit probation technical violations. Due process rules for parole violators are derived from the 1971 Supreme Court case *Morrissey v. Brewer* and they are similar to those set forth in *Gagnon v. Scarpelli*. A difference between probation and parole revocation is that either the state Parole Board or the county judiciary (depending on place of confinement) makes the determination as to whether an offender will receive an increased sanction or be returned to an institution. If an offender is returned to jail or prison by the Parole Board for a technical violation, they can only be remanded for the remainder of their original sentence that they have yet to serve on parole. If charged with a new offense, then a new sentence can be added to the time spent for a violation.

Correctional Policy Initiatives

In recent years, several major initiatives have been implemented by the Pennsylvania Department of Corrections (DOC) to reduce system crowding and decrease recidivism rates in the state. They include the implementation of a Boot Camp Program, Community Corrections Centers, State Intermediate Punishments programs, Recidivism Risk Reduction Incentive program, and, most recently, the Justice Reinvestment program.

Boot Camp

In 1990, the Pennsylvania legislature passed Act 215, which established a state motivational boot camp program to address the issue of overcrowding and to provide a sentencing alternative for the courts with the goal of crime reduction. Two years later, the Boot Camp Program opened in Quehanna, Clearfield County, Pennsylvania. This program is an alternative to a state incarceration sentence and allows eligible offenders (both male and female) to serve a reduced six-month sentence followed by intensive parole supervision. Boot camp programs for offenders started in 1983 in Georgia, whereby correctional programs borrowed the military concept of breaking existing habits and thought patterns and rebuilding offenders to be more disciplined through intensive physical training, hard labor, and rigid structure. Some boot camps include counseling and training programs.

Boot camps typically target youthful, non-violent offenders from urban areas who have been convicted of drug delivery offenses. Once sentenced to boot camp by the court, candidates go through an expedited classification process at either Camp Hill (males) or Muncy (females). If selected for the program by the Department of Corrections, the inmate must agree to the terms and conditions of the program. An inmate's participation in the motivational boot camp unit may be suspended or revoked for administrative or disciplinary reasons. Over the past ten years, the Boot Camp Program has averaged 479 admissions per year with a graduation rate of 87%. As a result of reducing the amount of time the Boot Camp offender is incarcerated by approximately six months, the program reportedly results in a cost savings of about $38,434 per graduate (Kempinen & Tinik, 2011).

Community Corrections Centers

The Pennsylvania DOC is also responsible for 14 community corrections centers (also known as halfway houses) and contracts for services with private vendors for nearly 50 community corrections centers throughout the Commonwealth. For the purposes of the administration of the centers, Pennsylvania is divided into three regions: Region I-East, Region II-Central, and Region III-West with centralized offices in each region. According to the Monthly Population Report provided by the DOC, as of April 2013 there were 390 inmates in state-operated community corrections facilities and another 914 offenders in privately contracted facilities (Pennsylvania Department of Corrections, 2013b).

Community correctional centers (halfway houses) provide a transitional living situation for offenders returning to society after a period of confinement. The centers play an essential role in the difficult adjustment from prison to society. Community corrections centers in Pennsylvania provide a wide range of employment, educational, and treatment opportunities. Staff members establish relationships with federal, state, and county agencies in an effort to have resources available to offenders upon their release from prison. Cultivating ties with volunteer, groups, faith-based organizations, and service providers is an ongoing effort. Once employed, inmates are required to pay fifteen percent of their pay for rent, while ten percent of their income is designated for other fees, such as court costs, fines, and restitution, and ten percent is placed in a savings account. Inmates pending parole to an approved residence, parole violators, and inmates serving state intermediate punishment can be placed into a community corrections center. Due to the limited number of centers and bed space available, community corrections centers are an option for only a small percentage of the inmate population.

State Intermediate Punishment Program

Pennsylvania's State Intermediate Punishment (SIP) Program was enacted by the legislature (Act 112 of 2004) in November of 2004 and became effective on May 18, 2005. The Act establishes the Commonwealth's first alternative sentencing program and attacks one of the underlying causes of criminal behavior—addiction. The goal of the program is to reduce recidivism by providing intensive drug and alcohol treatment to select offenders who have been convicted of a drug-related offense. A drug-related offense is a crime that is motivated by the offender's consumption of or addiction to alcohol or other drugs.

Offenders are referred by the court, prior to sentencing, to the Department of Corrections to undergo a risk assessment and alcohol/drug evaluation to determine whether they qualify for the program. This assessment is conducted within 60 days of the court's commitment of the offender to the Department of Corrections. If favorable, the Court will sentence the offender to a flat term of 24 months of State Intermediate Punishment. In many instances, the court may add a consecutive period of probation to the sentence, as long as the total sentence does not exceed the maximum sentence that could have been imposed upon the offender. Males sentenced to the SIP program are sent to the State Correctional Institute at Chester or to the Quehanna Boot Camp, while female offenders are housed at the State Correctional Institution at Cambridge Springs.

In order to qualify for the program, the offender must be convicted of a drug-related offense and in need of alcohol/drug addiction treatment. Further, the offender must not demonstrate a history of present or past violent behavior. The following offenses render an offender ineligible: personal injury crimes, incest, open lewdness, abuse of children, unlawful contact with a minor, sexual exploitation of children, and internet child pornography. The State Intermediate Punishment Program is structured into the following steps that the offender must follow for successful completion:

- a minimum of seven months in a state correctional institution of which not less than four months in an institutional therapeutic community,
- a minimum of two months in a community-based therapeutic community,
- a minimum of six months in treatment in an outpatient facility (the offender may spend part of the aftercare in a community corrections center or transitional residence), and
- a period of supervision in the community for the remainder of the sentence.

For the duration of the program, 24 months, the offender is supervised by the Department of Corrections (DOC). The DOC is permitted to suspend or expel offenders who commit a misconduct or are not fully participating in the program. At this juncture, the court may revoke the offender from the program and impose a new sentence. Since May of 2005, over 2,500 offenders have been evaluated and accepted into the SIP. Most of these offenders are white males, in their early thirties, who committed either a drug delivery offense or drunk driving. A large percentage of offenders accepted into the program have serious alcohol and drug addiction problems and prior involvement in the criminal justice system. Many have been involved in substance abuse treatment in the past only to relapse and recidivate. Research measuring the effectiveness of the program has indicated that offenders who successfully completed the SIP program were significantly less likely to recidivate than was a comparable group of offenders who were released from prison. Offenders expelled from the program (417) were significantly more likely to recidivate than offenders who completed the program or who were released from prison (Pennsylvania Commission on Sentencing, 2013a).

Recidivism Risk Reduction Incentive (RRRI)

In the effort to reduce the rate of recidivism by criminal offenders, Pennsylvania Act 81 was passed in November 2008 which allows certain nonviolent offenders who participate in a risk reduction program to receive reduced minimum sentences and earlier parole dates. Called the Recidivism Risk Reduction Incentive (RRRI), the stated purpose of the legislation is as follows:

> to create a program that ensures appropriate punishment for persons who commit crimes, encourages prisoner participation in evidence-based programs that reduce the risks of future crime and ensures prisoner participation in evidence-based programs that reduce the risks of future crime and ensures the openness and accountability of the

criminal justice process while ensuring fairness to crime victims (Pennsylvania Commission on Sentencing, 2013b).

Eligibility for the RRRI is very similar to the State SIP program in that offenders must be sentenced to a state facility, have no record of violent behavior, or be convicted/found guilty/adjudicated for personal injury crimes, weapons offenses, certain drug offenses, and sex offenses. At the time of sentencing the judge makes the determination as to whether an offender is eligible for RRRI. For those offenders deemed eligible, the court imposes two sentences: the "standard" or regular minimum and maximum sentence and the RRRI minimum. The RRRI minimum sentence is based upon a percentage of the standard minimum sentence: for minimum sentences three years or less, the RRRI sentence is three-fourths of the minimum; for minimum sentences over three years, the RRRI is five-sixths of the minimum sentence. For example, if the standard minimum sentence is 36 months, an offender sentenced to RRRI would receive the minimum sentence of 27 months. After an offender has been sentenced to the Department of Corrections (DOC) under RRRI, the Department evaluates the needs and risks of the offender. Based upon this assessment, a program plan is developed for each offender to lower his/her risk of recidivism.

As of December 31, 2011, there were 8,650 offenders sentenced to the Pennsylvania DOC with a RRRI minimum sentence reduction. RRRI offenders when compared to non RRRI offenders are more likely to be female, white, from rural areas, and have some drug violations. RRRI participants have a minimum sentence average length of 20 months as compared to 44 months for non-RRRI offenders, and they are much more likely to be low risk offenders. State reported research claims that recidivism rates (new arrests and technical violations of supervision) are slightly higher for RRRI offenders than a comparison group. However, RRRI offenders were more likely to have committed technical violations, while the non-RRRI offenders committed new arrests. Further, although the recidivism rate was slightly higher, the program was reported to reduce the state prison population through early releases and provided an estimated savings of 37.1 million dollars for the Commonwealth (Pennsylvania Commission on Sentencing, 2013b).

Justice Reinvestment

An initiative called justice reinvestment has spread across the United States and as of 2012 has become a reality in Pennsylvania. The idea behind justice reinvestment is that through the intelligent use of data, crime can be reduced, the cost of running the criminal justice system lowered, and eventually the savings reinvested back into communities. In July 2012, Gov. Tom Corbett signed into law legislation that government officials believe will provide justice reinvestment and also significantly alter the corrections system in Pennsylvania. Called the Criminal Justice Reform Act (Act 122 of 2012), the Act calls the following changes to the criminal justice system in Pennsylvania:

• providing law enforcement with additional funding to deter crime and provide victims information and resources to report crime,
• expanding the eligibility and use of intermediate punishments for offenses involving drugs and alcohol,
• encouraging technical parole violators be returned to community corrections centers rather than state prison,
• banning individuals convicted of certain (low level) misdemeanors from being sentenced to state prison, and
• creating a risk-assessment tool for judges to use when sentencing individuals.

Also, a major change in the Act is the elimination of pre-release. Until the passage of Act 122, offenders were able to gain parole prior to their mandatory minimum sentence, usually to be released to a halfway house or drug treatment program. Release would come from the Parole Board and it would be used for non-violent and/or minor drug offenders. Elimination of pre-release ensures that those who are in prison serve one-hundred percent of their minimum sentence. The changes in the correctional system called for by Act 122 are projected to save the Commonwealth up to an estimated $254 million over five years. According to a statutory formula, Pennsylvania will reinvest a portion of realized savings in local law enforcement, county probation and parole, and victim services (Justice Center, 2012).

Conclusion

Corrections systems in the United States and Pennsylvania have undergone many changes since the time of the Quakers and the Walnut Street Jail. Today, corrections, on all levels—federal state, and county—play a vital role in protecting society from violent offenders and punishing others who commit crimes. The current correctional system in the United States is a 70-billion-dollar industry with nearly 6 million offenders in jails, prisons, and community-based corrections. A reflection about corrections in the United States over the last 250 years cannot help but include the influence of corrections in Pennsylvania. The Commonwealth was responsible for a major contribution to American corrections with the advent of the Pennsylvania system. This system led to the formation of the penitentiary era in Pennsylvania and around the world. The penitentiary era gave way to other eras including the reformatory, rehabilitation, reintegration, and most recently the retributive era. In the past three decades, admissions to county, state, and federal prisons increased significantly, especially for drug offenders. In Pennsylvania alone, over the past 30 years, the Department of Corrections' budget has grown over 1,700% and is now the third largest department in the General Fund Budget. It is anticipated that the budget for fiscal year 2013–2014 will be approximately 2 billion dollars. The current Pennsylvania Department of Corrections is responsible for 51,000 inmates in jails and prisons and another 35,000 in community based programs like probation, parole and community correctional centers. In recent years, Pennsylvania has developed a number of initiatives such as intermediate sanctions, boot camp, risk reduction, and justice reinvestment with the goal of reducing crime and thereby lowering system costs. With prison overcrowding and skyrocketing costs, innovative initiatives such as these will continue to develop over the coming decades.

Key Terms and Definitions

Augustus, John (1784–1859): A Boston shoemaker who convinced judges in the Boston courts to allow him to help offenders live in the community and avoid incarceration. He is known as the "father of probation."

Boot camp: A short-term, institutional sentence, usually followed by a period of probation or parole, which puts the offender through a physical regimen designed to develop discipline and respect for authority.

Classification: The proper assignment of inmates to specific institutions for custody and treatment. Classification is based upon objective criteria such as the length/type of sentence, nature of the crime, prior record in the criminal justice system, the medical (physical and mental) needs of the offender, history of violence, and past substance abuse patterns.

Community corrections: Also called community-based corrections; non-incarcerative programs for offenders who remain within the community while serving their sentences.

Community corrections centers: Places where offenders can reside in the community and utilize rehabilitative services while they remain under some form correctional supervision, usually probation or parole.

County parole: A parole case supervised by a county probation/parole officer with a minimum of two years or less.

Determinate sentence: Is a sentence to confinement to be served by the offender that is fixed at the time of sentencing. The offender generally serves this specified time minus any good-time credits.

Federal Bureau of Prisons: Established in 1930 to provide for the care and custody of offenders who committed federal offenses

Good time: The reduction of a sentence based on the good behavior of an inmate based on his/her participation in rehabilitation programs.

Indeterminate sentence: A sentence that requires a minimum and maximum term (e.g., 2–4 yrs.) that allows for offenders to receive parole based on good behavior and successful completion of in-prison participation rehabilitation programs.

Intermediate punishments: Community-based sanctions for offenders that are more restrictive than probation, but less severe than confinement in jail or prison.

Jails: Facilities authorized to hold pretrial detainees, those awaiting transfer to other institutions, and offenders serving sentences on misdemeanor type crimes that are usually administered by local government.

Maximum sentence: The maximum amount of time spent imposed by the court that an inmate can be required to serve before being released from prison.

Minimum sentence: The minimum amount of time imposed by the court that an inmate must serve before eligible for release from prison. This sentence cannot exceed one-half of the maximum sentence under Pennsylvania statute.

New generation jails: This facility with a podular architectural design and management policies emphasizes interaction of inmates and staff and provision of services.

New York (Auburn) system: A penitentiary system in which inmates were held in isolation at night, but worked with other prisoners during the day under the rule of total silence. This system was developed in Auburn, New York, and replaced the Pennsylvania system.

Parole: The conditional release of an offender from incarceration under supervision in the community after part of the prison sentence has been served.

Penitentiary: An institution intended to isolate prisoners from society and from one another in order to reflect on their crimes, repent, and undergo reformation.

Pennsylvania system or **separate system:** A penitentiary system in which inmates were held in total solitary confinement for the duration of their sentence with all activities carried on in their cells.

Prison: An institution operated by the state or federal government for the confinement of offenders who are serving sentences of one year or more.

Probation: Both an agency that supervises people in the community who are convicted but not sentenced to jail or prison and a court ordered sentence that allows an offender to remain in the community and be placed on supervision with conditions.

Recidivism Risk Reduction Incentive (RRRI): A program in which certain nonviolent offenders participate in evidence-based programs to reduce recidivism while receiving reduced minimum sentences and earlier parole dates.

Special conditions of probation/parole: Conditions tailored to the criminogenic needs of a particular offender.

Standard conditions of probation/parole: Conditions or rules of conduct that apply to all probationers/parolees.

State parole: A parole case supervised by the Pennsylvania Board of Probation and Parole with a maximum exceeding two years or more.

Supervised release: The current term used to describe supervision in the community for federal offenders. In terms of control, supervised release is similar to parole with the exception of how the offender is released from prison.

Walnut Street Jail: The first jail in the United States; it housed offenders without regard to age, sex, or offense.

Websites

Pennsylvania Board of Probation and Parole (PBPP): http://www.pbpp.state.pa.us.
Pennsylvania Commission on Crime and Delinquency (PCCD): http://www.pccd.state.pa.us.
Pennsylvania Department of Corrections: http://www.cor.state.pa.us/.
Federal Bureau of Prisons: www.bop.gov.

Review Questions

1. What are the different forms of federal correctional supervision in Pennsylvania?
2. Describe the role that Pennsylvania had in the early development of corrections in America.
3. Summarize how and why the correctional budgets in Pennsylvania have changed over the last thirty years.
4. Explain the classification process for criminal offenders in Pennsylvania.
5. How is the new generation jail design different from the old style linear design?
6. What are the different options in Pennsylvania for supervision offenders in the community?
7. Summarize the recent state legislated correctional programs developed to reduce system crowding and to improve recidivism in Pennsylvania.

Critical Thinking Questions

1. What role did the state of Pennsylvania play in the development of corrections in America during its first 100 years?
2. Pennsylvania employed a system of solitary confinement that was later abandoned in favor of the New York (Auburn) style which favors work with other prisoners during the day. What factors to you feel contributed to the demise of the Pennsylvania system?
3. What factors over the past thirty years have contributed to the increase of the correctional population in the United States and Pennsylvania?
4. How do local and state politics affect jails, prisons, and parole boards? Should political influence be as extensive as it is? What could be done to limit political patronage, especially at the local level?
5. Probation is a sentencing option most often used by jurists throughout the country. Why do you think judges favor probation?
6. The federal system along with many states has phased out parole and parole boards. What are the advantages and disadvantages of this initiative?
7. Critique at least one of the new initiatives implemented by the Pennsylvania DOC. More specifically, do you think the one you choose will be successful or not? Why not?

References

Annual Statistical Report (2011). Pennsylvania Department of Corrections, Retrieved August 24th 2013 from http://www.cor.state.pa.us/portal/server.pt/community/research___statistics/10669/report s/1069947.

Barnes, H. E. (1968). The evolution of Penology in Pennsylvania: A study in American social History. Montclair, NJ: Paterson Smith. Reprinted from 1927 version.

Clear, T. R., Cole, G. F., Reisig, M. D. & Petrosino, C. (2012). *American corrections: In brief.* Belmont, CA: Wadsworth, Cengage Learning.

Cohn, E. G. (2006). Corrections in Pennsylvania. Upper Saddle River, NJ: Pearson Education, Inc.

Commonwealth of Pennsylvania Board of Probation and Parole (2012a). *County adult Probation and Parole Annual Statistical Report 2012.* Retrieved August 24, 2013 from http://www.pbpp.state.pa.us/portal/server.pt/community/reports_and_publications/5358/county_adult_probation_and_parole_information/502401.

Commonwealth of Pennsylvania Board of Probation and Parole (2013b). *Monthly Program Report.* Retrieved August 24, 2013 from http://www.pbpp.state.pa.us/portal/server.pt/community/reports_and_publications/5358/monthly_program_reports/502395.

Federal Bureau of Prisons (2013). About the Bureau of Prisons. Retrieved October 24, 2013 from http://www.bop.gov/about/index.jsp.

Glaze, L. E., & Parks, E. (2012). *Correctional Populations in the United States, 2011.* Retrieved August 24, 2013 from http://www.bjs.gov/index.cfm?ty=pbdetail&iid=4537.

Justice Center (2012). Justice Center: The Council of State Governments. Justice Reinvestment in Pennsylvania. May 2012. Retrieved November 1, 2013 from http://csgjusticecenter.org/jr/pa/.

Kempinen, C., & Tinik, L. (2011). The Pennsylvania Commission on Sentencing. *Pennsylvania's motivational boot camp program: What have we learned over the last seventeen years?* Retrieved September 24, 2013 from http://www.pcs.la.psu.edu.

Lategan, D., O'Neill, S., & Santore, A. (2011). *Pennsylvania department of corrections annual statistical report.* Retrieved August 24, 2013 from http://www.bing.com/search?q=Lategan%2C+D.%2C+O%27Neill%2C+S.%2C+%26+Santore%2C+A.+%282011%29&form=DLCDF8&pc=MDDR&src=IE-SearchBox.

Minton, T. (2013). *Jail inmates at midyear 2012—Statistical tables.* Retrieved May 22, 2013 from http://www.bjs.gov/index.cfm?ty=pbdetail&iid=4655.

Motivans, M. (2011). *Bureau of Justice Statistics, 2009* (NCJ 234184). U.S. Department of Justice. Retrieved August 24, 2013 from: http://www.bjs.gov/content/pub/pdf/fjs09.pdf.

Morris, Norval (2002). *Maconochie's Gentlemen: The Story of Norfolk Island and the Roots of Modern Prison Reform.* New York: Oxford University Press.

PCCD (2013). Pennsylvania Commission on Crime and Delinquency. *Corrections Reform Package: Acts 81–84.* Retrieved November 16, 2013 from http://www.portal.state.pa.us/portal/server.pt?open=512&objID=5294&&SortOrder=6&level=2&parentid=5257&css=L2&mode=2.

Pennsylvania Commission on Sentencing (2013a). *State Intermediate Punishment 2012 Report to the Legislature.* Retrieved August 24, 2013 from http://pcs.la.psu.edu/publications-and-research/research-and-evaluation-reports/state-intermediate-punishment.

Pennsylvania Commission on Sentencing (2013b). *Recidivism Risk Reduction Incentive.* Retrieved October 24, 2013 from http://pcs.la.psu.edu/publications-and-research/research-and-evaluation-reports/recidivism-risk-reduction-incentive.

Pennsylvania Department of Corrections (2013a). *About us—Department of Corrections.* Retrieved August 24, 2013 from http://www.cor.state.pa.us/portal/server.pt/community/about_us_our_mission/20857.

Pennsylvania Department of Corrections (2013b). *Monthly Population Reports.* Retrieved November 17, 2013 from http://www.cor.state.pa.us/portal/server.pt/community/research___statistics/10669/monthly_population_reports/1069959.

Pennsylvania Department of Corrections (2013c). *Persons Sentenced to Execution in Pennsylvania.* Retrieved June 3, 2013 from http://www.cor.state.pa.us/portal/server.pt/community/death_penalty/17351.

Pennsylvania Office of the Budget (2013). *2013–14 Budget in Brief.* Retrieved August 24, 2013 from http://www.budget.state.pa.us/portal/server.pt/community/current_and_proposed_commonwealth_budgets/4566.

U.S. Courts (2012). *Federal probation system: Persons under post-conviction supervision as of December 31, 2012.* Retrieved August 24, 2013 from http://www.uscourts.gov/Statistics/StatisticalTablesForTheFederalJudiciary/december-2.

U.S. Department of Justice, Federal Bureau of Prisons. (2013). *Weekly population report.* Retrieved August 24th 2013 from http://www.bop.gov/locations/weekly_report.jsp.

Wile, T. (1993). *Pennsylvania Law of Probation and Parole.* Rochester, NY: Lawyers Cooperative Publishing.

Chapter 7

The Death Penalty in Pennsylvania

Timothy R. Robicheaux

Learning Objectives

After reading the chapter, students will be able to:

- Explain the history of the use of the death penalty in Pennsylvania, including key state and federal cases influencing death penalty legislation.
- Identify aggravating and mitigating circumstances and explain how they are applied to death penalty decisions.
- Describe the death penalty process in Pennsylvania.
- Describe both public officials' and Pennsylvania citizens' opinions about the death penalty and the process.
- Describe key death penalty controversies, including fear of wrongful convictions, the state's large backlog of death row inmates, and the financial burden on the state.
- Explain the relevance of racial inequality to the death penalty conversation in Pennsylvania.

Key Terms

Aggravating circumstance	*Commonwealth v. Moody*
Bifurcated trial	First-degree murder
Capital punishment	*Furman v. Georgia*
Catchall mitigator	Mitigating circumstance
Commonwealth v. Heidnik	Torture

Introduction

According to the Pennsylvania criminal code, "A criminal homicide constitutes murder of the first degree [i.e., first-degree murder] when it is committed by an intentional killing" (18 Pa. C.S.A. §2502 [a]). First-degree murder is the only crime for which a defendant is eligible for the death penalty in Pennsylvania. Despite having the fourth-largest death row population in the United States, execution rarely is used in the state with only three executions in the past five decades. This chapter covers many of the major issues related to the imposition of the death penalty in Pennsylvania including the historical roots, legal procedures, and current controversies.

Historical Roots

Capital punishment, or the death penalty, has long been a part of the world's legal systems. The first formally established death penalty laws date as far back as 1780 B.C. through the Code of Hammurabi of Babylon (Reggio, 1997). The death penalty was also a staple of the British criminal justice system, inspiring its use throughout American history. The earliest recorded execution in Colonial America took place in Jamestown, the first permanent British settlement (DPIC History, n.d.). Accused of being a spy for Spain, Captain George Kendall was executed by firing squad in 1608.

Much like the colonists in Jamestown, Pennsylvania's first colonists also utilized the death penalty (ProCon.org, n.d.). Until 1913, the administration of the death penalty in the Commonwealth occurred through public hangings. However, Pennsylvania became the first in the union to abolish public hangings in 1834 (PA Dept. of Corrections, n.d.), and hangings were administered within the walls of county jails for the next eight decades. In 1913, the Pennsylvania legislature adopted electrocution as the official means of administering capital punishment, and the responsibility for carrying out executions shifted from individual counties to the state (Dept. of Corrections, n.d.).

The state legislature chose a newly built penitentiary, now known as State Correctional Institution (SCI) Rockview, in Centre County, as the home of the state's only electric chair. After two years to prepare the chair and the "death house," convicted murderer John Talap became the first Pennsylvania inmate executed by electrocution on February 15, 1915 (Dept. of Corrections, n.d.). Sixteen years later, on February 23, 1931, Irene Schroeder became the state's first female inmate executed by the electric chair (Fenton, 2010). The state allowed Schroeder to choose between death by the chair or life in prison; she chose the chair (Fenton, 2010). Convicted in the rape and murder of a 17-year-old Philadelphia girl, Elmo Smith became the last person to die in the chair in 1962. From 1915 to 1962, 350 inmates, including two women, died in Pennsylvania's electric chair (Dept. of Corrections, n.d.).

In November of 1990, lethal injection replaced the defunct electric chair as the official means of execution in Pennsylvania. Following Governor Robert (Bob) Casey's signing of the lethal injection legislation, the electric chair and all associated equipment was removed from SCI Rockview and turned over to the Pennsylvania Historical Museum Commission (Dept. of Corrections, n.d.). For several reasons elaborated upon later in the current chapter, no executions took place in the state from April 2, 1962, to May 2, 1995, when Keith Zettlemoyer became the state's first inmate to die by lethal injection. Zettlemoyer was convicted of the murder of a friend who intended to testify against him in a robbery trial. After firing his attorneys and testifying in front of the United States 3rd Circuit Court of Appeals, Zettlemoyer asked for execution, telling the court, "I see my execution as an end of suffering to my imprisonment—a blessed, merciful release from all these health symptoms that I'm constantly suffering with" (Heine, 1995).

Since Zettlemoyer's death, the state has executed only two other men: Leon Moser and Gary Heidnik. Moser, executed on August 15, 1995, was found guilty of killing his wife and two young daughters outside of a church in 1985 (Heine & Kim, 1995). Heidnik, discussed in more detail in a later section of this chapter, raped and tortured several women in his north Philadelphia "House of Horrors." Executed for the murder of two victims, Heidnik's crimes were considered particularly heinous and even inspired a character in the serial killer suspense movie *Silence of the Lambs* (Bovsun, 2013). Like Zettlemoyer, both Moser and Heidnik *voluntarily* waived their appeals and volunteered for execution.

Death Penalty Legal Factors[1]

As of June 1, 2013 there were 195 inmates on death row in Pennsylvania (Dept. of Corrections, n.d.). Some would find it surprising that only three men in Pennsylvania have been executed since the 1960s compared to 350 in the five decades preceding the 1960s. Some of the disparities can be explained by changes to the imposition of the death penalty following key decisions of the Supreme Court of the United States.

---

1. This section and most of the chapter emphasizes decisions made by the jury, but in a bench trial a judge would make all of the factual decisions. When juries are referenced in this chapter, judges would also be appropriate when the defendant opts for a bench trial.

In 1972 the Court held that "the imposition and carrying out of the death penalty [under the current law] constitute cruel and unusual punishment in violation of the Eighth and Fourteenth Amendments" (*Furman v. Georgia,* 1972, p. 239-240). The majority held that the way that the death penalty was carried out in Georgia was arbitrary and there was a potential for racial bias in death penalty decisions. The court felt that a problem with the administration of the death penalty was that Georgia and other states failed to give juries sufficient guidance on how to apply the death penalty. Justice Douglas felt that juries might act on their prejudices and that states needed to rewrite death penalty laws to give juries this guidance (*Furman v. Georgia,* 1972).

The *Furman* decision greatly influenced death penalty legislation throughout the United States, effectively abolishing the death penalty until states could rewrite their statutes. Hundreds of death row inmates throughout the country had their death sentences overturned to life sentences because of this decision (DPI History, n.d.). One such person was George Bradley, who appealed his death sentence to Pennsylvania's Supreme Court in the same year as the *Furman* decision. Bradley was one of three men found guilty for entering a Philadelphia bar on December 15, 1967, holding up the owner of the bar, and killing him in the process. Basing their decision on *Furman,* the Pennsylvania Supreme Court held that Pennsylvania's death penalty statute violated the Eighth and Fourteenth Amendments (*Commonwealth v. Bradley,* 1972).

In *Gregg v. Georgia* (1976) the Supreme Court of the United States ruled that Georgia's statute, which now included carefully specified aggravating and mitigating factors, was constitutional. Pennsylvania passed new death penalty legislation in 1974, despite an attempt to veto the law by then Governor Milton Shapp (Dept. of Corrections, n.d.). According to the statute, the jury was to consider both aggravating and mitigating circumstances when deciding a convicted murderer's sentence. An aggravating circumstance (e.g., criminal history, etc.) makes it more appropriate that the death penalty be imposed. A mitigating circumstance is the converse of an aggravating factor and makes the imposition of the death penalty less appropriate.

Pennsylvania's 1974 death penalty statute included three mitigating circumstances a jury might consider when determining a defendant's sentence in a capital murder trial. These factors were:

(i) The age, lack of maturity, or youth of the defendant at the time of the killing.
(ii) The victim was a participant in or consented to the defendant's conduct ... or was a participant in or consented to the killing.

(iii) The defendant was under duress although not such duress as to constitute a defense to prosecution ... (*Commonwealth v. Moody*, 1977).

This statute was also ruled unconstitutional by the Pennsylvania Supreme Court (*Commonwealth v. Moody*, 1977). The court reasoned that the mitigating factors in the 1974 statute were too narrow because they did not focus the jury's attention to the record and character of the defendant, a factor that was a key part of Georgia's statute ruled constitutional in the *Gregg* decision.

Following the *Moody* decision, the legislature once again considered the state's death penalty statute. Despite another attempt by Governor Shapp to veto the law, the legislature passed the most recent version of the death penalty statute in 1978 (Dept. of Corrections, n.d.). The law has survived judicial scrutiny and is still intact today. When writing the statute, the legislature relied in part on the *Gregg* decision and on the *Moody* decision. That statute (42 Pa C.S.A. § 9711) is still in effect today.

Under the current statute, the jury must consider the presence of aggravating and mitigating circumstances (discussed in more detail in the next section). Before the jury can render a verdict of death, the state must prove, beyond a reasonable doubt, the presence of *at least* one of eighteen statutorily defined aggravating circumstances. A jury must be *unanimous* in their finding of an aggravating circumstance or the verdict must be life. Thus, if even a single juror does not feel that the state has proven the presence of at least a single aggravating circumstance, the verdict must be life (42 Pa C.S.A. § 9711).

The unanimous finding of an aggravating circumstance is necessary, but not sufficient, for the jury to reach a verdict of death. The jury must also consider mitigating circumstances in the case. While the state must prove aggravating circumstances beyond a reasonable doubt, the defense must only prove mitigating circumstances by the preponderance of the evidence (i.e., a lower standard of proof) (42 Pa C.S.A. § 9711).

If the jury finds at least a single aggravating circumstance and *no* mitigating circumstances, they must render a verdict of death (see also, *Commonwealth v. Mitchell*, 2003). The jury also must render a verdict of death if they unanimously find that the state proved one or more aggravating circumstances which outweigh any mitigating circumstances proved by the defense (see also, *Commonwealth v. Heidnik*, 1991). If the unanimous decision of the jury is that there are no aggravating circumstances or that the aggravating circumstances fail to outweigh any mitigating circumstances, then the verdict must be life. Further, if the jury is unable to reach a unanimous sentence, the court may discharge the jury. If the jury is discharged for failure to reach a unanimous verdict, the court must sentence the defendant to life in prison (42 Pa C.S.A. § 9711).

Aggravating and Mitigating Circumstances

The prosecution must prove at least one of eighteen aggravating circumstances to reach a verdict of death. The jury is *only* permitted to consider these statutorily limited aggravating circumstances. Table 7.1 quotes these aggravating circumstances (i.e., factors adding to the seriousness of the crime); some have been truncated or summarized due to their length.

Some of these statutory aggravating circumstances are straightforward during consideration, such as the age of the victim or the criminal history of the victim. Other circumstances are not so objective. For example, some defendants have challenged the word torture as being too vague (*Commonwealth v. Pursell*, 1985). The Pennsylvania Supreme Court held that "torture is understood as the infliction of a considerable amount of pain and suffering on a victim which is unnecessarily heinous, atrocious, or cruel manifesting exceptional depravity" (*Commonwealth v. Pursell*, 1985, p. 239). Another circumstance that might seem vague concerns the grave risk of death to those other than the victim. The Pennsylvania Supreme Court has considered this part of the statute in several cases. For example, firing a gun at people other than the murder victim during a fight constituted a grave risk of harm to those other targets (*Commonwealth v. Miles*, 1996). Leaving a 9-month-old baby near the body of a murder victim for over a day after the killing put the child at a grave risk of harm and constituted an aggravating circumstance (*Commonwealth v. Wholaver*, 2006). The court has also specified that *actual* harm is not required, only the risk of it (*Commonwealth v. Scarfo*, 1992).

The defense attempts to prove the presence of mitigating circumstances, which jurors must consider and weigh against any aggravating circumstances they find. The Pennsylvania death penalty statute includes seven specific mitigating circumstances that the jury may consider. There is also an eighth factor, a "catchall mitigator," allowing the jury to consider other circumstances that they find might mitigate the sentence. Allowing jurors to consider circumstances beyond those explicitly listed in the statute distinguishes mitigating circumstances from aggravating circumstances. For the latter, the jury cannot consider any circumstances beyond those specified in the statute. Table 7.2 quotes the mitigating circumstances jurors must consider in death penalty cases.

Since the statute was written, the Supreme Court of the United States decided several cases that provide further guidance on these mitigating circumstances. For example, while jurors can consider the age of the defendant when weighing mitigating circumstances, those under the age of 18 are not eligible for the death penalty regardless of aggravating factors (*Roper v. Simmons*, 2005).

Table 7.1 List of Aggravating Circumstances in Pennsylvania's Death Penalty Statute

*1. The victim is one of several special categories, including but not limited to: the Governor, Lieutenant Governor, State Treasurer, Attorney General of Pennsylvania, a State law enforcement official, a firefighter or others who are killed in the performance of duties or as a result of his official position.

2. The defendant paid or was paid by another person or had contracted to pay or be paid by another person or had conspired to pay or be paid by another person for the killing of the victim.

3. The victim was being held by the defendant for ransom or reward, or as a shield or hostage.

4. The death of the victim occurred while defendant was engaged in the hijacking of an aircraft.

5. The victim was a prosecution witness to a murder or other felony committed by the defendant and was killed for the purpose of preventing his testimony against the defendant in any grand jury or criminal proceeding involving such offenses.

6. The defendant committed a killing while in the perpetration of a felony.

7. In the commission of the offense the defendant knowingly created a grave risk of death to another person in addition to the victim of the offense.

8. The offense was committed by means of torture.

9. The defendant has a significant history of felony convictions involving the use or threat of violence to the person.

10. The defendant has been convicted of another Federal or State offense, committed either before or at the imprisonment or death was imposable or the defendant was undergoing a sentence of life imprisonment for any reason at the time of the commission of the offense.

11. The defendant has been convicted of another murder committed in any jurisdiction and committed either before or at the time of the offense at issue.

*12. The defendant has been convicted of voluntary manslaughter ... or a substantial equivalent crime in any other jurisdiction, committed either before or at the time of the offense at issue.

*13. The defendant committed the killing or was an accomplice in the killing ... while in the perpetration of a felony under the provisions of ... The Controlled Substance, Drug, Device and Cosmetic Act....

*14. At the time of the killing, the victim was or had been involved, associated or in competition with the defendant in the sale, manufacture, distribution, or delivery of any controlled substance or counterfeit controlled substance ...

*15. At the time of the killing, the victim was or had been a nongovernmental informant or had otherwise provided any investigative, law enforcement or police agency with information concerning the criminal activity ... and the killing was in retaliation for the victim's activities ...

16. The victim was a child under 12 years of age.

17. At the time of the killing, the victim was in her third trimester of pregnancy or the defendant had knowledge of the victim's pregnancy.

*18. At the time of the killing the defendant was subject to a court order restricting in any way the defendant's behavior toward the victim ... or any other order ... to protect the victim from the defendant.

Source: 42 Pa C.S.A. §9711 (d).
 * Truncated or summarized (i.e., not directly quoted).

Table 7.2 List of Mitigating Circumstances in Pennsylvania's Death Penalty Statute

1. The defendant has no significant history of prior criminal convictions.
2. The defendant was under the influence of extreme mental or emotional disturbance.
3. The capacity of the defendant to appreciate the criminality of his conduct or to conform his conduct to the requirements of the law was substantially impaired.
4. The age of the defendant at the time of the crime.
*5. The defendant acted under extreme duress, although not such duress to constitute defense to prosecution …
6. The victim was a participant in the defendant's homicidal conduct or consented to the homicidal acts.
7. The defendant's participation in the homicidal act was relatively minor.
8. Any other evidence of mitigation concerning the character and record of the defendant and the circumstances of his offense.

Source: Source: 42 Pa C.S.A. §9711 (e).

   * Truncated.

Further, relevant to the ability to appreciate the magnitude of the crime, individuals who have mental retardation also are not subject to the death penalty (*Atkins v. Virginia*, 2002).

Although mitigating circumstances may not be sufficient to merit a successful defense to the crime, mitigating circumstances may be significant enough for consideration in determining the sentence. For example, if a defendant killed someone because the victim called and said, "I want you to come down here and shoot me," that would likely not be a sufficient defense to the premeditated murder. However, the jury might believe that such a statement were sufficient to be a mitigating circumstance. The jury would then weigh this mitigating circumstance against any relevant aggravating circumstances in reaching a verdict regarding the death sentence.

The final mitigating circumstance specified in the statute is often referred to as a "catchall mitigator." It is referred to as a catchall mitigator because the jury is allowed to consider "any evidence of mitigation concerning the character and record of the defendant and the circumstances of the defense." Thus, the jury can consider evidence of mitigation that the legislature might not have predicted when writing the statute but would still be relevant to sparing the life of the convicted murderer. Such catchall mitigating circumstances were considered important when the Supreme Court of the United States accepted changes to the Georgia statute (*Gregg v. Georgia*, 1977). The lack of a catchall mitigator was one reason why the Pennsylvania Supreme Court rejected the state's 1974 death penalty statute as well (*Commonwealth v. Moody*, 1977).

Circumstances that might fall under the catchall mitigating factor could include issues such as past abuse of the defendant (especially by the victim), remorse and apologies, past community involvement, and other aspects concerning the crime or the defendant's character. For example, in *Commonwealth v. Reid* (1994) the Pennsylvania Supreme Court held that a defendant can present evidence of his religious and moral values. However, the catchall mitigating circumstance does not mean that *any* information could be considered by a jury. For instance, the court did not allow evidence concerning how the execution of a defendant might impact the defendant's family (*Commonwealth v. Harris*, 2002). The court reasoned that family impact would not be relevant to the character or record of the *defendant* but instead of third parties. In addition, raising a catchall mitigator allows the prosecution to present evidence that might rebut, or dispute, the defendant's claim allowing the prosecutor to raise negative or damaging issues about the defendant that might not fall under the listed aggravating circumstances (*Commonwealth v. Koehler*, 1999).

The relationship between aggravating and mitigating circumstances can be a tricky one. Pennsylvania's death penalty statute specifies that when the jury finds an aggravating circumstance but no mitigating circumstance, the penalty is death. However, mitigating circumstances can occur in even the most heinous first-degree murder cases. When the jury finds at least one aggravating circumstance and at least one mitigating circumstance, the jury must weigh those circumstances to determine whether consideration leans them toward a particular decision.

Gary Heidnik: An Illustration

In the case of the last man executed in Pennsylvania, Gary Heidnik, the jury found a single mitigating circumstance but multiple aggravating circumstances. *Readers should be aware that some details of the case are particularly gruesome, but they are included because they illustrate how/why a jury might reach a decision of death even with the presence of a mitigating circumstance.*

On March 24, 1987, the Philadelphia Police Department responded to a phone call made from a pay phone and came across Josephina Rivera (*Commonwealth v. Heidnik*, 1991). The frantic woman told police that a man named Gary Heidnik held her captive in a basement for months and that other women were still trapped in his basement. Police went to the house and entered the basement. There they found two women in shackles on a dirty mattresses and a third woman in a hole in the basement floor that was covered with a board and bags of dirt. All three women were alive. Upon further search of the premises, the police learned of even more heinous acts that had occurred in Heidnik's home, as they found human body parts in bags in the refrigerator (*Commonwealth v. Heidnik*, 1991).

Police soon learned that Heidnik had murdered at least two women. His first known homicide victim was a woman named Sarah Lindsay, whom Heidknik had kidnapped. Heidnik would punish his victims for attempting to escape or screaming. As part of her punishment, Lindsay was forced to stand for several days with one hand shackled to a pipe above her head. During this time, Heidnik force-fed Lindsay bread and water and beat her as punishment for not eating or drinking fast enough. He also forced the other victims to beat her as well. After several days, Sarah Lindsay complained of not feeling well and collapsed. Heidnik then unshackled her arm and kicked her into the hole he dug in his basement floor. Later, he checked her pulse and determined that she was dead. To add to the depravity of the murder, Heidnik did several things to the corpse including removing Lindsay's head and boiling it in water and storing her body parts in the freezer (*Commonwealth v. Heidnik*, 1991).

A second woman, Debra Dudley, was also killed by Heidnik. After defying Heidnik's orders, Dudley was shown the boiled head of Lindsay. Dudley continued to disobey Heidnik and was punished as a result. Heidnik had removed insulation from an extension cord and used it to shock his victims. To punish Dudley, he placed her and two other women in the hole he dug in the ground. Heidnik then filled that hole with water and covered it with a board. He pushed the plugged cord through the hole until he hit the shackles he had on Dudley. She received the brunt of the shock with Heidnik electrocuting her until she stopped screaming. She died from these injuries (*Commonwealth v. Heidnik*, 1991).

The case illustrates several aggravating circumstances, such as two murders in the perpetration of a felony (in this case, kidnapping). The jury also found, unanimously, that there was significant torture due to the heinous nature of the killings. In the case of Dudley, the jury found that her murder occurred after Heidnik committed the prior murder of Lindsay and used that as an aggravating circumstance in sentencing for Dudley's death. Finally, the jury found that the killing created a grave risk to others, particularly because the two other women could have also been killed by the electric shock. The sole mitigating circumstance in the case came from Heidnik's lack of a significant criminal record. Thus, the jury was *not required* to return a verdict of death but felt that the aggravating circumstances did outweigh (in both quantity and magnitude) the single mitigating circumstance and rendered a death sentence (*Commonwealth v. Heidnik*, 1991).

The Death Penalty Process

If the district attorney chooses to seek the death penalty against a homicide defendant, he or she must present to a judge a list of aggravating circumstances present in the case to merit the death penalty. The defense has a right to view this list, along with other evidence and filings, prior to the start of trial. A death penalty case only moves forward if the prosecution can present relevant aggravating circumstances, as the death penalty would be moot in any case without aggravating circumstances. The following section illustrates many of the common procedural issues related to death penalty trials and the death penalty process in Pennsylvania.

Jury Selection

The *voir dire* process occurs in all jury trials, but it is an especially important part of death penalty trials. Jurors are individually questioned in the death penalty *voir dire* process to determine whether each potential juror is *death qualified* (Death Qualification, n.d.). A death-qualified juror is one who is able to objectively consider all sentencing options; in Pennsylvania these options are death and life in prison without possibility of parole.

The Supreme Court of the United States, in *Wainwright v. Witt* (1985), held that an individual juror is only death qualified when his or her views on capital punishment would not impair the juror's duty to follow death penalty instructions. The case provided more discretion to the trial judge to determine who might be biased to administer the death penalty when inappropriate or to not administer it when appropriate. Under the logic in *Wainwright* (1985), jurors can be excluded from serving on a death penalty jury for a variety of reasons including moral opposition to the death penalty, an inability to consider aggravating or mitigating circumstances, or general opinions that would otherwise bias decisions in either the merit or sentencing phase of a death penalty trial.

Each side can challenge an unlimited number of potential jurors for cause; these challenges will include those who are not death-qualified. However, each side also is still afforded preemptory challenges or can challenge for cause for other reasons not directly related to death qualification (e.g., the potential juror is related to one of the parties, etc.). Several researchers have expressed concern that death-qualified jurors are not always representative of the population (see Death Qualification, n.d.).

Bifurcated Process

Capital murder trials in Pennsylvania are bifurcated trials. Bifurcated trials have two parts: the guilt phase (also known as the merits phase) and the sentencing phase. The sentencing phase of the trial only occurs in a capital case when the defendant is found guilty of (or pleads guilty to) first-degree murder, as this is the only crime in which the death penalty is an option. If the jury finds the defendant guilty of first-degree murder, then the sentencing phase of the trial begins. In the sentencing phase, the jury no longer considers the guilt or innocence of the defendant. In Pennsylvania, a defendant has no right to testify about his innocence during the sentencing phase of the trial as the jury has already determined the defendant's guilt (*Commonwealth v. Fisher*, 2002).

In the sentencing phase, the jury considers evidence related to aggravating and mitigating circumstances in the case. Jury decisions in this phase of the trial do not affect the verdict from the merits phase, as guilt is established prior to the jury hearing sentencing-relevant facts. As discussed in a previous section, the jury must apply the proper standard when evaluating the prosecutor's proof of aggravating circumstances (beyond a reasonable doubt) and the defense's proof of mitigating circumstances (beyond a preponderance of the evidence). A failure to reach a unanimous verdict in this stage of the trial yields a verdict of life in prison.

Family members of the victim are also allowed to provide testimony about the impact of the murder on them (42 Pa C.S.A. §9711[e]). Under the statute, the jury can consider these statements when making their decision on the defendant's sentence as long as the jury first finds that at least one aggravating circumstance was present in the case. When considering the victim impact in sentencing deliberations, the jury can utilize it when *weighing* aggravating and mitigating circumstances. After considering the evidence in the sentencing phase of the trial, including weighing aggravating and mitigating circumstances, the jury then renders its decision.

After the Verdict

The court receives the jury's verdict and the sentence is announced. Judges in three states (i.e., Alabama, Delaware, and Florida) can override a jury's recommendation of life in prison to a death sentence, although the constitutionality of such policies have come into question (Equal Justice Initiative, 2011). However, judges in Pennsylvania do not have this power. Assuming a death sentence, the judge often hears a series of appeals from both sides in the case and might address whether all sides, including the jury, followed proper procedure. Frequently several days will pass between the jury's death sentence and a formal sentence by the judge (Dept. of Corrections, n.d.).

After the formal death sentence by the judge, the case is *automatically* reviewed by the Supreme Court of Pennsylvania (42 Pa C.S.A. §9711[h]). During this review, the court determines whether there were errors in either phase of the bifurcated trial and then either affirms the death sentence or vacates the sentence and sends the case back to the lower court for further proceedings. According to the death penalty statute, the state Supreme Court will affirm the death sentence unless they determine that:

> (i) the sentence of death was the product of passion, prejudice or any other arbitrary factor; or
> (ii) the evidence fails to support the finding of at least one aggravating circumstance specified in subsection (d) (42 Pa C.S.A. §9711[h]).

The statute further specifies:

> If the Supreme Court determines that the death penalty must be vacated because none of the aggravated circumstances are supported by sufficient evidence, then it shall remand for the imposition of a life imprisonment sentence. If the Supreme Court determines that the death penalty must be vacated for any other reason, it shall remand for a new sentencing hearing ... (42 Pa C.S.A. §9711[h]).

Following affirmation of the sentence by the Pennsylvania Supreme Court, the case then goes to the governor who is the only person who can sign a death warrant, which is a formal scheduling of the date of execution (Dept. of Corrections, n.d.). Before the warrant is signed, the Governor's legal department examines the case, and if it believes that the death penalty is the appropriate punishment the case goes to the Governor for review. The governor then has the authority to sign the death warrant.

Even after the governor signs the death warrant, inmates have many opportunities to appeal to both state and federal courts. Inmates can engage in post-conviction collateral appeals for any number of potential legal errors including jury misconduct, improper jury instructions, erroneous use of evidence, and for many other reasons. Once state appeals have been exhausted, the defendant can seek a federal habeas corpus proceeding, which apply to "any person in custody under a state-court judgment who seeks a determination that the custody violates the Constitution, laws, or treaties of the United States" (28 U.S.C. §2254). Through the federal habeas corpus proceeding, the defendant (petitioner) will assert *federal* claims on issues already considered by state courts. The possible results of habeas corpus claims include a new trial (to correct trial errors), a new sentence (to correct sentencing errors), other types of relief as applicable, or the federal court might affirm the sentence of the trial court. Any decision following a federal habeas corpus is also subject to appeal by both the inmate and the state. The state and federal appellate process can take years or even decades to complete.

From Sentencing to Death[2]

Once the death warrant is signed, the defendant is transferred to death row. Death row inmates are held in solitary confinement and separated from other inmates in a maximum security prison (Dept. of Corrections, n.d.). The rights of inmates are greatly diminished once on death row. Only family members, legal counsel, and clergy can visit the inmate. Inmates are limited to only a few personal and consumable items in their cells and are carefully monitored by correctional staff (Dept. of Corrections, n.d.).

As an inmate's execution date gets closer, he is transferred to the execution complex at SCI Rockview. The cells at the execution complex only hold inmates for a short time between arrival and scheduled execution and are not meant for long-term housing. In 1997, the Department of Corrections moved the execution complex from inside the prison building to a former field hospital on prison grounds. The move offers security of those involved in the execution process, including correctional staff, officials, members of the media, and execution witnesses from other inmates. As a further means of security, the Department does not disclose the exact times prisoners are moved to the execution complex and the routes they take from other prisons (Dept. of Corrections, n.d.).

On the day of execution, approved family members listed by the inmate are allowed to visit, as are the inmate's legal counsel and any designated spiritual advisor. According to the Department of Corrections, executions are presently scheduled at 7:00 PM on the day of execution, but the three most recent executions were scheduled for 10:00 PM and all occurred after this time. Inmates are provided a final meal from a selection of available items.

Immediately prior to execution, correctional staff transfer the inmate from the holding cell to an execution chamber where the lethal injection equipment is located (Dept. of Corrections, n.d.). The inmate is strapped to a gurney with an arm extended for the insertion of an IV. A viewing room, outside of

---

2. This section describes the process independent of state and federal appeals; few death row inmates in Pennsylvania make it to the execution complex, much less the execution chamber.

the execution chamber, separates the inmate from members of the victims' family, selected media, and a small number of community members (Dept. of Corrections, n.d.). Witnesses view the execution separately from victims' family members. A curtain between the viewing room and the execution room opens after the inmate is strapped to the gurney. Barring any last minute reprieves, the state proceeds with the death sentence. After the staff have fully prepared for execution and when the execution begins, a cocktail of chemicals enters the inmate's arm. Death typically occurs within minutes. According to a witness of Gary Heidnik's execution, after the chemicals entered his arm, "his face turned a deep red and then became ashen, close to the color of his salt-and-pepper beard" (Adamson & Smith, 1999). Following a medical examination, the inmate is declared dead and the next of kin receive any personal property. Due to the prospects of last minute reprieves, a phone line remains open between the Governor's office and SCI Rockview; a phone also sits in the execution chamber (Dept. of Corrections, n.d.).

Death Penalty Opinions and Attitudes

Opinions of Public Officials

The Department of Corrections does not take an official position on the ethics of the death penalty, as it is their job to administer punishment as deemed by the legislative, judicial, and executive branches (Dept. of Corrections, n.d.). Although former state Attorneys General have opposed the death penalty (Dept. of Corrections, n.d.), those who have held the position in the modern era have, at the very least, abided by the law. The current Attorney General, Kathleen Kane, supports the death penalty under certain conditions, though she desires safeguards in place (Murphy, 2012).

The Governor of Pennsylvania must sign the death warrant and has the power to commute sentences or even pardon inmates. As such, the governor's opinion on the death penalty can have the most impact on its imposition. Since 1971, six of the seven men who served as governor have issued death warrants during their time in office, although the number of warrants varied widely. Governor Milton Shapp, serving from 1971 to 1979, unsuccessfully tried to veto death penalty legislation twice and did not sign a death warrant. All Governors since then have signed multiple death warrants. Governor Thornburgh (1979–1987) supported the death penalty, issuing seven warrants as governor and even arguing in favor of the death penalty as United States Attorney General (Greenhouse, 1991). Governor Robert Casey (1987–1995), who was governor when lethal injection officially replaced the electric chair, issued 21 death warrants during his term (Dept. of Corrections, n.d.).

Perhaps the most ardent supporter of death penalty as Governor was Tom Ridge (1995–2001) who fought for a speedier death process (PBS NewsHour, 2001). Ridge signed 220 death warrants during his time in office, which is more than the number of death warrants signed by all other Governors since 1978, combined. He was also in office during the state's three modern executions (Dept. of Corrections, n.d.). Ridge released a statement on the date of Keith Zettlemoyer's execution, stating, "May Keith Zettlemoyer's soul rest in peace. May the soul of Charles DeVetsco [the victim] now rest in peace." (Heine, 1995). Ridge's words were not as kind when discussing the execution of Gary Heidnik, stating, "So horrible were his deeds, a jury of 12 Pennsylvanians determined unanimously that he must forfeit his life. Tonight, he paid that price. In doing so he suffered far less than the women he tortured" (Adamson & Smith, 1999).

Since Governor Ridge's time in office, 160 death warrants have been signed in Pennsylvania. Governor Ed Rendell (2003–2011) signed the majority of these at 119 warrants (Dept. of Corrections, n.d.). During his last week as Pennsylvania Governor, Rendell noted that there were problems with the death penalty process in the state, but he argued for a speedier process (Lappas, 2011). Governor Tom Corbett, currently serving, also supports the death penalty, issuing over 20 death warrants thus far.

Public Opinion

The majority of Americans support the death penalty, according to national polls. When asked if one is in favor of the death penalty for a person convicted of murder, 63% of Americans stated that they were in favor according to the latest Gallup survey at the time of this writing (December 19–22, 2012) (Gallup, 2012). However, death penalty support has decreased since the mid-1990s, when 80% were in favor (Gallup, 2012). Asking if one is in favor of the death penalty is not the only way to ask for opinions about the controversial topic. In addition to the standard death penalty question, Gallup asked respondents what they felt was the *best* punishment for murder between execution and life in prison without parole. When given these choices, respondents' support for the death penalty decreased to fewer than half of respondents believing a death sentence was the best punishment (Gallup, 2012).

In Pennsylvania, death penalty support is partially reflected through support of pro-death penalty political candidates. Throughout the past four decades, Pennsylvania voters have regularly elected Governors who have supported the death penalty. Residents have also elected other officials who have supported the death penalty, including legislators, prosecutors, and the current Attorney General. While political elections involve many issues other than the candidates' beliefs concerning the death penalty, Pennsylvania voters do continue electing these death penalty supporters to public office.

Penn State Harrisburg's Center for Survey Research conducted a widespread survey of Pennsylvanian's attitudes toward the death penalty in 2006. Respondents were asked, "What do you think should be the penalty for persons convicted of murder?" The largest group of respondents (42.9%) answered that they felt the death penalty should be the punishment, while 35.5% stated that it should be life in prison with no possibility of parole, 9.6% life in prison with the possibility of parole, and the remaining respondents either refused to answer the question or stated that they did not know or were not sure. Ignoring those in the latter group, just under half (48.8%) of Pennsylvania residents reported that the death penalty *should* be the punishment for murder (Center for Survey Research, 2006).

Similar to national poll findings, demographic variability exists among Pennsylvania residents in their death penalty attitudes. The figures discussed in the remainder of this section exclude those who refused to answer or stated they did not know or were not sure what the punishment should be for someone convicted of murder. Of those who expressed an opinion, males (59.4%) were more likely to support the death penalty than were females (38.6%). College-aged respondents showed the lowest support for the death penalty of all age groups with 37.2% of those aged 18–24 years selecting the death penalty. Those aged 35–44 years had the highest support (57.6%) (Center for Survey Research, 2006).

The data indicate large regional differences in death penalty support in the state. The researchers divided the state into nine distinct regions when summarizing the survey findings. The strongest death penalty support was among residents of South Central Pennsylvania, including Cambria, Blair, Huntington, and Bedford Counties. Almost 70% (67.9%) felt that the death penalty should be the punishment for murder; none of the respondents selected life in prison with possibility of parole. The lowest support was near Philadelphia, including Chester, Montgomery, Bucks, Delaware, and Philadelphia Counties. Here, only 34.4% of respondents felt that the death penalty should be the punishment for murder, with just under half (49.8%) believing that life without the possibility of parole was the most appropriate sentence (Center for Survey Research, 2006). While the majority of residents from the Philadelphia area did not feel that the death penalty was the appropriate punishment for murder, those counties account for nearly half of all inmates currently on death row in Pennsylvania (Dept. of Corrections, n.d.).

Large racial differences are present in attitudes toward the death penalty in Pennsylvania, as well as on the national level. In the Pennsylvania survey, a majority of White respondents (51.5%) responded that the death penalty was the most appropriate punishment. In contrast, more Black respondents felt that life in prison *with the possibility of parole* (26.1%) was the appropriate punishment for murder than felt that the death penalty (15.0%) was the appropriate punishment (Center for Survey Research, 2006).

Death Penalty Controversies

Proponents and opponents of the death penalty have raised several concerns about the imposition of the death penalty on both national and local levels. While the focus of this section is on wrongful conviction, a backlog of cases, and the high cost of the death penalty to the state, other controversies also exist. These include a concern about the quality of legal representation of poor capital murder defendants (Bookman, n.d.), the morality of the death penalty, the deterrent effect of the death penalty (if it exists), and the role of physicians in the death penalty process.

Wrongful Conviction

According to a 2011 national survey conducted by the Pew Research Center, 27% of those opposing the death penalty stated that their opposition was because they felt the justice system was imperfect and the state might execute the wrong person (Pew Research, 2012). More than half of Americans feel that someone who was innocent was wrongfully executed within the past five years (Gallup, 2012). Since 1973, over 140 death row inmates throughout the United States have been exonerated (i.e., the facts support their innocence).

Six exonerations of death row inmates have occurred in Pennsylvania since 2004 (Innocence Cases, n.d.) while hundreds more inmates have had their sentences commuted to life in prison due to flaws in the sentencing process (see PA Dept. of Corrections, n.d.). The six exonerated inmates served an average of 9.5 years in prison. Harold Wilson served 16 years on death row until exonerated by DNA evidence demonstrating that blood found at the scene did not belong to Wilson or three murder victims, suggesting someone else as the assailant (Innocence Cases, n.d.). Executing innocent individuals is a concern of many death penalty opponents, but even death row supporters have expressed this concern.

Case Backlog

With no one executed without waiving their rights to appeals since 1962, Pennsylvania currently has a large backlog of death penalty cases with many death row inmates having served nearly three decades on death row without being executed (Slobodzian, 2011). While several of these men are nearing the end of the appellate process, the reality is that many of Pennsylvania's death row inmates will die from old age rather than execution (Thompson, 2012). Several public officials in Pennsylvania, including former Governor Ed Rendell, have argued that the death penalty process in Pennsylvania is too slow. Terrance Williams, who committed a 1984 murder, has been on death row for almost three decades. He was scheduled for execution in 2012, but he was granted a last minute stay of execution to have a new sentencing trial to present evidence that he was abused by his victim as a teen (Dale, 2012). Fear of wrongful conviction, the lengthy state review and appellate process, and Pennsylvania's presence in the jurisdiction of the relatively liberal 3rd Circuit Court of Appeals all contribute to this backlog.

The High Cost of Death

The financial burden of capital murder cases on the state is quite high. Once sentenced to death, housing each death row inmate in Pennsylvania costs the Department of Corrections approximately $10,000 a year *more* than to house other inmates. These higher costs are associated with greater security and administrative expenses (Yates, 2011). As a result, the state spends more than $2 million more per year to house death row inmates than it would spend if the inmates had been sentenced to life in prison without parole. These are just the costs to house the inmates. The costs of the death penalty process, including the trial and appeals, are also likely higher for the state than are the costs of other cases, though exact costs are unknown (Yates, 2011).

Race and the Death Penalty

A striking characteristic of Pennsylvania's death row is that Blacks make up nearly two-thirds of the inmates currently on death row yet racial minorities make up only 11% of the state's population (Committee on Racial and Gender Bias, 2003). Only Louisiana has a death row with a higher percentage of Blacks than does Pennsylvania. Since 1985, governors have signed 238 death warrants for Black defendants and only 137 for White defendants (Dept. of

Corrections, n.d.). Prospective jurors who are Black are dismissed by prosecutors at a much higher rate than are White jurors, and Black capital murder defendants often rely on an overburdened public defender system (Committee on Racial and Gender Bias, 2003).

Eighty-three percent of Philadelphia death row inmates are Black. Research by David Baldus and colleagues (1998) suggests differential treatment of Black and White defendants in Pennsylvania, specifically in Philadelphia. The researchers found that in Philadelphia capital murder cases, the race of the defendant predicted legal decisions generally (e.g., verdict, sentence, etc.) and among jury analyses of aggravating and mitigating circumstances, Black defendants were at a disadvantage. The race of the victim in cases was also highly predictive of legal decisions; jurors were less likely to find mitigating circumstances when the murder victim was White (Baldus et al., 1998). The researchers concluded that "it would be extremely unlikely to observe disparities of both this magnitude and consistently if substantial equality existed in this system's treatment of defendants." (Baldus et al., 1998, p. 1715).

Based, in part, on testimony of Baldus on racial inequality in the state's death penalty system, the Pennsylvania Supreme Court's Committee on Racial and Gender Bias in the Justice System recommended a moratorium on imposing the death penalty. They stated that this moratorium should last "until policies and procedures intended to ensure that the death penalty is administered fairly and impartially are implemented." (Committee on Racial and Gender Bias, 2003). They further recommended that the state adopt a Racial Justice Act, legislation that would promote death penalty data collection and allow capital murder defendants to provide evidence of patterns of racial inequality.

Conclusion

Capital punishment was a fixture of Pennsylvania's justice system until 1962 when a series of legal battles on the local and national level changed the imposition of the death penalty in the state. After a series of changes to the death penalty statute, the current version of the law includes a list of 18 aggravating and eight mitigating circumstances, including the catchall mitigator, that death qualified jurors are allowed to consider when determining whether someone convicted of first-degree murder should be sentenced to death.

More than 200 defendants were sentenced to death in Pennsylvania over the past four decades, yet only three were actually executed. All three waived their rights to appeal, and at least one (Keith Zettlemoyer) explicitly asked the court to grant him mercy through execution. The death row complex, located at SCI

Rockview, has not been used in over a decade and might not be used any time soon due to concerns over the imposition of the death penalty in the state. Racial inequality has led at least one state commission to recommend a death penalty moratorium and others are examining whether the death penalty in Pennsylvania is worth the cost. The next several years are likely to lead to significant changes in the death penalty process in Pennsylvania—what changes and how they are implemented are yet to be seen.

Review Questions

1. How has the use of capital punishment changed over time in Pennsylvania, and how have federal and state court decisions influenced its imposition?
2. What are the circumstances that jurors must consider when determining the appropriate sentence for someone convicted of first-degree murder, and how are those circumstances guided through appellate court decisions?
3. What is the execution process in Pennsylvania for those who are actually executed?
4. What are the opinions of public officials and Pennsylvania residents about the death penalty and its imposition?
5. What is the relevance of race in the conversation about the death row in the state?

Critical Thinking Questions

1. Following decisions by the Supreme Court of the United States and the Pennsylvania Supreme Court, the Commonwealth adopted a "catchall mitigator" as part of the death penalty statute. However, there is no "catchall aggravator" in the law. Why do you think this is the case? Why might including a catchall aggravator lead to an arbitrary imposition of the death penalty?
2. Based on public opinion data, certain groups in Pennsylvania (e.g., women, those who are Black) are more likely than others to support the death penalty. How might the death qualification process, during *voir dire*, exclude these groups from being represented on a death penalty jury?
3. Consider information in this chapter related to the rarity of execution in Pennsylvania, the cost, public opinion, and racial disparities. Should the death penalty be abolished in the state? If not, what might help to make the process more efficient while continuing to protect the rights of the accused?

Key Terms and Definitions

Aggravating circumstance: An aspect of a criminal act that makes the crime more serious or outrageous; it can increase the severity of punishment for that crime. At least one aggravating circumstance must be present in a murder case to warrant execution.

Bifurcated trial: A trial that takes place in two phases. Under criminal law, bifurcated trials are generally associated with death penalty cases. If, and only if, the defendant is found guilty of first-degree murder, then a sentencing phase of the trial begins. In the sentencing phase, the jury (or judge in a bench trial) hears evidence relevant to aggravating and mitigating circumstances and then recommends a punishment of life or death.

Capital punishment: Punishment in which an individual is put to death for a criminal act; also referred to as the death penalty.

Catchall mitigator: As defined by Pennsylvania statute, "any evidence of mitigation concerning the character and record of the defendant and the circumstances of the defense" can be considered by the jury. This allows for a variety of evidence, possibly not originally anticipated by legislators, to be considered as mitigating factors in death penalty cases.

Commonwealth v. Heidnik: Appellate case relating to notorious murderer Gary Heidnik. Among the precedent from the case is the conclusion that Pennsylvania law allows for the execution of an individual when mitigating circumstances are present in the case as long as the aggravating circumstance(s) outweigh the mitigating circumstance(s).

Commonwealth v. Moody: The Pennsylvania Supreme Court case that held that the Commonwealth's 1974 death penalty statute was unconstitutional because it failed to draw the attention of the jury to the character and record of a defendant, two potentially mitigating circumstances.

First-degree murder: A criminal homicide committed by an intentional killing.

Furman v. Georgia: Case in which the Supreme Court of the United States held that the death penalty, as administered at the time, was arbitrary and thus unconstitutional.

Mitigating circumstance: An aspect of a criminal act that makes the crime less serious or outrageous; it can decrease the severity of punishment for a crime. In a capital murder case, the mitigating circumstances lessen the likelihood of a death verdict.

Torture: "[T]he infliction of a considerable amount of pain and suffering on a victim which is unnecessarily heinous, atrocious, or cruel manifesting exception depravity," according to *Commonwealth v. Pursell* (1985).

Websites

Capital Jury Project: information about the Capital Jury Project, a program of research studying jury decision making in capital cases including information concerning legal factors that juries often find difficult to understand. URL: http://www.albany.edu/scj/13192.php.

Death Penalty Pros and Cons: a look at controversies surrounding the death penalty from the side of supporters and opponents. URL: http://deathpenalty.procon.org.

Death Penalty Information Center: a plethora of information about the death penalty from this national non-profit center. URL: http://deathpenalty-info.org.

Pennsylvania's Death Penalty: information about the state's death penalty process from Pennsylvania's Department of Corrections. URL: http://www.cor.state.pa.us/portal/server.pt/community/death_penalty/.

References

Adamson, A., & Smith, J. (1999). Horrors' killer gets his wish: Victims' kin watch as Gary Heidnik gets lethal injection. *Philly.com.* Retrieved from: http://articles.philly.com/1999-07-07/news/25522531_1_gary-heidnik-lethal-injection-death-chamber.

Atkins v. Virginia, 536 U.S. 304 (2002).

Baldus, D.C., Woodworth, G., Zuckerman, D., Weiner, N.A., & Broffitt, B. (1998). Racial discrimination and the death penalty in the post-*Furman* era: An empirical and legal overview, with recent findings from Philadelphia. *Cornell Law Review, 83,* 1643–1770.

Bovsun, M. (2013). Philadelphia sicko Gary Heidnik inspired role of Buffalo Bill in 'The Silence of the Lambs.' *NY Daily News.* Retrieved from: http://www.nydailynews.com/news/justice-story/philly-sicko-death-dungeon-inspired-famous-movie-scene-article-1.1348191.

Center for Survey Research—Penn State Harrisburg (2006). 2006 Penn State Poll. Retrieved from: http://www.aclupa.org/downloads/PennStatePollD-Presults.pdf (cached copy).

Committee on Racial and Gender Bias (2003). *Final report of the Pennsylvania Supreme Court Committee on Racial and Gender Bias in the Justice System.* Retrieved from: http://www.pa-interbranchcommission.com/_pdfs/FinalReport.pdf.

Commonwealth v. Bradley, 449 Pa. 19 (1972).

Commonwealth v. Fisher, 813 A.2d 761 (2002).

Commonwealth v. Harris, 817 A.2d 1033 (2002).

Commonwealth v. Heidnik, 526 Pa. 458 (1991).

Commonwealth v. Koehler, 737 A.2d 225 (1999).

Commonwealth v. Miles, 545 Pa. 500 (1996).

Commonwealth v. Mitchell, 839 A.2d 202 (2003).

Commonwealth v. Moody, 476 Pa. 223 (1977).

Commonwealth v. Pursell, 555 Pa. 233 (1999).

Commonwealth v. Reid, 537 Pa. 167 (1994).

Commonwealth v. Scarfo, 611 A.2d 242 (1992).

Commonwealth v. Wholaver, 903 A.2d 1178 (2006).

Dale, M. (2012). Judge halts scheduled execution of Terrance Williams. Retrieved from: http://abclocal.go.com/wpvi/story?section=news/local&id=8828151.

Death Qualification (n.d.). Retrieved from: http://www.capitalpunishmentin-context.org/resources/deathqualification.

DPI History. (n.d.). Retrieved from: http://www.deathpenaltyinfo.org/part-i-history-death-penalty.

Equal Justice Initiative (2011). The death penalty in Alabama: Judge override. Retrieved from: http://www.eji.org/files/Override_Report.pdf.

Fenton, M. (2010). PA's big house. Retrieved from: http://pabook.libraries.psu.edu/palitmap/Rockview.html.

Furman v. Georgia, 408 U.S. 238 (1972).

Gallup (2012). Death penalty. Retrieved from: http://www.gallup.com/poll/1606/death-penalty.aspx.

Gregg v. Georgia, 428 U.S. 153 (1976).

Greenhouse, L. (1991). Court hears Thornburgh on the death penalty. *The New York Times.* Retrieved from: http://www.nytimes.com/1991/04/25/us/court-hears-thornburgh-on-the-death-penalty.html.

Heine, K. (1995). Zettlemoyer executed for 1980 killing of pal. *Philly.com.* Retrieved from: http://articles.philly.com/1995-05-03/news/25673982_1_keith-zettlemoyer-execution-warrant-pennsylvania-post-conviction-defender-organization.

Heine, K., & Kim, M.O. (1995). Leon Moser put to death. *Philly.com*. Retrieved from: http://articles.philly.com/1995-08-17/news/25710172_1_doris-schramm-death-warrants-linda-moser.

Innocence Cases (n.d.). Retrieved from: http://www.deathpenaltyinfo.org/innocence-cases-2004-present.

Lappas, S.T. (2011). Pennsylvania should end the death penalty. *PennLive.com*. Retrieved from: http://www.pennlive.com/editorials/index.ssf/2011/01/pennsylvania_should_end_the_de.html.

Murphy, J. (2012). Attorney general candidates offer mostly opposite views on election's hot topics. *PennLive.com*. Retrieved from: http://www.pennlive.com/midstate/index.ssf/2012/10/attorney_general.html.

PA Dept. of Corrections (n.d.). Pennsylvania's death penalty. Retrieved from: http://www.cor.state.pa.us/portal/server.pt/community/death_penalty/.

PBS NewsHour (2001). Pennsylvania's Tom Ridge appointed to Bush Cabinet. Retrieved from: http://www.pbs.org/newshour/updates/september01/ridge_bio.html.

Pew Research (2012). Continued majority support for the death penalty. Retrieved from:

ProCon.org. (n.d.). Historical timeline. Retrieved from: http://www.people-press.org/2012/01/06/continued-majority-support-for-death-penalty/. http://deathpenalty.procon.org/view.resource.php?resourceID=003096.

Reggio, M.H. (n.d.). History of the death penalty. Retrieved from: http://www.pbs.org/wgbh/pages/frontline/shows/execution/readings/history.html.

Roper v. Simmons, 543 U.S. 551 (2005).

Slobodzian, J.A. (2011). Rarely used, Pennsylvania's death penalty remains a headache on both sides of the debate. *Philly.com*. Retrieved from: http://articles.philly.com/2011-05-15/news/29545856_1_death-penalty-capital-punishment-first-degree-murder-cases.

Wainwright v. Witt, 469 U.S. 412 (1985).

Yates, R. (2011). Killer costs. *The Morning Call*. Retrieved from: http://articles.mcall.com/2011-07-23/news/mc-pennsylvania-death-row-costs-20110723_1_death-row-death-penalty-death-penalty-opponents.

Chapter 8

The Juvenile Justice System in Pennsylvania

Maria L. Garase

Learning Objectives

After reading this chapter, students will be able to:

- Discuss the history of the juvenile justice system in Pennsylvania.
- Explain the major components of the Balanced and Restorative Justice Model and how the philosophy informs decision-making throughout the juvenile justice process.
- Identify the circumstances in which a juvenile may be detained and discuss how the process proceeds from that juncture.
- Identify the various agencies that are involved in the operation of the juvenile justice system.
- Describe the process by which a juvenile is waived to adult court in Pennsylvania.
- Discuss the juvenile crime statistics in Pennsylvania as compared to the adult crime statistics.

Key Terms

Adjudicatory Hearing
Aftercare
Balanced and Restorative Justice (BARJ) Model

Commonwealth v. Fisher
Community Protection
Competency Development
Consent Decree

Decertification Hearing
Dependent Youth
Detention
Disposition
Diversion
Ex parte Crouse
Hearing Master

Informal Adjustment
Intake
McKeiver v. Pennsylvania
Offender Accountability
Petition
Parens Patriae

Introduction

Although most states have a "Department of Juvenile Justice" which is responsible for all juvenile justice issues, Pennsylvania is not one of these states.
Pennsylvania has a highly decentralized juvenile justice system, which essentially gives an unusual amount of local control to the counties' juvenile court
judges as well as allows for a diverse mix of private delinquency service providers
to supplement the public services network (PA Juvenile Court Judges Commission (JCJC), 2008). This means that juvenile intake, detention facilities,
probation supervision, and aftercare services are all under county level supervision and under the administrative purview of the juvenile court judges
(NCJJ, 2011).

Although each of the 67 counties' day-to-day operations are independent of
each other, they all fall under the Department of Public Welfare's Office of
Children, Youth and Families (DPW) and are all bound by the Pennsylvania
Juvenile Act. The DPW advises the courts regarding institutional placement
decisions, approves and licenses many local and private institutions for juveniles, and sets the county's "needs-based budgets" for purposes of state reimbursement (JCJC, 2008). DPW also runs state's non-secure youth forestry
camps and secure youth development centers (NCJJ, 2011). It is important to
note that in this decentralized system, Pennsylvania uses reimbursements to
counties to create incentives for how juvenile justice services are provided at the
county level (Schwartz, 2013). Pennsylvania's county based, public/private approach to delinquency has produced a model juvenile justice system; it is generally considered a model for the nation (JCJC, 2008).

History of Juvenile Justice in Pennsylvania

Juvenile justice in Pennsylvania has roots that date back to the 19th century.
In 1826, one of the nation's first "Houses of Refuge" for children was estab-

lished in Philadelphia; this was the nation's second institution of its kind after the New York House of Refuge (McCarthy, 1984). Subsequent years saw the creation of separate correctional institutions for children who were convicted of crimes and vagrancy (JCJC, 2008). In 1835, legislation was enacted to include "incorrigibility" as a reason for commitment (Anderson, 1999). The Houses of Refuge became the precursors to the state run "reform schools" and industrial schools. With the *Ex parte Crouse* decision (1838), the Pennsylvania Supreme Court ruled that "*parens patriae*" is sufficient basis for intervening in the lives of juveniles without parental consent. *Crouse* was the first delinquency case in the country to use the phrase "*parens patriae*" (McCarthy, 1984). By 1893, Pennsylvania law already required separate trials and trial dockets for children and prohibited their confinement with alleged or convicted adult criminals (Anderson, 1999).

In 1899, the first juvenile court was established in Cook County, Illinois. Two years later Pennsylvania passed the Juvenile Court Act of 1902, which was almost identical to the Illinois Act; however, it was deemed unconstitutional by the Superior Court (McCarthy, 1984). So although processes were in place for handling children differently than adults in Pennsylvania, it wasn't until the adoption of the Pennsylvania Juvenile Court Act of 1903 that " … all minor crimes, or those specifically certified by a magistrate or justice of the peace as not requiring criminal conviction, could fall within the jurisdiction of the juvenile court" (Anderson, 1999, p. 2). Furthermore, this Act as well as the United States Supreme Court case *Commonwealth v. Fisher* (1905) formalized the rules that the court can intervene without impunity when the objective is to help the youth (i.e., if the intent is good, the Juvenile Court can act). With the passage of the 1933 Juvenile Court Law, the juvenile court extended its jurisdiction to include all crimes, except murder, committed by children under the age of 16 (Anderson, 1999). It further expanded its reach to include "ungovernability and truancy" concerns (Anderson, 1999). A 1939 amendment increased the ceiling of the juvenile court's jurisdiction from age 16 to include individuals up to age 18 (McCarthy, 1984).

Although juvenile justice has steadily progressed over the years, its critics acknowledged that juveniles lacked the same legal safeguards as their adult counterparts. It was during the 1960s that a series of United States Supreme Court cases [*Kent v. United States* (1966); *In re: Gault* (1967)] formalized the procedural protections of juveniles. The *Kent* and *Gault* decisions informed the development of the Uniform Juvenile Court Act, by the National Conference of Commissioners on Uniform State Laws (Anderson, 1999). The Pennsylvania legislature responded to the Uniform Juvenile Court Act with the passage of the Juvenile Act of 1972. This Act redefined the definition of a "delinquent act" as well as codified the rights of juveniles in proceedings. The Act provided the following constitutional safeguards for juveniles: right to receive written notice of charges against them, to be assisted by counsel, to confront accusers, and to be convicted with proof beyond a reasonable doubt. Consistent with the sentiment of the Juvenile Act of 1972, the *McKiever v. Pennsylvania* (1972) found that since juvenile prosecutions are not considered either civil or criminal, the Sixth Amendment does not necessarily apply. As such, there is no requirement for a jury trial in juvenile cases.

Throughout the 1970s and 1980s, amendments were added to the Juvenile Act of 1972 to include changes in definitions, booking processes, confidentiality, and access to juvenile proceedings (JCJC, 2008). In 1977, a significant change was made to the age threshold for the juvenile court; age 10 was the new lower limit to be considered delinquent and thus eligible for juvenile court. At the same time, "ungovernable behavior" was eliminated from the definition of delinquent acts and would now be handled as a dependency case instead of a delinquent case. Throughout the 1980s the Juvenile Act was amended to relax confidentiality restrictions concerning juvenile offenders' records (JCJC, 2008). In 1986, victims and their counsel and their supporters gained the right to attend juvenile hearings (JCJC, 2008).

In response to the spike in juvenile violent crime in the 1990s, many states were competing with each other to treat children more like adults and to make their juvenile justice systems more responsive to the needs of the community. It was in 1995 that Governor Tom Ridge signed into law one of the most significant reforms in the history of Pennsylvania's juvenile justice system (Anderson, 1999). Pennsylvania lawmakers forged a path between rehabilitation, which had been the heart of the juvenile justice system for nearly a century, and retribution (Schwartz, 2013). In terms of retribution, Act 33 of Special Session of 1995 effectively redrew the jurisdictional boundaries between the juvenile and criminal courts, placing a number of violent felonies on the criminal side of the line. Thus, Act 33 redefined the definition of "delinquent act" thereby expanding the number and types of offenses that were excluded from the jurisdiction of juvenile court.

In terms of rehabilitation, Act 33 essentially redefined the purpose of Pennsylvania's juvenile justice system to incorporate the principles of the Balanced and Restorative Justice (BARJ) philosophy. Unlike its counterparts in other states, Act 33 made a more fundamental and thoughtful change—reorienting the juvenile justice system itself, expanding the circle of clients whose interests it serves, and broadening its stated purposes to include more comprehensive goals. The Act 33 amendment of the Juvenile Act changed the purpose clause to:

Consistent with the protection of the public interest, to provide for children committing delinquent acts programs of supervision, care and rehabilitation which provide balanced attention to the protection of the community, the imposition of accountability for offenses committed and the development of competencies to enable children to become responsible and productive members of the community (PA Juvenile Act 42 PA CSA §6301, 1999).

The newly defined purpose gives priority to repairing the harm done to crime victims and communities, defining offender accountability in terms of assuming responsibility, and taking action to repair harm (Maloney, Romig, & Armstrong, 1988). The foundation of this mandate is the concept that crime victims and the community, as well as juvenile offenders, should receive balanced attention and gain tangible benefits from their interactions with Pennsylvania's juvenile justice system. (*See section on The Balanced and Restorative Justice Model for a more detailed review of the BARJ Model*).

As a response to the new purpose clause in the Juvenile Act, the Pennsylvania Commission on Crime and Delinquency funded the first BARJ Specialist positions at the Juvenile Court Judges Commission (JCJC). BARJ coordinator positions were created and funded at the county level in 1999 (Griffin, 2006). In 2000, victims of juvenile offenders advocate positions were created and the "Bill of Rights" law for crime victims was extended to include victims of delinquent acts (Griffin, 2006). According to the JCJC's 2005 Juvenile Justice Report Card more than $2.5 million dollars was collected from Pennsylvania juveniles, whose cases were closed that year, in the form of victim restitution and Crime Victim's Compensation Fund payments. Furthermore, those same juveniles completed more than a half a million of hours of community service (Griffin, 2006). From that same report "about 87% of cases statewide were closed without a new offense that year, which means that in almost nine out of 10 cases, juvenile courts and probation departments succeeded, through supervision, monitoring, and enforcement of firm expectations" (Griffin, 2006, p. 5). In terms of competency development, more than 77% of juveniles were employed or engaged in an education or vocational activity at case closing (Griffin, 2006).

By early 2003, the John D. and Catherine T. MacArthur Foundation had decided to invest in Pennsylvania as its first Models for Change Core State. Pennsylvania was chosen "because of the state's leadership, structure, commitment to system-wide change, and likelihood to influence reforms through the state" (Puzzanchera, Knoll, Adams, & Sickmund, 2012, p. 1). Models for Change collaborates with selected states to advance juvenile justice reforms that effectively hold juveniles accountable for their actions, provide for their rehabilitation, protect them from harm, increase their life changes, and manage the risk they pose to themselves and to public safety (Schwartz, 2013). Pilot projects were implemented in various counties throughout the state that focused on these issues. Evaluation of these objectives as well as the BARJ model is constantly being undertaken. Virtually all components of Pennsylvania's juvenile justice system are engaged in employing evidence-based practices as well as measuring the results of these efforts.

The Balanced and Restorative Justice Model (BARJ)

Because the juvenile justice system is based on principles of BARJ, it is important to have basic understanding of the philosophy and its application in Pennsylvania's juvenile justice system. BARJ ideals focus on protecting communities, restoring victims, and developing youth competencies that enable youth to become responsible citizens in the community (Maloney, Romig, & Armstrong, 1988; Seyko, 2001). The BARJ model pays balanced attention to the three components: Community Protection, Offender Accountability, and Competency Development. Community Protection means that citizens have a right to feel safe and secure in their communities through prevention, supervision, and control (Torbet, 2008). This includes conducting timely investigations and processing of juveniles, using a wide range of diversion, control, and placement programs, and creating partnerships with the community that emphasize deterrence of crime (Torbet, 2008). Under this model, weight is also given to repeat offenders or those "known" to law enforcement to monitor subsequent decisions in court.

The second component to this model is Offender Accountability/Victim Restoration. Offender Accountability/Victim Restoration is seen through restoring victims by holding the juvenile responsible for the harm caused to the victim and the community, thereby, taking action to repair the harm and restore the victim (PA Council of Chief Juvenile Probation Officers, 2012). Some of the ways that this goal has been implemented are through the use of victim impact statements, victim community awareness classes, apology statements, restitution, group conferencing, community service, and payment to the crime victims' compensation fund (Torbet, 2006). The last component is Competency Development. Under Competency Development, the juvenile is afforded opportunities to acquire skills, get a job, develop personal relationships, and form attachments to pro-social groups and institutions in the community (PA Council of Chief Juvenile Probation Officers, 2012). Some of the programs designed to improve competency development include requiring youth to participate in classes that promote learning pro-social, moral reasoning, academic, workforce development, and independent living skills (Torbet, 2008).

Purpose and Jurisdiction of the Juvenile Court

Pennsylvania operates two separate and distinct justice systems: the criminal court (i.e., adult court) and a juvenile court. The jurisdiction of the juvenile court is found in 42 PA C.S. §6301-6365 (1999) also known as the Juvenile Act. The purpose clause of the Pennsylvania Juvenile Act §6301, includes the following:

(1) To preserve the unity of the family whenever possible or to provide another alternative permanent family when the unity of the family cannot be maintained.

(1.1) To provide for the care, protection, safety and wholesome mental and physical development of children coming within the provisions of this chapter.

(2) Consistent with the protection of the public interest, to provide for children committing delinquent acts programs of supervision, care and rehabilitation which provide balanced attention to the protection of the community, the imposition of accountability for offenses committed and the development of competencies to enable children to become responsible and productive members of the community.

(3) To achieve the foregoing purposes in a family environment whenever possible, separating the child from parents only when necessary for his welfare, safety or health or in the interests of public safety.

(4) To provide means through which the provisions of this chapter are executed and enforced and in which the parties are assured a fair hearing and their constitutional and other legal rights recognized and enforced.

The juvenile justice system has jurisdiction over delinquent youth who are ages 10 to 17 at the time that the crime was committed. The juvenile court also has jurisdiction over dependent youth. Dependent youth are youth who are habitually, without justification, truant; youth who have committed a specific act or acts of habitual disobedience of the reasonable and lawful commands of his parent, guardian or other custodian; and/or youth who are ungovernable and found to be in need of care, treatment, or supervision (PA Juvenile Act). There are provisions in the Juvenile Act that allow the juvenile justice system to maintain "instruction and treatment" until the youth's 21st birthday. There are also provisions that allow for the automatic transfer of a juvenile to adult court depending on certain criteria *(See section on Juveniles in Adult Court).* No one may be processed in the juvenile justice system for a crime he/she is alleged to have committed as an adult.

Additionally, the juvenile court differs from the criminal court in procedure as well as terminology. In juvenile court, most hearings are not open to the public. Juvenile court hearings can be open to the public if a 12 or 13 year old child is adjudicated delinquent of certain very serious offenses, or if a child who is 14 years old or older is adjudicated delinquent of any felony offense (PA Council of Chief Juvenile Probation Officers, 2012). Juvenile hearings are presided over by a judge or a Hearing Master. Hearing Masters are attorneys, in good standing with the Bar Association, who are appointed to serve in Juvenile Court to conduct certain types of hearings (e.g., detention hearings, detention review hearings, shelter-care hearings, uncontested dispositional review hearings, or uncontested probation revocation hearings in both misdemeanor and felony cases); however, they are not to preside over adjudication hearings in felony cases (PA Council of Chief Juvenile Probation Officers, 2012). A judge must review and approve the Master's decisions and recommendations. Juveniles do not have the right to a jury trial; thus, all proceedings are conducted by either a Hearing Master or a Judge, who will make the final outcome determination.

The terminology used in the juvenile justice system differs from terms used in the adult criminal court. Offenses committed by juveniles are considered "delinquent acts" whereas in the criminal justice system they are referred to as "crimes." Prior to a hearing, youth who are considered to be a danger to themselves or others, may be placed in "preventative detention." The equivalent to this in adult court would be "in jail awaiting trial." Youth have "adjudication hearings" while adults go to "trial." Children in juvenile court are "adjudicated delinquent" rather than are "convicted" or "found guilty." Juveniles who are adjudicated delinquent have a "dispositional hearing" instead of a "sentencing hearing" and will receive a "disposition" instead of a "sentence." Youth who are released from placement (i.e., youth correctional facility) are involved in "aftercare" programs, which is similar to adult "parole" programs. The juvenile justice system is intended to focus on treatment, rehabilitation, and supervision, while the criminal justice system has various, and sometimes, conflicting goals.

Juvenile Justice Process and Structure

Pennsylvania's juvenile justice system is designed to achieve its balanced and restorative mission by employing evidence-based practices at each stage in the process, from arrest/referral to case closed. Given the BARJ model, the juvenile justice system has processes in place to help children learn from their mistakes and make positive changes that will help them become responsible and productive citizens in society.

Arrest/Referral

Juveniles can come into contact with the juvenile justice system in a few different ways. The majority of the time, the juvenile is arrested for a suspected offense; however, the juvenile may be referred to the Court by non-law enforcement. Once an arrest is made, the juvenile may be released to his/her parent or legal guardian or taken to the police station or juvenile processing center. If taken to the police station, the juvenile may be photographed and fingerprinted, and his or her information entered in the police computer system (PA Council of Chief Juvenile Probation Officers, 2012). If released to a parent or guardian, a meeting will likely be scheduled with a probation intake officer. A written allegation may be filed against the juvenile; this is the document that starts the delinquency proceedings. A written allegation is not a petition, in that it does not necessarily mean that formal court action will occur. It does set in motion the process of determining whether the court has jurisdiction and if formal proceedings are warranted (JCJC, 2008).

Intake

Following the receipt of a written allegation, the juvenile probation officer entrusted with intake decisions must determine if the matter described in the written allegation should continue with formal court action (JCJC, 2008). Two basic questions are asked: "Are the allegations within the jurisdiction of the juvenile court?" and "If so, is it appropriate to schedule an intake conference to determine what further action, if any, should be taken?" (JCJC, 2008, p. 34). At the intake conference, the juvenile may have his/her parents or guardians present as well as his/her attorney and he/she has the right to remain silent. The juvenile is given a copy of the written allegation. The immediate purpose of the intake conference is to gather information for applying decision-making guidelines. Subsequent to the intake conference, it will be determined by the juvenile intake officer if the matter should be dismissed, informally adjusted/diversion, or petitioned. The intake screening is guided by criteria, guidelines, policies, and procedures established by the administrative judge and chief probation officer, and the recommendations are subject to review and approval by the administrative judge or a designee (JCJC, 2008).

For less serious offenses, juveniles may have the allegations dismissed or be given an informal adjustment. For juveniles who receive a dismissal, it is usually because it is a minor offense, it is a juvenile with no history of previous arrests, it is a juvenile who does not need any referral services or who is currently receiving adequate services, the victims do not want to pursue further, and/or the parents are able to provide needed supervision (JCJC, 2008). In lieu of filing a petition, an informal adjustment or diversionary program may be used. In this case, all parties have to consent to the informal adjustment and it must be in the best interests of the child and the public and also be approved by the administrative judge and the chief probation officer (JCJC 2008). In this case, the juvenile and his/her parents may or may not be referred to outside service agencies for services that are consistent with the BARJ mission of community protection, offender accountability, and competency development. Some examples of diversion programs may include participation in restitution programs, victim-offender mediation, community-based dispute resolution programs, or restorative group conferencing (JCJC, 2008).

Cases that are likely to be petitioned to the court are ones that include serious offenses or cases where there is a denial of involvement or a dispute regarding the facts of the case. In these instances, formal processing is warranted especially if services and corrective measures are required to resolve the matter, the juvenile has a prior record, the public may be as risk, and/or the juvenile and/or parents are unwillingly to participate in the informal adjustment (JCJC, 2008). These cases will proceed to either an adjudicatory or transfer hearing or a consent decree.

Consent decrees can be negotiated at any time before the adjudicatory hearing. Consent decrees are mutually agreed upon terms and conditions set forth in accordance with the juvenile probation department, the judge, and the juvenile. The juvenile must abide by all conditions set forth; these conditions are consistent with the philosophy of the BARJ model. For example, a consent decree may require the juvenile attend school, cooperate in therapy or counseling, and/or participate in activities that aid in their competency development (JCJC, 2008).

Detention and Detention Hearing

After arrest, some juveniles may be detained in a juvenile detention facility, shelter, or other placement facility. Detention provides safe, short-term care and custody to juvenile offenders who, for a variety of reasons, cannot remain in the community while awaiting juvenile court processing (JCJC, 2008). If a child is arrested and the police wish to detain, they must contact the Juvenile Probation Officer (JPO) on duty or the Intake Probation Officer to see if he/

she will authorize detention. Before authorizing detention, the JPO must interview the police officer, and others if necessary, to determine if the child meets the criteria set forth in the Standards Governing Secure Detention under the Juvenile Act. Some of these criteria include if the juvenile needs to be protected from himself/herself; if persons and property need to be protected; if there is a need to ensure attendance at a hearing; or other reasons (e.g., no parent or responsible guardian can house him/her until the hearing).

If an individual is detained, an informal detention hearing must be conducted before a judge or a hearing master within 72 hours of admission (JCJC, 2008). The narrow focus of this hearing is to determine that probable cause exists and there is a need for detention. The outcome of the hearing may be to 1) continue detention until the next hearing or 2) to release the juvenile to his/her parents or to a less restrictive environment (e.g., home detention, shelter care). As of 2012, there are 16 detention facilities statewide, that range in size from eight to one-hundred-thirty beds (JDCAP, 2012). Shuman Detention Center is the largest of the facilities; this 130-bed facility is located in Allegheny County, where Pittsburgh is the county seat.

Adjudicatory Hearing

The next step in the process after a petition is filed is an adjudicatory hearing. If the juvenile is held in detention or in shelter care, the Juvenile Act requires that the adjudicatory hearing be scheduled no later than ten days from when the petition is filed (JCJC, 2008). Under certain circumstances, this time frame can be extended by an additional ten-day period. If a juvenile is not in detention, the hearing must be held within ninety days of the date the petition was filed. This hearing is similar to the bench "trial" in adult court, in that the adjudicatory hearing is in front of a judge (or a hearing master) and the juvenile is entitled to legal representation at this hearing. All adjudicatory hearings are recorded. However, the general rule is that juvenile hearings are closed to all except "the parties, their counsel, witnesses, the victim and counsel for the victim, other persons accompanying a party or a victim for his or her assistance, and any other person as the court finds have a proper interest in the proceeding or in the work of the court" (JCJC, 2008, p. 89). The victim has a right to be present and heard at this hearing.

The focus of the hearing is for the judge (or hearing master) to determine if the juvenile court has jurisdiction of the matter, to maintain that all constitutional safeguards are afforded to the juvenile, to engage in fact finding, to hear evidence and accept admissions, and to adjudicate delinquent, if warranted (JCJC, 2008). At the adjudicatory hearing, the juvenile may admit to the allegations (pleads guilty) or deny the allegations (pleads not guilty) in which case both the prosecution and the defense present their cases. The adjudicatory hearing is not an adversarial forum, but rather one in which there is an overall concern for the juvenile and the most appropriate outcome.

According to the Juvenile Court Judges' Commission (JCJC) Standards Governing Hearing Procedures:

> The atmosphere of the hearing should encourage the maximum participation of all concerned. It should be evident that it is the intent of the judge to determine the facts of the case and provide for a forum that is consistent with the public interest and is intended to arrive at a disposition that provides balanced attention to the protection of the community, imposition of accountability for offenses committed and development of competencies to enable the child to become a responsible and productive member of the community (JCJC, 2008, p. 87).

Possible outcomes of the adjudicatory hearing are that the juvenile is found to be delinquent and "in need of treatment, supervision or rehabilitation," or the case is dismissed. If it is dismissed, the youth is discharged from the juvenile justice system. If the juvenile is adjudicated delinquent, a disposition hearing will be held at a later date.

Disposition Hearing and Placement

Prior to the disposition hearing, a social study report is generated by the juvenile probation department. This report includes information about the severity of the offense, the juvenile's current and prior behavior patterns, the family's, community's, and school's role in the juvenile's life, court ordered evaluations (e.g., psychiatric evaluation), victim impact statements, and the overall rehabilitative potential of the juvenile (JCJC, 2008). The disposition hearing, for youth who are detained, must occur within twenty days of the adjudication hearing; however, for cases where the juvenile is not detained, the dispositional hearing must occur within sixty days of the adjudication hearing. The goal of the dispositional hearing is to determine the most appropriate treatment, supervision, or rehabilitation for the juvenile that it is consistent with the BARJ model philosophy of balanced attention with community protection, offender accountability, and competency development (JCJC, 2008). Dispositions range from probation supervision to residential placement.

Juveniles may receive probation supervision, which requires the juvenile to adhere to any special conditions (e.g., mental health counseling, drug and alcohol counseling, anger management classes, sex offender program) deemed appropriate by the court. Probation can also be used in conjunction with other programs, such as restitution programs, community service programs, and victim awareness classes, to name a few. Juveniles may also be committed to out-of-home placement programs. These programs include non-secure (i.e., not securely locked) placements and secure (i.e., locked) placements. Examples of non-secure placements include day or evening treatment programs, group homes, wilderness camps, and training schools. Secure placements are usually reserved for the most serious offenders; these placements are referred to as Youth Development Centers. Youth Development Centers are secure treatment units that resemble a jail setting. Generally, it is standard practice for juveniles to be committed to programs that are least restrictive and can be moved to more restrictive environments depending on the circumstances of the case and their individual progress or lack of progress.

Although the disposition is considered to last for an indefinite period of time, review hearings are required every six months to determine the rehabilitative progress of the youth (JCJC, 2008). Using the BARJ principles as a guide, the judge presiding over the review hearing will make a determination as to when the juvenile has fulfilled the orders of the court and can be released from probation and/or placement. In some instances, once youth are released from placement they are to begin an aftercare program.

Aftercare

The purpose of an aftercare program is to build a bridge between institutional and community environments by providing a smooth transition period for the juvenile (JCJC, 2008). The aftercare plan must also address the BARJ principles related to accountability to the victim and the community and show continuous progress toward competency development. A motion to terminate court supervision can be made by the juvenile probation department when the juvenile has completed the terms of the disposition, paid in full all restitution, court costs and fines, and refrained from committing any new offenses for which delinquency or criminal proceedings are warranted (JCJC, 2008).

Key Juvenile Justice
Agencies and Personnel

Due to the decentralized nature of the juvenile justice system in Pennsylvania, it is important to understand the roles of various agencies that are involved with the operation and evaluation of the system. There are four state

Figure 8.1 Pennsylvania Juvenile Justice Flowchart

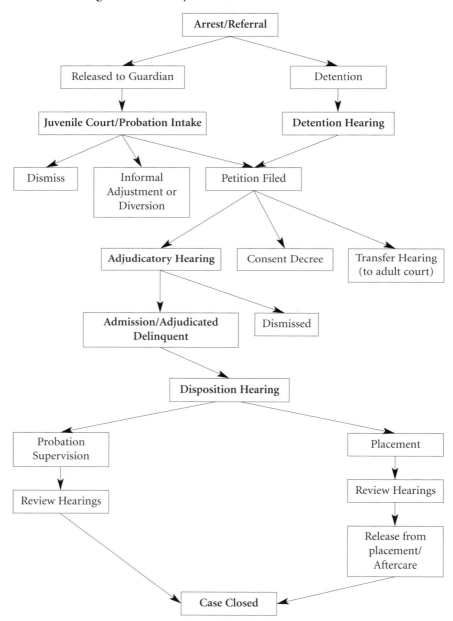

Source: PA Council of Chief Juvenile Probation Officers, Family Involvement Committee (2012).

agencies that provide leadership to the juvenile justice system in Pennsylvania: the Department of Public Welfare (DPW), the Pennsylvania Commission on Crime and Delinquency (PCCD), the Juvenile Court Judges' Commission (JCJC), and the Pennsylvania Council of Chief Probation Officers (Chiefs' Council).

DPW through the Office of Children, Youth and Families oversees the state's secure treatment institutions, youth forestry camps, and youth development centers. The Bureau of Juvenile Justice Services, which is housed within the Office of Children, Youth and Families, administers and manages 12 state-operated facilities and contracts with a private entity for another facility (JCJC, 2008). These facilities have an overall capacity of 618 beds (365 secure and 253 non-secure, including a 30 bed facilities for females) (JCJC, 2008). In addition to operating these facilities, the DPW is responsible for overseeing and auditing the private providers that contract with counties.

DPW sets the "needs-based budget" for purposes of state reimbursement for "county-purchased services" for each of the 67 counties in Pennsylvania (JCJC, 2008, p. 23). This is an extremely important function of the DPW. There are federal, state, and local dollars that pass through the DPW for the operations of the juvenile justice system. Federal dollars come in the form of Title IV-E funding and Medicaid funding if the juvenile meets certain criteria (e.g., behavioral and mental health treatment services) (JCJC, 2008). The majority of the funding is derived from Act 148 funding. Act 148 funds are distributed to counties for reimbursement for county-purchased services for juveniles (i.e., day treatment, counseling, foster and institutional care). Interestingly, the Act 148 funds are reimbursed at various levels starting from 50% to a high of 90% reimbursement for different types of services. The varying rates are a way to encourage counties to use least restrictive types of placements. For example, reimbursement rates are Shelter Care (90%); Community Residential Care (80%); Community-Based Alternative Treatment Programs (80%); Institutional Services (except Detention) (60%); and Juvenile Detention (50%) (PA Three Year Juvenile Justice Plan, n.d.). County tax dollars pay for everything that is not covered in the above funding categories and any expenses over the reimbursement cap.

The PCCD is a statewide agency that is "responsible for juvenile justice system planning, coordination, and policy analysis" as well as provides "data analysis, research and legislative recommendations to the Governor's Office and the General Assembly" (JCJC, 2008, p. 23). It is actively involved in spearheading and funding initiatives (e.g., Victim/Witness Assistance Program, Crime Victim's Compensation Fund) that benefit local governments (JCJC, 2008). The JCJC is a "statutorily created body that collects and disseminates Pennsylvania juvenile court statistics, established administrative and procedural standards for juvenile courts, and sets personnel practices and employment standards for juvenile probation departments" (JCJC, 2008, p. 24). This Harrisburg-based organization's members are appointed by the Chief Justice of the Pennsylvania Supreme Court and are appointed by the Governor for three year terms (JCJC, 2008). Lastly, the Chiefs' Council is an organization comprised all of the Chief (and Deputy Chief) Juvenile Probation Officers in the state. The organization works closely with the JCJC "on probation training, education and planning issues" (JCJC, 2008, p. 24).

In addition to these statewide agencies, there are various components of the juvenile justice system that are integral to its operation. The Juvenile Court employs a number of juvenile court judges who have a tremendous amount of autonomy and power over juvenile court matters. Each of the state's 67 counties have "unlimited original jurisdiction in all cases except as may otherwise be provided by law" (JCJC, 2008, p. 22). The president judge of the county functions as the administrative judge of the juvenile court and is responsible for the direction of the juvenile court. In Allegheny County and Philadelphia County, the administrative judge is appointed by the Pennsylvania Supreme Court (JCJC, 2008). The role of the administrative judge is to oversee the policies on intake, diversion guidelines, detention, probation, aftercare supervision, and crime notifications (JCJC, 2008). The judge also has oversight over the adequacy of the services available to the juvenile court and seeks out additional services when there is an unfilled need. They are also required to work with the community and probation department to help the court understand the community's problems and priorities (JCJC, 2008).

The Juvenile Probation Department is the primary point of contact with court-involved youth and is responsible for managing cases from intake through the case closing process. They are required to have a least a bachelor's degree and are directed to undergo forty hours of continuing training annually. Probation officers make regular reports to juvenile courts about a youth's progress at all points in the system. Probation officers must ensure that residential services meet courts' expectations, and that services anticipate a youth's release (JCJC, 2008). As previously noted, Pennsylvania's juvenile justice system relies on many private agencies to administer delinquency programming to its juvenile offender population. There are more than 500 separate programs that include group homes, day treatment programs, alternative schools, wilderness programs, sex offender treatment programs, mental health programs, and secure placements. Each of these programs are inspected and approved by the Department of Public Welfare (JCJC, 2008).

Juvenile Crime and Outcomes in Pennsylvania

Because the Juvenile Justice System is decentralized in Pennsylvania, there are various agencies that are responsible for keeping track of statistical data on juvenile justice issues. The Pennsylvania Department of Public Welfare, Office of Children, Youth, and Families (DPW) maintains budgetary information for the juvenile justice system. The Pennsylvania State Police is the central repository for collecting statistical data on the number of arrests. The Juvenile Court Judges' Commission (JCJC) is responsible for collecting and analyzing data on statewide dispositions and outcome data.

For 2012, the Pennsylvania Uniform Crime Reports (PA State Police, 2013) reveals that juveniles represented 15.2% of individuals arrested for Index Offenses. Similar to the adult arrests, in 2012, the majority of juvenile arrests are for larceny offenses and the least frequent is for murder. It is interesting to note that from 2011 to 2012, the number of juvenile arrests for index offenses decreased (15,112 to 13,467). The exception is for arson, which increased by 41.8% (177 to 251) from 2011 to 2012. The number of arrests for murder stayed the same; there were 28 juvenile arrests for murder in both 2011 and 2012. The largest decrease is with forcible rape, which decreased by 27.9% (179 to 129).

The most recent data on dispositions in Pennsylvania, compiled by JCJC in the *2011 Pennsylvania Juvenile Court Dispositions* report, illustrate that there were 34,990 delinquency-related dispositions in Pennsylvania during 2011, which represents a 4.5% decrease from 2010, and a 23.2% decrease since 2007. A majority (57%) of the total dispositions occurred in the eight jurisdictions (Lancaster, Berks, Lehigh, Delaware, York, Montgomery, Allegheny, and Philadelphia counties) reporting more than 1,000 dispositions each. In the Commonwealth's largest jurisdictions, Allegheny County reported a decrease from 2010 of 15.3%, while Philadelphia reported an increase of 30.6% (JCJC, 2011). "Seventeen year olds represented the most dispositions for any age group in 2011, accounting for 26.8% of all dispositions, followed in descending order by sixteen year olds (21.9%) and fifteen year olds (16%)" (JCJC, 2011, p. 26).

The 2011 report shows that Consent Decree, Probation, and Informal Adjustment continued to be the most frequent dispositions, representing approximately half (49.2%) of all dispositions. Informal Adjustment, Fines/Costs Ordered, and Complaint Withdrawn each decreased from 2010 levels of 15.6%, 10.6%, and 5.9%, respectively. Dispositions of Dismissed increased from 3.5% in 2010 to 5.8% in 2011, while Placement utilization remained relatively sta-

Table 8.1 2011 Delinquency Placements by Type

2011 Delinquency Placements by Type	Percentage
Private Institution	46.7%
Group Home	13.6%
Drug and Alcohol	11.4%
Wilderness-Based	5.8%
Private Secure	4.8%
Boot Camp	4.0%
DPW Secure Youth Development Center (YDC)	3.2%
DPW Youth Forestry Camp (YFC)	3.0%
DPW Open Youth Development Center (YDC)	2.3%
Other Placement	1.8%
Foster Care	1.7%
Independent Living	1.6%

Adapted from: JCJC, 2011.

ble—6.8% to 6.7%—from 2010 to 2011 (JCJC, 2011). Statewide, delinquency placements declined each year from 2007 to 2011, and decreased by 29.4% from 2007 to 2011 (JCJC, 2011, p. 19). The number of placements as a percentage of total dispositions, including disposition reviews, decreased from 2010 (8.7%) to 2011 (8.0%). The largest decrease occurred in Philadelphia, 7.4% to 5.6% (JCJC, 2011).

Delinquency placements to private institutions continue to represent the most frequent type of delinquency placements in 2011-more than 46% of all placements. Commitments to group homes, as well as drug and alcohol programs, represented 25% of all delinquency placements, while wilderness-based, boot camp and all secure programs (private and DPW/YDC) comprised another 17.8% (JCJC, 2011, p. 23). These statistics are consistent with the 2010 placements.

Juvenile courts in Pennsylvania conduct review hearings at least every six months from the time of disposition until a case is closed to monitor a youth's progress (Schwartz, 2013). The majority of delinquency placement review proceedings resulted in an order of "Continued in Previous Placement." In the small percentage of placement reviews in which a transfer to another placement was ordered, most transfers were to a "private institution" (JCJC, 2011).

JCJC also publishes *Statewide Outcome Measures* on the BARJ model. According to this report, the evaluation of the Community Protection component of the BARJ model showed that it was successful with respect to closing cases without a new offense occurring. "Since 2004, county juvenile probation departments have supervised and closed cases involving approximately 137,111 juvenile offenders" (JCJC, 2012). The proportion of cases closed successfully is 85.7% which is an excellent rate of success and compares favorably with other states collecting similar data (Utah—67%, Arizona—70%, and South Carolina—86%)" (JCJC, 2012, p. 1). Furthermore, the statistics in this report reveal that in 2011, 12,642 (85.1%), of juveniles successfully completed supervision without a new offense resulting in a Consent Decree, Adjudication of Delinquency, ARD, Nolo Contendere, or finding of guilt (JCJC, 2012).

In evaluating the success of Offender Accountability/Victim Restoration, the JCJC (2012, p. 3) found that "over the last eight years, juvenile offenders have completed 4,334,176 hours of community service." The value of the community service hours completed equates to services worth approximately $31,422,776 based upon a minimum wage of $7.25 per hour. Over that same time period, victims of juvenile crime have received $19,486,029 in restitution from juvenile offenders. In 2011, of the "3,779 juveniles with a restitution obligation, 77.4% made full restitution to their victims" (JCJC, 2012, p. 4). Additionally, in 2011, 96.5% of the 5,910 juveniles who were required to participate in victim awareness curriculums while under supervision successfully completed the program (JCJC, 2012). Of those juveniles who were ordered to participate in a Competency Development activity, 91.4% of them successfully completed the activity while under supervision in 2011 (JCJC, 2012). Overall, Pennsylvania has experienced a decline in juvenile arrests, seen a decrease in the number of dispositions, and engaged in a greater use of least restrictive placements. Even with this decline, there are still juveniles who commit crimes that will be handled in adult criminal court.

Juveniles in Adult Court: Waiver and Statutory Exclusion

The juvenile justice system in Pennsylvania has original jurisdiction over youth ages 10 to 17. Individuals who are adjudicated delinquent in juvenile court can be held under juvenile court supervision up to their twenty-first birthday. Depending on the seriousness of the offense, the prior record of the offender, and the age of the offender at the time of the offense, being held until one's twenty-first birthday may not be the most appropriate punishment for the individual. For these types of cases, some youth may be transferred to the adult criminal justice system and some youth who meet certain criteria (such as a committing a murder) as defined by legislative statute will be excluded from juvenile court altogether. The rationale behind both waiver and statutory exclusion is to enhance public safety and offender accountability.

There are two ways in which a juvenile can be transferred to adult court in Pennsylvania. Juvenile cases can be waived to adult criminal court through a judicial waiver and/or statutory exclusion. The judicial waiver laws allow the juvenile courts to transfer jurisdiction to adult court on a case-by-case basis. Although the case is initially filed in juvenile court, it may be waived over to adult court with a judge's approval, based on specific standards and following a formal hearing. Within the judicial waiver there are two options: discretionary waiver and presumptive waiver.

According to 42 Pa. C. S. §6355, a discretionary waiver may be used "if a child of at least 14 years of age is accused of a felony, and the juvenile court, after a hearing, transfers the case for criminal prosecution if it finds that (1) there is a prima facie case that the child committed the offense alleged and (2) there are 'reasonable grounds to believe' that (a) 'the public interest is served' by the transfer and (b) the child is not subject to commitment to a mental institution. The law specifies a number of factors that must be considered in making the public interest determination—including the child's amenability to treatment, supervision, and rehabilitation, which must in turn be determined with reference to a long list of sub-factors. Except under certain special circumstances (see Presumptive Waiver), the Commonwealth has the burden of establishing by a preponderance of the evidence that the public interest would be served by a transfer and that the child is not amenable to treatment, supervision, and rehabilitation. The court's decision to grant or deny a transfer is not immediately appealable."

Another type of judicial waiver is the presumptive waiver. A presumptive waiver can be used when certain offense(s) are committed and are serious enough that it warrants the case be heard in adult court. The circumstances for this type of waiver include that the Commonwealth has a prima facie case that (1) a child of at least 14 used a deadly weapon in the commission of a felony or (2) a child of at least 15 committed any offense that would be excluded from the definition of "delinquent act" (see Statutory Exclusion) if it had been committed with a deadly weapon (See 42 Pa. C. S. §6355(g)). In this case a hearing is held before a juvenile court judge to determine if this case will be bound over to adult court. In this hearing, the defense has to show by a preponderance of the evidence that the public interest would not be served by a transfer, and that the child is amenable to treatment, supervision, and rehabilitation.

There are certain offenses that are determined by statute, that if a juvenile commits one of these enumerated offenses, he/she will be automatically handled as an adult, regardless of age. Thus, under statute, certain cases will originate in adult criminal court. This is referred to a legislative waiver, statutory exclusion, or in the case of Pennsylvania, it is also known as a Fisher Bill case. These cases are directly filed in adult criminal courts, and they have also been referred to as direct file cases. The prime sponsor of Act 33 of 1995 was D. Michael Fisher, who was a PA senator at the time, and the following year was elected as the Pennsylvania Attorney General, under then Governor Tom Ridge.

According to Judicial Code 42 Pa C.S. §6322 (2) (ii), otherwise known as the *Fisher Bill*, youth would be excluded from juvenile court jurisdiction if the youth met all of the following criteria: (1) The youth was 15 years or older at the time of the alleged crime; (2) The youth was charged with rape; involuntary deviate sexual intercourse; aggravated assault; robbery; robbery of a motor vehicle; aggravated indecent assault; kidnapping; voluntary manslaughter; or an attempt, conspiracy, or solicitation to commit murder or any of the crimes listed; or (3) The youth used a deadly weapon during commission of the crime. Additionally the act also excludes any youth 15 years or older at the time of the alleged crime who committed any of the above offenses, except for aggravated assault, and who had previously been adjudicated delinquent for one of the offenses [42 Pa. C.S. §6302 (2)(iii)]. In these cases, individuals are considered "convicted" rather than "adjudicated delinquent." These convictions are not subject to expungement.

A case transferred to adult criminal court does not necessarily have to stay there. Pennsylvania has a mechanism in place for juveniles to petition the criminal court to have their case heard in juvenile court. This is known as a reverse waiver or decertification. In a decertification hearing, the burden of proof is on the defendant to show that the juvenile is "amenable to treatment, supervision, and rehabilitation." According to 42 Pa. C. S. §6322, if a child accused of an excluded offense (see Fisher Bill offenses) files a petition requesting a transfer from criminal to juvenile court and establishes by a preponderance of the evidence that a transfer will serve the public interest, the court may order such a transfer. The court must make the transfer determination after considering the same factors that bear on a juvenile court's decision to transfer a case for criminal prosecution. Any transfer order must be supported by "specific references to the evidence," and is subject to expedited appellate review. Once a case has been transferred from adult criminal court, the juvenile court may not retransfer it to adult court.

It is also important to note that Pennsylvania has a "Once an Adult, Always an Adult" provision (NCJJ, 2011). This provision essentially states that if a juvenile is found guilty in a criminal proceeding, a subsequent offense that is a misdemeanor or felony will automatically be filed in criminal court (See 42 Pa. C.S. §6302 (v)). For example, let's say there is a 15-year-old juvenile who was tried in adult court for robbery of a motor vehicle. He received a two-year state prison sentence. He is now 17 years old, out of prison, and commits a misdemeanor simple assault. Due to this provision, his simple assault case would automatically be heard in adult court, thus bypassing the juvenile court.

In light of the passage of Act 33 of 1995 as well as the perceived continued statewide increase in youth violence, a Young Adult Offender Program (YAOP) was initially established at State Correctional Institute (SCI) Houtzdale in 1996. Subsequently, SCI-Pine Grove was opened in 2001 as the state designated maximum security facility to incarcerate male Young Adult Offenders (YAOs), between the ages of 15–22 convicted as adults. The YAOP within the facility is designed to meet the YAOs' special needs of education, adolescent development, and recreational activity, while providing a safe environment for the offenders (PA Department of Corrections). When SCI-Pine Grove opened in 2001, there were approximately 150 inmates who were classified as YAOs; soon after opening, the facility also housed adult offenders. Currently, the facility maintains two housing units for the YAOP. According to the PA Department of Corrections, as of June 2013, there are only 18 inmates under the age of 18 in the facility, which makes up only 1.47% of the population of SCI-Pine Grove (N=1,218). It is important to note that this facility was designed for the YAO population, yet, it was quickly realized that there was not a large wave of YAOs to fill the prison.

In addition to juveniles being tried as adults and serving adult time sentences, juveniles who had been tried and convicted in adult criminal court were eligible to receive the death penalty. In 2005, the United States Supreme Court case *Roper v. Simmons* held that the Eighth and Fourteenth Amendments to the U.S. *Constitution* forbid execution of offenders who were under the age of 18 years old when their crimes were committed. The Court's ruling affected 72 juveniles in 12 states (Streib, 2004). Pennsylvania was one of the states that housed two juveniles, Kevin Hughes and Percy Lee. Kevin Hughes was a Black male, aged 16 at the time of the crime, who was convicted of the rape and murder of a nine-year-old black female in Philadelphia and sentenced on October 27, 1983. Hughes' death sentence was vacated in 2005 and the court imposed a sentence of life imprisonment without the possibility of parole for the murder conviction (*Hughes v. Beard et al.*, 2013).

Percy Lee was a black male, aged 17 at crime, who was convicted of the murder of two black females, ages 17 and 33, in Philadelphia and sentenced on January 28, 1988 (Streib, 2004). Lee's death sentence was later vacated under

Roper v. Simmons (2005), and replaced with two consecutive life sentences, one for each of the two murders (*Percy Lee v. Shirley Smeal*, 2011). According to Streib (2004), December 4, 1916, was the last time a juvenile was executed in Pennsylvania.

Current Issue Facing Pennsylvania's Juveniles in Adult Court

The U.S. Supreme Court cases *Graham v. Florida* (2010) and *Miller v. Alabama* (2012) essentially redefined sentencing options for juveniles who are convicted and sentenced as adult in adult court. The decision in the *Graham v. Florida* case stated that juvenile life without parole sentences is unconstitutional for crimes, excluding murder. The *Miller v. Alabama* decision expanded on the *Graham v. Florida* ruling and found that mandatory juvenile life without possibility of parole sentences are unconstitutional for juveniles. According to the Pennsylvania Department of Corrections, as of June 2013, there are 462 inmates housed in Pennsylvania prisons who were under the age of 18 at the time when they were sentenced to life in prison without possibility of parole. That number (N= 462) is nearly 20 percent of the nationwide total (N=2,574), placing Pennsylvania at the top of all states for life-without-parole sentences for crimes committed by those under 18. In November 2013, the Pennsylvania Supreme Court ruled that the *Miller* decision is not retroactive.

Conclusion

Pennsylvania has a long and rich tradition which has served as a model throughout the country. Starting in the 1800s, Pennsylvania was on the forefront with treating juveniles differently than adults; furthermore, it has been progressive in its treatment, supervision, and rehabilitation services available to juveniles. A significant change in the mission of the Juvenile Court came in 1995 when the Balanced and Restorative Justice model permeated all aspects of the juvenile justice system. The Juvenile Court became more focused on protecting the community, making the offender accountable for his/her actions, and developing competencies in the juvenile. The acknowledgement of the offender, victim, and community needs provides a balanced approach to justice. As seen in the most recent juvenile crime statistics and outcome measures, it appears that Pennsylvania is on the right path in successfully handling juvenile crime problems. Lastly, the Juvenile Court is constantly forming new partnerships with community organizations and providers to further the BARJ mission of the court.

Key Terms and Definitions

Adjudicatory Hearing: Similar to the bench trial in adult court, it is a hearing in front of a master or a judge to determine if there is sufficient evidence to find a youth to be a delinquent.

Aftercare: Similar to parole in the adult criminal justice system, it is court mandated programming that is designed to provide a smooth transition for the youth from placement to the community.

Balanced and Restorative Justice (BARJ) Model: A philosophy that focuses on community protection, offender accountability, and competency development.

Commonwealth v. Fisher: A 1905 United States Supreme Court case that formalized the rules that the court can intervene without impunity when the objective is to help the youth.

Community Protection: A component of the BARJ model that means that citizens have the right to be safe and secure in their communities.

Competency Development: A component of the BARJ model where the juvenile is given opportunities to acquire skills, to hold a job, and to develop pro-social skills.

Consent Decree: Mutually agreed upon terms and conditions that are in accordance with the BARJ model, which are imposed upon the juvenile by the probation department and the judge.

Decertification Hearing: It is a hearing in which the juvenile and his attorney request the case be moved back to juvenile court from adult criminal court.

Dependent Youth: Youth who are habitually, without justification, truant; youth who have committed a specific act or acts of habitual disobedience of the reasonable and lawful commands of his parent, guardian or other custodian; and/or youth who are ungovernable and found to be in need of care, treatment, or supervision.

Detention: Similar to pretrial detention in adult court, the juvenile remains in custody to await further court action.

Disposition: Similar to the sentence in adult court, it is the intervention, program, and/or treatment designed to rehabilitate the juvenile.

Diversion: It is an informal remedy that is used to bring the case to a resolution.

Ex parte Crouse: An 1838 decision, where the Pennsylvania Supreme Court first used the phrase *parens patriae*.

Hearing Master: An attorney who is appointed to serve in juvenile court to conduct certain types of hearings; however, they are not to preside over adjudications in felony cases.

Informal Adjustment: It is the informal handling of an offense without filing a petition.

Intake: Following the receipt of a written allegation, the juvenile probation officer is entrusted to make intake decisions to determine if formal court action is needed.

McKeiver v. Pennsylvania: A 1972 United States Supreme Court case that decided it was not constitutionally required for juveniles to have a jury trial in delinquency proceedings.

Offender Accountability: A component of the BARJ model where the juvenile is held responsible for restoring the harm caused to the victim and the community.

Petition: The written document that is filed in juvenile court that alleges that a juvenile is delinquent, a status offender, or a dependent child.

Parens Patriae: A legal doctrine in which the state is viewed as the parent.

Websites

Frontline Program: When Kids Get Life. 2009 documentary. http://www.pbs.org/wgbh/pages/frontline/whenkidsgetlife/.

PA Commission on Crime and Delinquency website: http://www.pccd.state.pa.us/portal/server.pt/community/pccd_home/5226.

PA Council of Chief Probation Officers. http://www.pachiefprobationofficers.org.

PA Juvenile Court Judges Commission website: http://www.jcjc.state.pa.us/portal/server.pt/community/jcjc_home/5030.

PA Department of Public Welfare website: http://www.dpw.state.pa.us/dpworganization/index.htm.

Review Questions

1. Discuss the history of the Juvenile Justice System in Pennsylvania.
2. What are the major components of the Balanced and Restorative Justice Model and how do they inform decision-making throughout the Juvenile Justice Process?
3. What are some of the reasons that a juvenile may be detained, and how does the process proceed from that juncture?
4. Discuss the role of the administrative court judge in the juvenile justice system.
5. How has Act 33 impacted the ways that juveniles may be tried in adult criminal court?
6. Discuss the implications that waiving juveniles to adult criminal court has had on the adult correctional system.

Critical Thinking Questions

1. You find out that a friend from high school, who is younger than you and who is still a juvenile, has been arrested for a felony burglary. You want to inform him as to what to expect from the process. Write a one-page letter to him describing the process he is about to encounter. Detail each of the steps of the process, points in the process where his case may be dismissed, and possible dispositional options if he is adjudicated delinquent.
2. Using the BARJ model, you are responsible for making a disposition recommendation for a juvenile who was adjudicated delinquent of breaking and entering, burglary, receiving stolen property, and possession of a small amount of marijuana. Discuss how you will incorporate the 3 components of the BARJ model as you make your specific treatment recommendations to judge. Discuss your rationale for why you chose these treatment options.
3. Should Act 33 of 1995 be revisited to include or exclude certain offenses? Identify and discuss any new offenses that you would add and identify any offenses that you would delete from the list of excluded offenses. Should the minimum age (i.e., 15 years old) for the Fisher bill change? Why or why not?
4. In 2001, SCI-Pine Grove opened and was designated as a maximum security facility to house the Young Adult Offender program (YAO). Initially, it housed 150 YAOs. As of June 2013, there are only 18 YAOs housed in SCI-Pine Grove. What are some possible explanations for this?

References

Anderson, J. (March 1999). Pennsylvania's juvenile justice system: A rich heritage, clear mission, and bright future. *Pennsylvania Juvenile Justice, 8*(3). Shippensburg, PA: Center for Juvenile Justice Training and Research. Pennsylvania Juvenile Court Judges' Commission.

Griffin, P. (2006). Ten years of balanced and restorative justice in Pennsylvania. *Pennsylvania Progress: A Juvenile Justice Research, Policy, and Practice Series.* National Center for Juvenile Justice.

JCJC (Juvenile Court Judges' Commission). (2008). *Pennsylvania's Juvenile Delinquency Benchbook* Harrisburg, PA: Pennsylvania Juvenile Court Judges' Commission.

JCJC (Juvenile Court Judges' Commission). (2011). *Pennsylvania Juvenile Court Dispositions 2011.* Harrisburg, PA: Pennsylvania Juvenile Court Judges' Commission. Center for Juvenile Justice Training and Research.

JCJC (Juvenile Court Judges' Commission). (2012). *Statewide Outcome Measures* Harrisburg, PA: Pennsylvania Juvenile Court Judges' Commission. Retrieved from http://www.jcjc.state.pa.us/portal/server.pt/community/publications/5037.

JDCAP. (2012). Juvenile Detention Centers Association of Pennsylvania Membership Brochure. http://www.jdcap.org/SiteCollectionDocuments/JDCAPBrochureRevised2011.pdf.

Maloney, D., Romig, D., & Armstrong, T. (1988). Juvenile probation: The balanced approach. *Juvenile and Family Court Journal, 39* (3), 1–63.

McCarthy, F. B. (1984). *Pennsylvania juvenile delinquency practice and procedure.* The Harrison Company, Norcross: GA.

NCJJ (National Center for Juvenile Justice). (2011). *Pennsylvania State Juvenile Justice Profiles.* Pittsburgh, PA: NCJJ. Online. PA Council of Chief Juvenile Probation Officers, Family Involvement Committee. (2012). *A Family Guide to Pennsylvania's Juvenile Justice System.* Retrieved from http://www.pachiefprobationofficers.org/library.php.

PA Juvenile Act 42 Pa CSA § 6301, 1999. Retrieved from http://www.pachiefprobationofficers.org/docs/Juvenile%20Act.pdf

PA State Police (2013). 2012 Summary Report: Uniform Crime Reporting (UCR) Program. Harrisburg, PA.

PA Three Year Juvenile Justice Plan (n.d.). Juvenile Justice and Delinquency Prevention Committee, Pennsylvania Commission on Crime and Delinquency. http://www.google.com/url?sa=t&rct=j&q=&esrc=s&frm=1&source=web&cd=4&ved=0CEAQFjAD&url=http%3A%2F%2Fwww.portal.state.pa.us%2Fportal%2Fportal%2Fserver.pt%2Fdocument%2F895366%2

Fpa_three_year_juvenile_justice_plan_pdf&ei=Bj6BusqwLJLD4AOd4IHQ
AQ&usg=AFQjCNHfhXRgvX-igwZ4xu31Ksp2SHuokQ&bvm=bv.561468
54,d.dmg.

Puzzanchera, C., Knoll, C, Adams, B., & Sickmund, M. (2012). *Allegheny County Detention Screening Study.* Pittsburgh, PA: National Center for Juvenile Justice.

Schwartz, R.G. (2013). *Pennsylvania and MacArthur's Models for Change: The Story of a Successful Public-Private Partnership.* Juvenile Law Center. Retrieved from http://www.modelsforchange.net/publications/457.

Seyko, R. (2001). Balanced approach and restorative justice efforts in Allegheny County, Pennsylvania. *The Prison Journal, 81,* 187–205. DOI: 10.1177/0032885501081002004.

Streib, V. (2004) *Juvenile Death Penalty Today: Death Sentences and Executions for Juvenile Crimes, January 1, 1973 to April 30, 2004.* Ohio Northern University, The Claude W. Pettit College of Law. NCJ Report 206332. Retrieved from http://www.internationaljusticeproject.org/pdfs/JuvDeath April2004.pdf.

Torbet, P. (2008). *Advancing Community Protection—A White Paper for Pennsylvania.* Pittsburgh, PA: National Center for Juvenile Justice.

Cases Cited

Commonwealth v. Fisher, 213 PA. 48 (1905).

Ex parte Crouse, 4 Wheaton (PA) 48 (1838).

Graham v. Florida, 560 U.S. ___ (2010).

Hughes v. Beard et al., No. 06-250 (3d Cir. Apr. 30, 2013).

Kent v. United States, 383 U.S. 541, 86 S. Ct. 1045, 16 L. Ed. 2d 84 (1966).

In re Gault, 387 U.S. 1, 87S. Ct. 1428, 18 L.Ed. 2d 527 (1967).

McKeiver v. Pennsylvania, 403 U.S. 528 (1971).

Miller v. Alabama, 567 U.S. ___ (2012).

Percy Lee v. Shirley Smeal, No. 06-250 (3d Cir. April 30, 2012).

Roper v. Simmons, 543 U.S. 551 (2005).

Statutes Cited

Juvenile Act, 42 PA C.S. §6302 (v)

Juvenile Act, 42 PA C.S. §6302 (2) iii

Juvenile Act, 42 PA C.S. §6222 (2) ii

Juvenile Act, 42 PA C.S. §6355

Juvenile Act, 42 PA C.S. §6355 (g)

Chapter 9

Crime Victims in Pennsylvania

Mary P. Brewster and Jane M. Tucker

Learning Objectives

After reading the chapter, students will be able to:

- Describe the role of the Pennsylvania Commission on Crime and Delinquency's Office of Victims' Services (OVS) in assisting victims of crime.
- Describe the role of the Office of the Victim Advocate in advocating crime victim's rights.
- Identify and explain the various rights of victims that are available throughout the criminal and juvenile justice processes.
- Identify special types of victims and corresponding special services and protections afforded to them.
- Identify and describe some of the state's programs that are focused on benefitting the offender and victim and/or community.

Key Terms

Address Confidentiality Program	Full faith and credit
Area Agency on Aging	Impact of Crime Classes
Balanced and Restorative Justice (BARJ)	Mandatory reporters
ChildLine and Abuse Registry	Mediation
Conferencing Programs	Mural Arts Program
Contemporaneous Alternative Method	Office of Victims' Services (OVS)

Older Adults Protective Services Act (OAPSA)

Pennsylvania Coalition against Domestic Violence (PCADV)

Pennsylvania Coalition against Rape (PCAR)

Pennsylvania Commission on Crime and Delinquency (PCCD)

Pennsylvania's Crime Victims Act

Pennsylvania Department of Aging

Pennsylvania Office of the Victim Advocate

Pennsylvania Statewide Automated Victim Information and Notification (PA SAVIN)

Protection from Abuse Database (PFAD)

Protection from Abuse Order (PFA)

Restitution

Sexual Assault Forensic Examiner (SAFE)

Sexual Assault Nurse Examiner (SANE)

Sexual Assault Response Team (SART)

Sex Offender Registry

Victim Advocate

Victims Compensation Assistance Program (VCAP)

Victim Impact Statement

Victim Offender Dialogue Program

Introduction

Much of this text focuses upon the criminal suspect, defendant, and convicted offender throughout the criminal justice process, and the role of police, courts, and corrections in addressing crime. This chapter, on the other hand, will focus on the victims of crime and will address:

- various agencies and organizations involved in helping victims;
- crime victims' rights within the criminal and juvenile justice processes;
- the special considerations made for child victims in the criminal and juvenile justice systems;
- the special considerations made for domestic violence victims in Pennsylvania;
- the special considerations made for sexual assault victims in Pennsylvania;
- the special protections afforded to elderly victims in Pennsylvania; and
- several victim-offender programs that attempt to benefit and restore both parties.

Defining Crime Victims

The term "victim" is legally defined (18 P.S. §11.103) in Pennsylvania to include:

(1) "a direct victim" (i.e., the person against whom the crime was committed);

(2) "a parent or legal guardian of a direct victim who is a child, except when the parent or legal guardian of the child is the alleged offender";

(3) "a minor child who is a material witness to" attempted or completed criminal homicide, aggravated assault, or rape "against a member of the child's family";

(4) "a family member of a homicide victim, including stepbrothers or stepsisters, stepchildren, stepparents or a fiancé ... except [in situations in which] the family member is the alleged offender."

Extent of Crime Victimization

In 2011, there were an estimated nearly 23 million serious crime victimizations in the United States, including 5.8 million violent victimizations and 17.1 million property victimizations (Truman & Planty, 2012, p. 1). As was highlighted in Chapter 1, there were 329,627 Part I Index crimes reported to the police in Pennsylvania in 2011, a rate of more than 2,500 per 100,000 Pennsylvania residents (Federal Bureau of Investigation, 2012). As is the case in every other state, most of the reported incidents were property crimes, not violent crimes (Federal Bureau of Investigation, 2012). Personal and property index crimes, as well as many less serious crimes, incur varying degrees and types of harm to victims. For this reason, there are a variety of agencies and organizations that provide many services to crime victims. Additionally, Pennsylvania statutes afford a number of protections and rights to victims of crime.

Victim Support Agencies and Organizations

Office of Victims' Services

The Pennsylvania Commission on Crime and Delinquency's Office of Victims' Services (OVS) is charged with ensuring "that the voices, needs and perspectives of all crime victims/survivors will be considered in the development of services, service standards, policies, funding priorities legislation and outcomes" (Pennsylvania Commission on Crime and Delinquency, 2012, p. 3). Two programs are administered by OVS—the Victims Compensation Assistance Program and the Victims' Services Program.

The Victims Compensation Assistance Program

The Victims Compensation Assistance Program (VCAP) was established following the passage of Act 139 of 1976, and assists victims who have suffered a financial burden due to the crime committed against them. The program is funded predominantly by fines paid by convicted offenders. Victims may file compensation forms to cover reimbursement of transportation expenses (for travel to court, medical appointments, counseling appointments, trips to the pharmacy, etc.), loss of earnings, loss of support, medical expenses, counseling expenses, funeral expenses, childcare, crime-scene cleanup, home health-care expenses, and, in some cases, stolen cash. All expenses must be verified with receipts and/or documents from employers, doctors, or school administrators. Generally, awards may not exceed $35,000; there are a few exceptions to this cap, including crime-scene cleanup and counseling.

In the 2010–11 fiscal year, the Victim Compensation Assistance Program received 8,771 new claims and awarded payment to victims totaling nearly $15 million. A fraction of these were emergency awards (335 awards totaling over $348,000), while others were supplemental awards (5,347 awards totaling over $4.5 million). Since the processing of regular claims by the program may take up to 8 weeks, victims may file emergency award applications for up to $2,500 to cover immediate losses and expenses including "loss of earnings, loss of support, stolen benefit cash or money for crime-related bills that [the victim has] already personally paid" (Pennsylvania Commission on Crime and Delinquency). In many cases, victims realize additional expenses following their initial filing of applications. Nearly one-third of the awards made are "supplemental awards" (Pennsylvania Commission on Crime and Delinquency, Office of Victims' Services).

Victims may not receive compensation for property damage (except for the replacement of stolen or damaged medical equipment), although they may file insurance claims for such losses, or file a civil lawsuit against the offender who caused the damages. Additionally, any payments received by victims for expenses already covered by the Victim Compensation Assistance Program must be repaid to the program. This includes payments received from insurance companies, worker's compensation, and those ordered by the court such as awards in a civil case or victim restitution in a criminal case. In addition to the property damage exclusion, the Victim Compensation Assistance Program will not make payment for pain and suffering. Payments made by the program are not subject to IRS reporting (i.e., they are not taxable).

Victims' Services Programs

The Victim Compensation Program is only one of the services that fall under the umbrella of the Pennsylvania Commission on Crime and Delinquency's Office of Victims' Services (OVS). The OVS also oversees locally operated victims' services programs. There are over 250 victim service agencies through-out Pennsylvania, each providing services to victims in one or more of the Commonwealth's 67 counties. Residents of every county throughout Pennsylvania have access to crime victim services through one or more of these agencies. Victims may visit agencies intended to serve those within their county of residence, or they may seek assistance from agencies intended to serve other counties. Victim service providers, typically called "victim advocates," are found within criminal justice agencies (e.g., district attorney's office, probation department, etc.) and within the community. Community-based victim service agencies are typically private, non-profit organizations.

The services provided to victims "range from accompaniment and court-room orientation to notification, restitution, victims compensation assistance, transportation, child care, counseling, assistance with Victim Impact Statements and victim communication with the offender" (Pennsylvania Commission on Crime and Delinquency, 2012, p. 3). Most of these agencies provide services to all types of victims, while others focus on domestic violence and/ or sexual assault victims, and some on victims of drunk driving. In 2010, 56,479 victims of juvenile offenders and 170,583 victims of adult offenders received one of more of these services (Pennsylvania Commission on Crime and Delinquency, 2012, p. 3).

Victims' services are partially supported by state and federal grants, and by private donors. The exceptions to this are public agencies that provide services exclusively to elderly or child victims. Many victims' service agencies also rely heavily upon volunteers for much of the agencies' staffing and for 24-hour hot-line coverage. The Pennsylvania Commission on Crime and Delinquency's Office of Victims' Services "administers state and federal funds in order to provide grants, training, and technical assistance to community-based and system-based programs that work to serve victims of crime" (Pennsylvania Commission on Crime and Delinquency, 2012, p. 3). In recent years, victim services have faced "unprecedented state and federal funding cuts" and the PCCD formed a Victims' Services Advisory Committee and charged it with "studying and making recommendations related to the organizational capacity and sustainability of victim services over the next 5–10 years" (Pennsylvania Commission on Crime and Delinquency, 2012, p. 4).

Office of the Victim Advocate

The Pennsylvania Office of the Victim Advocate (OVA) was created in 1995 and is charged with "representing, protecting, and advancing the individual and collective rights and interests of crime victims" (Pennsylvania Of-

fice of the Victim Advocate, 2013). Nominated by the governor and confirmed by the Senate, the Victim Advocate serves a term of six years, during
which he or she will collaborate with various other state and local agencies
to serve the needs of crime victims. The work of the Victim Advocate (currently Jennifer Storm) involves post-sentencing protections of victims and
represents their "rights and interests ... before the Pennsylvania Department
of Corrections (DOC) and the Pennsylvania Board of Probation and Parole
(PBPP)" (Pennsylvania Office of the Victim Advocate, 2013). The Victim
Advocate is responsible for notifying victims of various post-sentencing events
and providing opportunities for victim input at numerous points in the post-
sentencing stage of the criminal justice process. Rights to notification and
input will be described later in this chapter.

Other State Organizations Involved in Helping Crime Victims

While the Pennsylvania Commission on Crime and Delinquency's Office of
Victims' Services (OVS) and the Pennsylvania Office of the Victim Advocate play
a large role in the provision of victim services, other state agencies and organizations also contribute to the protection of prospective and actual victims.
For example, the Pennsylvania Department of Public Welfare's Office of Children, Youth and Families oversees the ChildLine and Abuse Registry. The
agency maintains information regarding child abuse, and conducts background
checks for prospective employees (e.g., teachers, coaches), school and church
program volunteers, foster and adoptive parents, and others who in their role
would have access to others' children. The purpose of this registry is to protect prospective victims from harm at the hands of a known offender (Pennsylvania Department of Public Welfare. Child Abuse History Clearance).
Similarly, the Pennsylvania State Police provides a general criminal background
clearance (Pennsylvania State Police. Request for Criminal Record Check).

Another Department of Public Welfare role is that of notifying crime victims of the transfer or release of offenders residing in mental health institutions
(discussed later in this chapter). The Pennsylvania Department of Aging oversees local agencies throughout the Commonwealth that seek to protect older
adults from various types of "abuse, neglect, exploitation, and abandonment"
(Pennsylvania Department of Aging). The Pennsylvania Department of Education's Office for Safe Schools provides assistance to local schools in terms of
security and violence prevention (Pennsylvania Department of Education).
The Elder Abuse Unit of the Pennsylvania Attorney General's Office is charged
not only with investigating and prosecuting scams and abuse aimed at the eld-

erly, but also with educating the public about fraud against seniors and protective measures (Pennsylvania Attorney General, Elder Abuse Unit; Pennsylvania Attorney General, Filing a Complaint). In sum, there are a variety of state agencies and organizations, only some of which are highlighted here, that play a role in preventing and responding to crime victimization.

Crime Victims' Rights

In each state, the rights of crime victims are included in constitutional amendments, state statutes, or both. While Pennsylvania does not have a crime victims' rights amendment to its constitution, Pennsylvania's Crime Victims Act (18 P.S. § 11.101) and other statutes afford victims in Pennsylvania several rights. Some rights are granted to the victim automatically upon reporting the crime, others must be requested, and still others require a registration process.

Pennsylvania Crime Victims Act

Pennsylvania Act 11 of 1998 codified many victims' rights within a single act known as the Crime Victims Act. The Pennsylvania Crime Victims Act provides a number of basic rights including: the right to receive basic information regarding crime victim services; the right to be notified about various actions, proceedings, and decisions throughout the criminal justice process; the right to be accompanied to criminal and juvenile proceedings; the right to restitution in certain circumstances; and the right to provide input to decision-makers at various stages of the criminal justice process.

The Right to Receive Basic Information

Pennsylvania's Crime Victims Act gives victims the right "to receive basic information concerning the services available for victims of crime" (18 P.S. § 11.101). The responsibility for providing this information generally falls upon law enforcement agencies, and the information must be provided to the victim with 24 hours of first contact between the alleged victim and the police. In cases in which there has been some financial harm to the victim, the police must, within 48 hours of the crime having been reported, provide the direct victim (or the parent or guardian of a child victim) with written information regarding the availability of crime victim's compensation. An application form for compensation is also provided to the victim by the police. The information provided to crime victims upon contact with the police typically will include a list of rights and services available to crime victims.

Rights to Notifications Regarding the Offender

Crime victims in Pennsylvania have the right to be notified of certain events that take place in the criminal justice process. For example, the police must make a reasonable effort to notify a victim of a personal (i.e., violent) crime of the arrest of a criminal suspect. Such notification should occur within 24 hours of the arraignment of the defendant. Victims are responsible to provide a valid address and phone number for this and any other type of notification. It is the victim's responsibility to notify the police (and/or other criminal justice offices) of any updates to their address and phone number. The victim's contact information that is provided to the police is kept confidential, and not released to anyone other than law enforcement agencies, corrections agencies, and/or prosecutors' offices. Additionally, a law enforcement officer, sheriff, deputy sheriff, or constable will notify assault victims of an inmate's escape from custody.

Following the arrest of a suspect, the victim has the right to be informed of other events throughout the criminal justice and juvenile justice processes. The victim has the right, for example, to be informed of whether or not bail has been granted, whether an arrested juvenile has been detained or released, whether a "petition alleging delinquency has been filed," if an offender has escaped from a local correctional facility while awaiting trial or from a facility while serving a sentence, if an offender has been recommended by the judge for a motivational boot camp, if an offender is granted work release, the disposition of a juvenile, if an offender is released from incarceration for medical reasons, when a parole hearing is scheduled to take place, if an offender is released on parole, pardon, or through other means, if a juvenile offender has escaped from a juvenile facility, if a juvenile or adult offender is being transferred to other facilities, and when the court's jurisdiction over the case has been terminated. For example, Pennsylvania offers a boot camp program for young (under 35), minimum-custody level, male and female offenders sentenced to between 2 and 5 years of confinement under the jurisdiction of the State Department of Corrections. Participation in the program requires the recommendation of the judge at sentencing or the Department of Corrections. Quehanna Motivational Boot Camp (QBC) provides a rigorous six-month disciplinary and training program. Upon successful completion, offenders are "release[d] on parole to a 30-day stay at a community corrections center" (Pennsylvania Office of the Victim Advocate. Quehanna Boot Camp, 2013). Victims have a number of rights during this process, including the right to be notified of the judge's recommendation that the offender be sent to QBC, the offender's transfer to QBC, the offender's failure at QBC and transfer back to a state prison, and the offender's anticipated graduation date.

Victims may receive notification regarding offenders throughout the criminal justice and juvenile justice processes through various means, including phone calls or letters from the police, victim-witness coordinator in the prosecutor's office, juvenile probation officers, or other criminal justice professionals. For example, if a person is incarcerated in the county jail for violation of a Protection from Abuse order (PFA), the victim will be notified by telephone by the victim-witness coordinator in the district attorney's office or by a representative of the county jail in the event of the defendant's release from jail on bail. Victims may also receive notification through automated systems. One means through which crime victims may be notified of changes in an offender's custody is through the Pennsylvania Statewide Automated Victim Information and Notification (PA SAVIN) service. Victims may register for this free service to receive information regarding the status of offenders in state custody (i.e., those in jail, in prison, or on parole). Information may also be received by crime victims through VINELink, a mobile app. PA SAVIN will automatically inform victims via email or phone call of "an inmate's release, transfer, or escape" (Pennsylvania Department of Corrections, 2013). Victims' SAVIN registration is confidential; offenders have no knowledge of anyone's participation in the program. While PA SAVIN is available to *any* Pennsylvania resident, victims of crimes resulting in a state prison sentence of 24 months or longer may register with the Office of the Victim Advocate for special notifications including "when an offender is being considered for release" from prison (Pennsylvania Department of Corrections, 2013). Victims who would like to be notified about an offender who is residing in a mental health facility can register with the Pennsylvania Department of Public Welfare.

Right to Input

Victims are provided the right to submit input prior to key decisions being made throughout the criminal justice and juvenile justice processes. For example, victims of personal injury crimes (i.e., assault, sexual assault, arson and related offenses, robbery, kidnapping, victim witness intimidation, the violation of a protection from abuse order, some driving under the influence offenses, homicide by vehicle or homicide by watercraft while under the influence, as well as hit and run crashes resulting in injury) or burglaries have the right "to give prior comment on the potential reduction or dropping of charges or any changes of a plea in the criminal … case" or the diversion of a juvenile or adult case, "to offer prior comment on the sentencing of a defendant or the disposition of a delinquent child," to receive assistance in preparing the oral and/or written victim impact statement (VIS) "detailing the physical, psychological and economic effects of the crime," which will be considered by

Table 9.1 Victims' Rights to Notification and Input Post-Sentencing

Event Type	Registered Victim Receives Notification?	Registered Victim Has Right to Provide Input?
Prerelease review for Community Corrections Center (CCC)	Yes	Yes
Release to CCC	Yes	Opportunity for input provided earlier. Registered victim will receive information on offender's location
Prerelease review for Education Release review	Yes	Yes
Release to Education Release	Yes	Opportunity for input provided earlier. Registered victim will receive information on program duration and location.
Furlough review	Yes	Yes
Furlough release	Yes	Opportunity for input provided earlier. Registered victim will receive information on offender's location
Transfer to Mental Health Facility	Yes	No. Responsibility for victim notification transfers to DPW.
Transfer to Quehanna Boot Camp (QBC)	Yes	Victim can provide statement if DOC requests that the sentencing court reconsider the offender's sentence for QBC
State Intermediate Punishment (SIP)	Yes	Victim can provide statement to court if DOC requests that the sentencing court reconsider the offender's sentence for SIP
Prison Escape/Recapture	Yes	No
Transfer to other authorities (county, other state)	Yes	No
Inmate Death	Yes	No
Automatic Parole upon Completion of QBC	Yes	No input option-however, registered victim can request parole conditions
Parole Review when offenders is eligible	Yes	Yes

Table 9.1 Victims' Rights to Notification and Input Post-Sentencing,
continued

Event Type	Registered Victim Receives Notification?	Registered Victim Has Right to Provide Input?
PBPP Decision to approve/refuse parole	Yes	No
Parole Revocation	Yes	No
Parolee Death	Yes	No

Source: Pennsylvania Office of the Victim Advocate. OVA Services for Crime Victims. http://www.ova.state.pa.us/portal/server.pt/community/assistance_and_services/.

the courts. Victims of violent crimes or burglary are permitted "to submit prior comment … on the potential reduction or dropping of any charge or changing of a plea in a criminal or delinquency proceeding" (18 P.S. § 11.201).

Victim Input and Sentencing

As mentioned in Chapter 2, a judge may order a pre-sentence investigation (PSI) following a conviction or guilty plea. The PSI is conducted by a probation officer and the PSI report includes information about "the circumstances of the offense," "the character of the defendant," and "a victim impact statement" (234 Pa Code Rule 702). The victim impact statement is voluntary, and may be submitted to the probation officer in writing or verbally. Victim advocates are available to provide assistance to victims in preparing their victim impact statements (VIS). The VIS generally includes information about the physical, psychological, emotional, and/or financial consequences of the crime on the victim. The PSI report is used by the judge to help him or her to determine an appropriate sentence for a convicted offender.

Victim Input and Changes to an Offender's Sentence

In circumstances in which the Department of Corrections (DOC) is requesting that an adult offender be resentenced to an intermediate sanction, the victim has the right to submit a victim impact statement. Similarly, a victim may provide input prior to the judge's decision regarding recommendation that the offender be sent to the Quehanna Boot Camp (Pennsylvania Office of the Victim Advocate. Quehanna Boot Camp, 2013).

Victim Input and Parole

Victims are notified of upcoming parole board hearings at least 90 days before such hearings. The Crime Victims Act permits a crime victim or a member of the victim's family to submit to the victim advocate an oral, written, or video-recorded pre-parole statement within 30 days of notification of an inmate's parole hearing. The statement is to be considered by the parole board. On June 18, 2013, Pennsylvania House Bill 492 was passed into law (Act 14), amending the law to more explicitly state the right of the victim to provide direct testimony before the board. The passage of the bill gave "the victim or the victim's representative, at his or her election" the right "to appear in person before the board [or hearing examiner] or, in the alternative, the [victim's testimony may be presented by conference call] victim or victim's representative may elect to present testimony by electronic means as provided by the board." As had been the case previously, "the testimony of a victim or victim's representative before the board shall be confidential. Records maintained by the department and the board pertaining to victims shall be kept separate. Current address, telephone number and any other personal information of the victim, victim's representative and family members shall be deemed confidential" (General Assembly of Pennsylvania, PA HB 492).

Victim Input and Pardons

The Board of Pardons in Pennsylvania makes recommendations to the Governor regarding clemency or pardon for offenders who have been convicted of crimes ranging from summary offenses to homicide. Act 5 of 1995 requires that the Board of Pardons provide victims/survivors the opportunity to provide written or oral comment that will be considered by the five-member Board of Pardons prior to its making a recommendation to the governor.

Any victim comments submitted to the Board of Pardons will be shared with the Office of the Victim Advocate, so that the OVA can reach out to the victim and offer accompaniment and assistance during the Board of Pardons public hearing, offer to attend the public hearing on behalf of the victim, and/or make referrals for the victim to receive other victim services (Pennsylvania Office of the Victim Advocate. Board of Pardons). Table 9.1 summarizes victims' post-sentencing rights to notification and input.

Victims' Right to Attend and Be Accompanied to Proceedings

Victims have the right to be present at various court hearings, including murder trials. Additionally, victims have the right to be accompanied at many criminal and all juvenile court proceedings by a family member, a victim advocate, or other support person (42 Pa.C.S. §6336(d). Victim service agencies may provide a victim advocate for support purposes, if the victim so chooses.

Reimbursement of Victims' Losses

Victims of crime in Pennsylvania have the right

> "... to be restored, to the extent possible, to the precrime economic status through the provision of restitution, compensation and the expeditious return of property which is seized as evidence in the case when in the judgment of the prosecutor the evidence is no longer needed for prosecution of the case (18 Pa. C.S. 1106(c))" (Pennsylvania Office of the Victim Advocate. Pennsylvania Crime Victims' Rights, 2013).

In addition to having their property returned to them, crime victims may recover some of the costs resulting from the crime through the Victim Compensation Assistance Program, court-ordered restitution, and/or civil lawsuits. The VCAP has been described in a previous section of this chapter. It is important to note that victim compensation is made from a general fund, meaning that the capture, identification, and prosecution of an offender are not necessary in order for a victim to obtain compensation. Restitution, on the other hand, is an order made at the time of the sentencing of the offender to pay the victim for unrecovered property, property that has decreased in value due to the offender, and/or expenses incurred by the victim due to the crime. Pennsylvania legislation calls for the sentencing judge to order full restitution to the victim (18 Pa C.S.A. 1106(c)). During the pre-sentence investigation, juvenile and adult probation officers will often be proactive in soliciting input from victims regarding restitution. A final means through which victims may seek to recover from financial losses due to crime is through a civil lawsuit. Unlike restitution and compensation, a civil lawsuit is the only legal option that enables a victim to potentially receive a monetary award for pain and suffering in addition to tangible losses. As mentioned earlier in this chapter, if an award in a civil case covers damages already covered through the state Victim Compensation Assistance Program (VCAP), the victim must reimburse VCAP for the duplicate payments received.

Other Crime Victims' Rights

In addition to the rights that comprise/constitute the Crime Victim Act, there are a number of other rights that are afforded through other Pennsylvania statutes. For example, even if homicide survivors will be providing testimony or presenting an impact statement during the sentencing phase, they may not be excluded from the trial (42 Pa. C.S. Section 9738). Additionally, upon registration with and selection by the Victim Advocate of the Pennsylvania Office of the Victim Advocate, up to four homicide survivors may be present at the execution of an offender in their case (61 Pa. C.S. Section 4305). Victims of domestic violence also have a number of additional rights (to be discussed shortly).

Special Types of Victims

Historically, there has been special attention paid to certain groups of crime victims perceived to be particularly vulnerable or especially harmed by the crimes committed against them. These crime victims include children, the elderly, domestic violence victims, sexual assault victims, and families of murder victims.

Child Victims

Unlike most adult victims, special considerations are given to child victims. The state provides a child abuse hotline and maintains records related to reports of abuse (Child Line and Abuse Registry). ChildLine offers a 24-hour per day hotline for reports of suspected child abuse. The intake specialist who handles the call will determine whether to report the suspected abuse to the county child protective services agency for investigation or to the police. Other options include referring the caller to other local agencies for assistance. Calls to ChildLine may be made by anyone suspecting abuse and may be made anonymously, although professionals who encounter children during their work are mandatory reporters who may be prosecuted for the failure to contact the authorities. Mandatory reporters (also known as required reporters) include doctors, nurses, funeral directors, social workers, members of the clergy, school employees, and others who, "in the course of their employment, occupation or practice of their profession come into contact with children and have reasonable cause to suspect, on the basis of their medical, professional, or other training and experience, that a child coming before them in their professional or official capacity is a victim of child abuse" (55 PA Code § 3490.4).

Local child protective service agencies are overseen by the Department of Public Welfare's Bureau of Child Welfare Services. The local (usually county) agencies are generally responsible for investigating allegations of child abuse and neglect, assessing the risk to the child(ren) involved, contacting law enforcement when appropriate, developing a service plan, providing in-home services, and arranging for temporary and permanent out-of-home placement for endangered youth. The focus of the local agencies should be on the safety and welfare of the child, and reunification of the family only if deemed appropriate.

Child Victims in the Courtroom

Due to their cognitive and emotional immaturity and their relationship to, and possible dependence on, the perpetrator, child victims are particularly vulnerable to intimidation in the courtroom. For this reason, most states have passed legislation allowing for special protections for young victims. Pennsylvania law allows for the use of recorded testimony or contemporaneous alternative methods in cases involving child victims under the age of 16. These two alternatives to traditional testimony in court are to be used in situations in which the court has determined that "testifying either in an open forum in the presence and full view of the finder of fact or in the defendant's presence will result in the child victim ... suffering serious emotional distress that would substantially impair the child victim's ... ability to reasonably communicate" (42 Pa. Cons. Stat. Ann § 5984.1 (2012)).

The statute makes admissible in court the presentation of a child victim's recorded testimony "that accurately captures and preserves the visual images, oral communications and other information presented during such testimony" (42 Pa.C.S.A. § 5984.1(a)). The testimony, taken under oath or affirmation, may be recorded "in chambers or in a special facility designed for taking the recorded testimony of children." Only the prosecutor and defense attorney, technical equipment operator, shorthand reporter, and "any person whose presence would contribute to the welfare and well-being of the child ... may be present in the room with the child during testimony." The defendant can hear and see the testimony, but the child shall not see or hear the defendant. "Examination and cross-examination of the child victim ... shall proceed in the same manner as normally permitted" (42 Pa. Cons. Stat. Ann § 5984.1 (2012)). Testimony by contemporaneous alternative method is also permitted by the statute (42 Pa. Cons. Stat. Ann § 5985 (2012)). This testimony would involve a "live feed" rather than prerecorded testimony. The same restrictions as for recorded testimony would hold for this contemporaneous alternative method. The "testimony of a parent or custodian or any other person, such as a person who has dealt with the child victim … in a medical or therapeutic setting" is also permitted. During this testimony, the defendant has the right to be present (42 Pa. Cons. Stat. Ann § 5984.1 (2012)).

Expert Witnesses in Child Sexual Assault Cases

Other recent legislation related to criminal cases involving child victims pertains to the use of expert testimony when a child is alleged to have been sexually assaulted. Although HB 1264 was introduced in 2006, it was not passed until 2012 following the Penn State University scandal involving football assistant coach and youth camp director Jerry Sandusky sexually abusing boys under his care in the camp program. Expert testimony regarding the behavior of sexual assault victims was not permitted during Sandusky's trial, so jurors may have been unaware of typical behavior of these victims. For example, they might not understand why one alleged victim had sent a Father's Day card to the defendant. HB 1264 amended Title 42 (Judiciary and Judicial Procedure) to allow for expert testimony to enlighten jurors of the psychological impact of sexual abuse and victim behavior during and subsequent to the crime (Tully, 2012). It may help jurors to understand why a victim of sexual abuse may not fight off the perpetrator or report the offense immediately, or why the victim may continue to associate with a perpetrator. This new legislation is also relevant in sex crime cases involving adult victims. The passage of this legislation made Pennsylvania the final state in the United States to enact legislation that allows for expert testimony to enlighten jurors about the "dynamics of sexual assault" (Bass, 2012).

Domestic Violence Victims

A number of services are available for victims of domestic violence in Pennsylvania. In 1976, a group of nine domestic violence agencies joined together to form the Pennsylvania Coalition against Domestic Violence (PCADV), the first coalition of its type in the United States. At present, PCADV serves nearly 100,000 domestic violence victims each year. They manage approximately 60 community-based domestic violence services, including a 24-hour hotline, crisis centers, individual and group counseling programs, shelters, and a wide variety of other services (Pennsylvania Coalition against Domestic Violence, 2013a).

The PCADV, in compliance with federal and state requirements, provides public education, school-based programs, and training for criminal justice professionals (e.g., police, prosecutors, judges) and policy-makers (Pennsylvania Coalition against Domestic Violence, 2013a). The PCADV also acts as an advocate for battered women. This advocacy includes lobbying the Pennsylvania legislature, on behalf of battered women, for improvements to domestic violence laws and enforcement of existing laws (Pennsylvania Coalition against Domestic Violence, 2013a). The Coalition also administers state contracts for domestic violence services, distributes funding to community programs, distributes public awareness materials, and supports research on public attitudes toward domestic violence (Pennsylvania Coalition against Domestic Violence, 2013b).

In April 2013, the ACLU filed a lawsuit against the Borough of Norristown (PA) challenging a local ordinance (Borough of Norristown §245-3) that penalized landlords when police responded to calls to a residential rental property for disorderly behavior (Zara, 2013). Unfortunately, "disorderly behavior" included "domestic disturbances that do not require that a mandatory arrest be made" (Borough of Norristown §245-3). Concerns were raised regarding domestic violence victims' hesitation to call police repeatedly for fear of eviction. The threat of eviction might discourage some domestic violence victims from calling the police. The ACLU argues that the municipal ordinance is a violation of the Violence Against Women Act (VAWA), federal legislation that "protects many domestic violence victims from eviction based on the crimes committed against them" (American Civil Liberties Union). The PCADV advocated for the victim in this case through the filing of an amicus brief.

Protection from Abuse Act

Pennsylvania's Protection from Abuse Act (23 Pa. C.S. §6105 et seq.) offers special protections and rights to victims of domestic violence. Upon encountering a domestic violence victim, it is incumbent upon the police to notify the victim (both verbally and in writing) of available services and rights (23 Pa. C.S. §6105). This includes providing information related to the availability of hotlines, safe shelters, and other services. Written notice must be provided in English and Spanish and must include the following statement:

> If you are the victim of domestic violence, you have the right to go to court and file a petition requesting an order for protection from domestic abuse pursuant to the Protection from Abuse Act (23 Pa. C.S. Ch. 61), which could include the following:
> (1) An order restraining the abuser from further acts of abuse.
> (2) An order directing the abuser to leave your household.
> (3) An order preventing the abuser from entering your residence, school, business or place of employment.
> (4) An order awarding you or the other parent temporary custody of or temporary visitation with your child or children.

(5) An order directing the abuser to pay support to you and the minor children if the abuser has a legal obligation to do so (23 Pa. C.S. §6105).

Those who have been physically abused, raped, sexually assaulted, threatened with physical harm, or stalked by a current or former intimate partner may apply for a Protection from Abuse order (PFA). The PFA is a civil restraining order that is issued by either a district court justice or a court of common pleas judge. Emergency Orders may be issued by a district justice after hours or on weekends when the court of common pleas is closed. An Emergency Order is usually only valid until the next business day. An Ex Parte Temporary Order is usually issued by the district justice or common pleas judge and will remain in effect until a hearing for a Permanent Order is held. Generally, the sheriff will serve the defendant with the order, although in some counties, someone else may serve the defendant. A Permanent Order may be in effect for a matter of months or up to three years.

Although the PFA is a civil order, its violation can constitute indirect criminal contempt. Depending upon the circumstances, the police may make an arrest and/or file a complaint, or the victim may file a private complaint. The defendant may also be prosecuted for other crimes associated with the violation of the PFA (assault, stalking, etc.).

In 1994, Act 85 was signed into law. The bill called for amendments to Pennsylvania's Protection from Abuse Act, including the creation and maintenance of a statewide protection order registry. The Protection From Abuse Database (PFAD), created in 1997 and managed by the Pennsylvania State Police, is an archive that not only includes all PFA proceedings in the Commonwealth, but allows authorized users (e.g., law enforcement officers, courts, legal agencies, private attorneys) to access PFA records via a secured Internet website, 24 hours a day/365 days of the year (Pennsylvania. Protection From Abuse Database). The availability of this information assists law enforcement in enforcing these civil orders.

The current version of the PFA law (23 Pa. C.S. §6101 *et seq*) affords victims of domestic violence a number of protections. PFAs issued in one jurisdiction within the Commonwealth are valid and enforceable throughout the state. As a centralized archive of PFAs, the PFAD makes this possible. Under the full faith and credit clause of the Protection From Abuse Act, domestic violence victims who have had comparable protection orders granted within a jurisdiction outside of the Commonwealth are also protected by such orders. The victim may file the foreign protection order with the prothonotary in the Pennsylvania county within which the plaintiff "believes enforcement may be necessary." Once filed, the prothonotary will transmit the information to the Pennsylvania State Police for inclusion in the statewide database (23 Pa. C.S.

§6104). Even if the victim chooses not to file the foreign order with the prothonotary, the order (when presented to police) is still enforceable by police in Pennsylvania.

Sexual Assault Victims

Just as domestic violence programs joined together to form the PCADV, the state's 50 rape crisis centers that serve all 67 Pennsylvania counties form the Pennsylvania Coalition Against Rape (PCAR). PCAR was created in 1975 and has, since then, advocated for victims of sexual violence. The organization actively attempts to "raise public awareness" and "effect changes in public policy," hoping to eliminate sexual violence. The Coalition also oversees the fifty rape crisis centers throughout the state (Pennsylvania Coalition Against Rape).

Post-Assault Treatment of Sexual Assault Victims

Due to the traumatic impact of sexual assault, it is important that the law enforcement and medical professionals with whom the victim interacts be especially sensitive to the victim's needs. Medical professionals who are specially trained to care for sexual assault victims are known as sexual assault forensic examiners (SAFE) or sexual assault nurse practitioners (SANE). These registered nurses, medical doctors, or physicians' assistants collect forensic evidence, and provide the victim with medication to prevent pregnancy and sexually transmitted diseases. SAFE or SANE programs can be found throughout Pennsylvania in various hospitals and within the community. Sometimes the SANE or SART programs are part of a sexual assault response team (SART), a collaborative group consisting of "a sexual assault forensic examiner, sexual assault counselor/advocate, a law enforcement representative, ... a prosecutor," and sometimes "other members of the community" (Pennsylvania Coalition Against Rape. SAFE/SANE/SART).

Pending Legislation Related to Sexual Assault Victims

As in a dozen other states, Pennsylvania rape victims who bear children from the rape can request that the court terminate the parental rights of the rapist to his biological child. Unfortunately, under Pennsylvania law, when this termination occurs, the rapist is no longer obligated to pay child support. A 2013 bill (H.B. 836) would require that rapist fathers pay child support even in the event of termination of paternal rights. As of December 16, 2013, the bill had not yet been acted upon.

Another pending bill (written with the assistance of PCAR) that was on the House Calendar for action as of December 16, 2013 was Senate Bill 681, a bill that seeks to protect victims of sexual violence in the same way as victims of domestic violence. At the time of this writing, protection orders could only be obtained by victims who had been harmed or threatened by someone with whom they had had an intimate relationship. Senate Bill 681 calls for making protection orders available to victims of sexual violence, regardless of the relationship between perpetrator and victim. The standard of proof for obtaining the protection order would be a preponderance of the evidence. If the protection order were granted, the defendant would be ordered to stay away from the sexual assault victim.

Sex Offender Registry

Each state throughout the United States maintains a sex offender registry. Pennsylvania's Megan's Law (42 Pa.C.S. § 9799.10 et seq.) "exists solely for the purpose of providing a means of protecting the public, especially our children, from victimization by sexual offenders" (Pennsylvania State Police. Megan's Law Website). A database of convicted sex offenders is maintained by the Pennsylvania State Police. The publicly accessible database is searchable by county, municipality, zip code, address, and name. It also contains a mapping feature that allows the user to map the residences of registered offenders and to search within a specified radius of a given address. Information included in sex offender's online profiles includes name, date of birth, home address, school address, work address, a photograph, physical description, identifying marks (e.g., scars, tattoos, etc.), vehicle information, type of offense, date of conviction, and whether the victim was a minor. Offenders' profiles remain on the site for 15 years, 25 years, or life, depending upon the seriousness of the crime. Offenders are required to register at the time of sentencing (or upon arrival in the state for residence, school, or work, if convicted in another state), and are mandated to report any changes to address, employment, etc. for the length of their registration period.

In addition to the website, Pennsylvania's Megan's Law calls for community notification when the offender is classified as a Sexually Violent Predator or Sexually Violent Delinquent Child. In such cases, the police notify people who live or work within 250 feet of the offender's residence or "the 25 most immediate residences and places of employment, whichever is greater" (Pennsylvania State Police. Megan's Law Website). Flyers are distributed or posted that include the offender's name, address, type of offense, photo, and a statement indicating that the offender is a Sexually Violent Predator (Pennsylvania State Police. Megan's Law Website).

Address Confidentiality Program

Another protection afforded to domestic violence, sexual assault, and stalking victims in Pennsylvania is the Address Confidentiality Program (ACP) administered by the Office of the Victim Advocate (OVA). This service is used by victims who have moved to a new residence unknown to the perpetrator of the crime against them. The OVA will provide the victim with a confidential substitute address that state and local agencies are required by law to use. The staff at a local victim service agency will help the victim complete the necessary paperwork as part of an overall safety plan. Once established, the victim will file a change of address form at the post office, and the alternative address will be used for all mail. Upon enrollment, a victim's residential and work addresses must be kept confidential (23 Pa. C.S.A. §6701) unless disclosure is mandated by court order, a participant is under investigation, a governmental agency requests and is granted a waiver, or the participant or his or her family members are in danger. Participation in the alternative address program lasts for three years unless cancelled prior to the expiration date. Participants may file a renewal application to extend participation in the program (Pennsylvania Office of the Victim Advocate. Address Confidentiality Program, 2013).

Elderly Victims

Persons aged 60 and over are protected by all of the laws described earlier in this chapter, however, there are additional protections afforded to older Pennsylvanians. Elder abuse includes physical, financial, and sexual abuse, and neglect. Additionally, the elderly may be targets of identity theft, fraud, and various scams. Pennsylvania's Department of Aging oversees the state's 52 Area Agencies on Aging (AAA), each of which serves the residents of one or more counties. The Pennsylvania Department of Aging's Consumer Protection Division is responsible for services that protect older Pennsylvanians against "fraud, abuse, neglect, exploitation and abandonment, and for managing the Criminal History Background Check process"—a requirement for employment at specific types of facilities such as nursing homes and home health care agencies (Pennsylvania Department of Aging, 2013).

Specifically, complaints regarding the financial exploitation of senior citizens are handled by the State Attorney General's Elder Abuse Unit. These complaints may include scams and frauds. The role of the State Attorney General's Elder Abuse Unit is to investigate and prosecute those who attempt to financially victimize Pennsylvania senior citizens. Other state agencies tasked with protecting elderly victims include the Pennsylvania Department of Aging and the Pennsylvania Consumer Protection Division.

The Older Adults Protective Services Act (OAPSA) (P.L. 1125, No.169) mandates services for older adults who are unable to protect themselves and may be at imminent risk of victimization (i.e., abuse, neglect, exploitation). These "protective services must safeguard the rights of older adults while protecting them from abuse, neglect, exploitation and abandonment" (Pennsylvania. Older Adult Protective Services Act, 2013). In 1997, the Act was amended to require both criminal background checks for employment in the elder care industry, as well as mandatory reporting of suspected abuse of the elderly (Act 13-1997). Specifically, the Act mandates that any employee or administrator report suspected abuse of the elderly to the local Area on Aging (AAA) (Pennsylvania. Older Adult Protective Services Act, 2013). Incidents involving serious bodily injury, sexual abuse, or suspicious death must be immediately reported to additional agencies, including local law enforcement, the Department of Aging, the facility's licensing agency, and the coroner (where applicable) (Pennsylvania. Older Adult Protective Services Act, 2013).

Elderly victims may also have access to national, regional, or local resources, which may be publicly funded or privately funded non-profit organizations. An example would be the Center for Advocacy for the Rights and Interests of the Elderly (CARIE), a Philadelphia-based non-profit organization that offers a variety of services to the elderly. Among the services available are advocacy and assistance to elderly victims of crime and abuse. One of the services maintained by CARIE is the Elderly Victims Emergency Security Fund (EVESF). This fund provides services for victims 60 and over who may need assistance in securing their residence (e.g., replacing locks, security bars on windows, etc.) to prevent further criminal victimization (Center for Advocacy for the Rights and Interests of the Elderly).

Families of Murder Victims

In addition to special programs and services available to child victims, sexual assault victims, domestic violence victims, and elderly victims, there are also programs available for Families of Murder Victims (FMV) in Pennsylvania. These programs are often available in urban areas where murder rates are higher, and offer services such as up-to-date information on criminal justice proceedings (e.g., investigation, arrest, hearings, etc.), support in the courtroom, counseling, assistance with victim's compensation claims, and support groups.

Victim and Offender Programs

Most states offer a variety of victim-offender programs that attempt to restore the victim and/or community while simultaneously rehabilitating the offender. Some programs involve face-to-face contact between offender and victim that allow the two parties to interact and better understand one another's perspective, while others involve symbolic restitution on the part of the offender through community service projects. Pennsylvania offers several victim-offender programs such as the Victim Offender Dialogue Program, Impact of Crime classes, Balanced and Restorative Justice (BARJ), community conferencing, and the Mural Arts Program.

Victim Offender Dialogue Program

Pennsylvania's Victim Offender Dialogue Program is a victim-offender mediation program that allows victims or survivors (i.e., family members of a homicide victim) to meet with the perpetrators of crime. The Victim Offender Dialogue (VOD) Program provides victims with the opportunity to ask perpetrators questions about the crime (e.g., motivation, feelings of remorse) and express to the perpetrators how the crime has impacted the victims' lives. The program provides the perpetrator an opportunity to "accept responsibility" and victims the possibility of empowerment. The VOD Program can entail actual face-to-face meetings between victim and perpetrator, or the exchange of letters between the parties. Prior to the meeting or letter-writing, the victim and perpetrator each work with "trained volunteer facilitators" who help them prepare for the meeting or help them to "compose and exchange letters" (Pennsylvania Office of the Victim Advocate, Victim Offender Dialogue Program, 2013). The VOD Program is victim-initiated; victims must contact the VOD Program Coordinator at the Office of the Victim Advocate. Unfortunately, as of the time of this writing, the waiting list for the VOD Program was "approximately one year" (Pennsylvania Office of the Victim Advocate, Victim Offender Dialogue Program, 2013).

Impact of Crime Classes

Similar to the Victim Offender Dialogue Program, Pennsylvania state prisons offer an opportunity for victims to share with inmates their stories related to crime victimization and its impact. Unlike victim-impact statements at sentencing and input at parole hearings, victim participation in Impact of Crime

Classes (ICC) is not intended to affect the type or length of sentence served by offenders. Instead, the program attempts to "increase the inmate's level of accountability and empathy for those they have harmed" (Pennsylvania, 2013).

Balanced and Restorative Justice

The importance of the victim and community is a central theme within the juvenile justice system. In 1995, legislation was passed in Pennsylvania that established a new purpose of the state's juvenile justice system based upon the philosophy of Balanced and Restorative Justice (BARJ). The principles of BARJ include community protection, juvenile offender accountability and repair/restoration of the harm to the victim and community, and competency development (i.e., improvements in the juvenile offender's ability to live as productive members in the community (Family Involvement Committee). The BARJ approach is based upon the belief that "justice is best served" when the community, victim, and offender "receive balanced attention" (Family Involvement Committee, nd, p. 18). More about BARJ can be found in Chapter 8 of this text.

Conferencing and Mediation Programs

Similar to the BARJ approach, community conferencing and victim-offender conferencing/mediation allow for face-to-face interaction between victim and offender, allowing both parties to share their thoughts, experiences, motivations, and emotions. Unlike victim-offender conferencing or victim-offender mediation which seek resolution between the offender and his or her victims, community conferencing programs offer the offender and community members (symbolic victims) from the community in which an offense has taken place to meet and share their experiences, perspectives, and the impact of the perpetrator's behavior. Typically, community conferencing offers the perpetrator the opportunity to make amends or repair the harm that he or she may have caused to the community.

Mural Arts Program

Similar to community conferencing programs, Philadelphia's Mural Arts Program does not put offenders in direct contact with their victims. Rather, the Mural Arts Program provides offenders with an opportunity to repair the harm they have caused the community by "creating large outdoor murals" (City of Philadelphia. Mural Arts Program). Considered to be a Restorative Justice program, the Mural Arts Program emphasizes "re-entry, reclamation of civic spaces, and the use of art to give voice to people who have consistently felt disconnected from society" (City of Philadelphia. Mural Arts Program). Over 300 adult prison and jail inmates, probationers, and parolees, and over 200 juvenile delinquents, participate each year. The offenders make a positive contribution to the community through the collaborative outdoor artwork.

Summary and Conclusion

Pennsylvania offers a number of services to crime victims at the local level, most of which are overseen by a state organization. Additionally, various Pennsylvania statutes provide rights to victims of crime, and offer special considerations to child victims, elderly victims, domestic violence victims, and sexual assault victims. Finally, several programs exist that emphasize the restoration of crime victims in conjunction with changing the offender for the better.

Key Terms and Definitions

Address Confidentiality Program: A service offered by the Pennsylvania Office of the Victim Advocate which provides a confidential substitute address to victims of domestic violence, sexual assault, and stalking.

Area Agency on Aging: Pennsylvania county-level agencies, overseen by the Department of Aging, tasked with providing services for older Pennsylvanians, including elderly victims of crime.

Balanced and Restorative Justice (BARJ): The purpose of the Commonwealth's juvenile justice system (as established by Pennsylvania legislation passed in 1995). The principles of BARJ include community protection, juvenile offender accountability and repair/restoration of the harm to the victim and community, and competency development.

ChildLine and Abuse Registry: ChildLine, maintained by the Pennsylvania Department of Public Welfare's Office of Children, Youth and Families is the 24/7 hotline for the purpose of reporting suspected child abuse. Each call is followed up by either a state or local agency designed to investigate child abuse. The Office of Children, Youth and Families also maintains records on abuse for the purpose of processing background checks.

Conferencing Programs: A voluntary face-to-face encounter between the victim, offender, and sometimes community members, in support of the restorative justice philosophy.

Contemporaneous Alternative Method: The capture of the testimony of child victims (particularly in sexual abuse cases) through video/audio from a room other than the courtroom to protect the child from emotional distress that could result from testifying in front of the defendant.

Full Faith and Credit: A clause of the Protection from Abuse Act that ensures that domestic violence victims who have had comparable protection orders granted within a jurisdiction outside of the Commonwealth are also protected by such orders.

Impact of Crime Classes: Classes designed to educate offenders with regard to the impact their offenses have had on the victim and the community.

Mandatory Reporters: One who is legally obligated to report suspected child abuse based on his/her occupational position and/or regular contact with children in the course of his/her occupation.

Mediation: Programs which allow for face-to-face interaction between victim and offender, allowing both parties to share their thoughts, experiences, motivations, and emotions.

Mural Arts Program: Programs which provide offenders with the opportunity to repair the harm that they have caused the community through the creation of large outdoor murals.

Office of Victims' Services (OVS): Part of the Pennsylvania Commission on Crime and Delinquency that is charged with helping state agencies to meet the needs of victims and administering the Victims Compensation Assistance Program and the Victims' Services Program.

Older Adults Protective Services Act (OAPSA): Pennsylvania law that provides a wide range of services for older Pennsylvanians, including those who are susceptible to, or have been victimized by, crime.

Pennsylvania Coalition Against Domestic Violence (PCADV): Formed in 1976, a group of nine domestic violence agencies, which has since grown to include over 60 community-based domestic violence programs serving victims of domestic violence in Pennsylvania. It was the first of its type in the United States.

Pennsylvania Coalition Against Rape (PCAR): Founded in 1976, the PCAR's mission is to provide a voice for victims of sexual assault and eliminate sexual violence through raising public awareness, and advocating for changes in public policy and response to sexual violence.

Pennsylvania Commission on Crime and Delinquency (PCCD): A commission, formed in 1978, designed to bring improvements to the Pennsylvania criminal justice system.

Pennsylvania's Crime Victims Act: A Pennsylvania statute that enumerates specific rights afforded to victims of crime in Pennsylvania.

Pennsylvania Department of Aging: A state-level agency that facilitates services for older Pennsylvanians. While the agency operates some direct services for senior citizens, they are also an information clearinghouse and provide funding to the 50 county-level Area Agencies on Aging throughout the Commonwealth.

Pennsylvania Office of the Victim Advocate: An office formed in 1995 to represent the rights and interests of crime victims in Pennsylvania.

Pennsylvania Statewide Automated Victim Information and Notification (PA SAVIN): A program, instituted in 2006, which provides victims the opportunity to obtain real-time information on the status of offenders, including notification of release from custody and/or escape.

Protection from Abuse Database (PFAD): An electronic archive which not only includes all PFA proceedings in the Commonwealth, but allows authorized users (e.g., law enforcement officers, courts, legal agencies, private attorneys) to access Protection from Abuse via a secured Internet website, 24 hours a day/365 days of the year.

Protection From Abuse Order (PFA): A civil order filed by a victim on his or her own behalf against a family or household member that protects a victim and his/her children from an abuser.

Restitution: A court-ordered payment by an offender to a victim (or community) to compensate the victim for a loss caused by the criminal actions of the offender.

Sexual Assault Forensic Examiner (SAFE): A medical professional who is specially trained to care for sexual assault victims.

Sexual Assault Nurse Examiner (SANE): A forensic nurse who is specially trained to care for sexual assault victims.

Sexual Assault Response Team (SART): A collaborative group consisting of individuals who respond to sexual assaults. The SART generally includes a sexual assault forensic examiner or nurse, a sexual assault counselor/advocate, a law enforcement representative, a prosecutor, and sometimes other members of the community.

Sex Offender Registry: A system designed to document the residence and work addresses of individuals who have been convicted of crimes that would designate them as sex offenders. Per federal requirements, each state must have a sex offender registry database.

Victim Advocate: An employee/volunteer working in a criminal justice agency or in a community-based victim service agency whose role may include accompanying victims (to court or medical exams), guiding victims through the criminal justice process, counseling victims, and assisting victims with restitution, victims compensation assistance, transportation, child care, and preparing Victim Impact Statements.

Victims Compensation Assistance Program (VCAP): a state program administered by PCCD to which victims may file claims for reimbursement of some crime-related losses and expenses.

Victim Impact Statement: A written or oral statement presented by the victim or victim's family at sentencing to express the impact that the crime has had on the victim and/or his or her family.

Victim Offender Dialogue Program: A victim-offender mediation program that allows victims or survivors (i.e., family members of a homicide victim) to meet with the perpetrators of crime.

Websites

National Crime Victim Law Institute. (2013). Pennsylvania Victims' Rights Laws. http://law.lclark.edu/live/files/4976-pennsylvania.

Pennsylvania. Pennsylvania Crime Victims. Your Detailed Rights as a Crime Victim. http://www.portal.state.pa.us/portal/server.pt/community/your_rights_as_a_crime_victim/14555/detailed_rights/606722.

Pennsylvania. Pennsylvania Crime Victims. Meeting the Needs of Victims of Crime. http://www.portal.state.pa.us/portal/server.pt/community/pcv_home/14554.

Pennsylvania Juvenile Court Judges' Commission. Balanced and Restorative Justice http://www.portal.state.pa.us/portal/server.pt/community/balanced_and_restorative_justice/5032.

Pennsylvania Office of the Victim Advocate (2013). http://www.ova.state.pa.us/portal/server.pt/community/ova/20938.

Victim Services

All Victim Services Programs in state of Pennsylvania organized by county. Contact information including phone numbers, email, and/or web addresses provided http://www.portal.state.pa.us/portal/server.pt/community/clickable _map/11201/victim_services_in_pennsylvania/585088.

All statewide victim services organizations. http://www.portal.state.pa.us/portal/ server.pt/community/clickable_map/11201/statewide_organizations/585419.

Victim/Witness Services of South Philadelphia, Inc. http://www.vwssp.org/.

Archive of OVS Annual Reports http://www.portal.state.pa.us/portal/server. pt?open=512&objID=5255&&PageID=495596&level=2&css=L2&mode=2.

Crime Rate

PA Uniform Crime Reporting System—Annual Crime Reports 2000–2011. http://ucr.psp.state.pa.us/UCR/Reporting/Annual/AnnualSumArrestUI.asp.

Review Questions

1. Describe the role of various agencies and organizations in assisting victims of crime in Pennsylvania.
2. Explain the key rights of victims at each stage of the criminal justice process.
3. Identify and describe the special considerations and services afforded to domestic violence victims.
4. Identify and describe the special considerations and services afforded to sexual assault victims.
5. Identify and describe the special considerations and services afforded to child victims.
6. Identify and describe the special considerations and services afforded to elderly victims.
7. Explain mandatory reporting of child and elder abuse and neglect.

Critical Thinking Questions

1. The trend in recent decades has been to afford many rights to victims of crime. Do any of these rights infringe upon the constitutional rights of criminal defendants or offenders? If so, explain.

2. Various mediation and restorative justice programs are available throughout the Commonwealth. For what types of victims and offenders are these types of programs most appropriate? Are there cases in which these programs should not ever be considered? Justify your response.
3. Funding for many victim service agencies is dependent upon grants, unlike criminal justice agencies. Does this indicate a lack of prioritization of victims? Why or why not?

References

American Civil Liberties Union. Briggs v. Borough of Norristown et al. Retrieved from https://www.aclu.org/womens-rights/briggs-v-borough-norristown-et-al.

Bass, A. (2012). And then there were none. Pennsylvania bill to permit expert testimony in sexual assault cases lands on the governor's desk. Women's Law Project (6/25/2012). Retrieved from http://womenslawproject.wordpress.com/2012/06/25/and-then-there-were-none-pennsylvania-bill-to-permit-expert-testimony-in-sexual-assault-cases-lands-on-the-governors-desk/.

Center for Advocacy for the Rights and Interests of the Elderly. Retrieved from http://www.carie.org/.

City of Philadelphia. Mural Arts Program. Retrieved from http://muralarts.org/programs/restorative-justice.

Family Involvement Committee. Pennsylvania Council of Chief Juvenile Probation Officers. A Family Guide to Pennsylvania's Juvenile Justice System. Retrieved from www.pachiefprobationofficers.org/library.php.

Federal Bureau of Investigation. (2012). *Crime in the United States 2011.* Retrieved from http://www.fbi.gov/about-us/cjis/ucr/crime-in-the-u.s/2011/crime-in-the-u.s.-2011/tables/table-1.

General Assembly of Pennsylvania. House Bill No. 492. Session of 2013. Printer's No. 968.

Pennsylvania Attorney General. Elder Abuse Unit. Retrieved from http://www.attorneygeneral.gov/seniors.aspx?id=296.

Pennsylvania Attorney General. Filing a Complaint with the Attorney General's Elder Abuse Unit. Retrieved from http://www.attorneygeneral.gov/complaints.aspx?id=3093.

Pennsylvania Department of Aging, 2013. Retrieved from http://www.aging.state.pa.us/portal/server.pt/community/department_of_aging_home/18206.

Pennsylvania. Older Adult Protective Services Act, 2013. Retrieved from http://www.portal.state.pa.us/portal/server.pt?open=512&objID=4984&&PageID=482051&level=2&css=L2&mode=2.

Pennsylvania (2013). Pennsylvania Crime Victims. Impact of Crime Class. Retrieved from http://www.portal.state.pa.us/portal/server.pt/community/empowering_the_victim/14769/impact_of_crime_class/664536.

Pennsylvania. Protection From Abuse Database. Introduction to the PFAD Project. Retrieved from http://www.pfad.state.pa.us/pfadinfo.html.

Pennsylvania Coalition against Domestic Violence (2013a). About Us. History. Retrieved from http://www.pcadv.org/About-Us/History/.

Pennsylvania Coalition against Domestic Violence (2013b). About Us. What We Do. Retrieved from http://www.pcadv.org/About-Us/What-We-Do/.

Pennsylvania Coalition against Rape (PCAR). Retrieved from http://www.pcar.org/.

Pennsylvania Coalition Against Rape. SAFE/SANE/SART. Retrieved from http://www.pcar.org/healthcare/safe-sane-sart.

Pennsylvania Commission on Crime and Delinquency. Office of Victims' Services. Retrieved from http://www.pccd.state.pa.us/portal/server.pt/community/victims_of_crime/5255.

Pennsylvania Commission on Crime and Delinquency. Office of Victims' Services. (2012). Office of Victims' Services. Annual Report, 2010–11. Retrieved from http://www.portal.state.pa.us/portal/server.pt?open=512&objID=5255&&PageID=495585&level=2&css=L2&mode=2.

Pennsylvania Crime Victims. Retrieved from http://www.pacrimevictims.org/portal/server.pt/community/pcv_home/14554.

Pennsylvania Department of Aging. Report Elder Abuse. Retrieved from http://www.portal.state.pa.us/portal/server.pt/community/abuse_or_crime/17992/report_elder_abuse/616645.

Pennsylvania Department of Corrections (2013). PA SAVIN/VINELink. Retrieved from http://www.portal.state.pa.us/portal/server.pt/community/inmate_information/7278/pa_savin_vinelink/787744.

Pennsylvania Department of Education. Office for Safe Schools. Retrieved from http://www.portal.state.pa.us/portal/server.pt/community/office_of_elementary_secondary_education/7209/office_of_safe_schools/1152067.

Pennsylvania Department of Public Welfare. Child Abuse History Clearance Forms. Retrieved from http://www.dpw.state.pa.us/findaform/childabusehistoryclearanceforms/.

Pennsylvania Office of the Victim Advocate (2013). Retrieved from http://www.ova.state.pa.us/portal/server.pt/community/ova/20938.

Pennsylvania Office of the Victim Advocate. Address Confidentiality Program (2013). Retrieved from http://www.portal.state.pa.us/portal/server.pt/community/acp_home/11193.

Pennsylvania Office of the Victim Advocate. Board of Pardons. Retrieved from http://www.ova.state.pa.us/portal/server.pt/community/victim_notification_and_input/20954/board_of_pardons/1455339.

Pennsylvania Office of the Victim Advocate. Crime Victims' Rights (2013). http://www.ova.state.pa.us/portal/server.pt/community/information_and_victim_rights/9243.

Pennsylvania Office of the Victim Advocate. Quehanna Boot Camp (2013). Retrieved from http://www.ova.state.pa.us/portal/server.pt/community/information_and_victim_rights/9243/quehanna_bootcamp/540361.

Pennsylvania Office of the Victim Advocate. Victim Notification and Input (2013). Retrieved from http://www.ova.state.pa.us/portal/server.pt/community/victim_notification_and_input/20954.

Pennsylvania Office of the Victim Advocate. Victim Offender Dialogue Program (2013). Retrieved from http://www.ova.state.pa.us/portal/server.pt/community/victim_notification_and_input/20954/victim_offender_dialogue_program_%28vod%29/1180442.

Pennsylvania State Police. Request for Criminal Record Check. Retrieved from http://www.dpw.state.pa.us/ucmprd/groups/webcontent/documents/form/s_001769.pdf.

Pennsylvania State Police. Megan's Law Website. Retrieved from http://www.pameganslaw.state.pa.us/FAQ.aspx?dt.

Truman, J.L., & Planty, M (2012). Criminal Victimization, 2011. U.S. Department of Justice, Bureau of Justice Statistics. October 2012, NCJ 239437. Retrieved from http://www.bjs.gov/ content/pub/pdf/cv11.pdf.

Tully, J. (2012) Pennsylvania to allow expert testimony in sex abuse trials. *USA Today* (6/29/2012). Retrieved from http://usatoday30.usatoday.com/news/nation/story/2012-06-29/pennsylvania-sex-abuse-experts-trial/55920378/1Zara, C. (2013). Domestic violence victims threatened with eviction? ACLU sues Norristown, Pa, over so-called nuisance ordinance. International Business Times (July 24, 2013). Retrieved from http://www.ibtimes.com/domestic-violence-victims-threatened-eviction-aclu-sues-norristown-pa-over-so-called-nuisance.

Chapter 10

Training and Educating Criminal Justice Personnel in Pennsylvania

Robert J. Boyer

Learning Objectives

After reading the chapter, students will be able to:

- List the minimum requirements for many criminal justice positions.
- Identify motivations for seeking employment in law enforcement.
- Describe various positions available in courts and corrections.
- List the stages in seeking law enforcement employment.
- Understand key topics addressed in various criminal justice training programs.
- Explain the functions of the Pennsylvania Commission on Crime and Delinquency.
- Discuss the role of the Municipal Police Officers' Education and Training Commission in setting training standards for Pennsylvania Police Officers.

Key Terms

Act 120
Minor Judiciary Education Board
Municipal Police Officers' Education and Training Commission (MPOETC)
Pennsylvania Commission on Crime and Delinquency

Introduction

This chapter will explore the training and educational requirements of several positions within the Pennsylvania criminal justice system. Most of the positions covered here are "sworn" positions such as police officer and trooper, or operational positions in the courts and corrections components. Supportive positions such as administrative or clerical staff are not included as a part of this discussion.

The requirements for many criminal justice system professions are regulated by statute, departmental policy, and agency rules. Most positions require, at a minimum, that the applicant be 21 years of age, have a valid driver's license, possess a high school diploma, and have no prior criminal record. Some positions require additional intensive training and even a college degree.

It is important to note that an applicant's background and past criminal record are key considerations in applying for work in the criminal justice system. For example, convictions in the adult court system of any "*disqualifying criminal offense*" (i.e., "a criminal offense for which more than 1 year in prison can be imposed") will bar an individual from certification as police officer in Pennsylvania (MPOETC, 2013). This would apply to any felony or misdemeanor of the first or second degree. This provision would generally not apply to offenses resulting in an A.R.D. (Accelerated Rehabilitative Disposition) as this is not considered a conviction of a criminal offense. It should be noted that adverse interactions with the justice system such as citations, convictions of misdemeanor of the third-degree offenses, license suspensions, and civil judgments might later become an issue for the applicant during the background investigation. As a criminal justice employment-seeker, one must realize that it is critical to keep one's criminal record clean.

The requirement of a college education often varies from position to position. However, considering the often fierce competition for these positions, a college degree offers several distinct advantages:

- the potential to have better overall scores on written exams;
- improved oral/written communication skills; and
- educational background in academic areas such as psychology and sociology.

Applicants for criminal justice employment should expect to see more agencies increase their educational requirements. Years ago, a college education wasn't a requirement to apply for a position as a Pennsylvania State Trooper. Today, the agency generally requires an Associate's Degree or 60 credit hours from an accredited agency of higher education. There are provisions for waiving part of this requirement for prior military service and law enforcement experience (Pennsylvania State Police, 2013). It is suggested that applicants pursue a Bachelor's Degree to aid in their job search, to increase personal marketability and to improve opportunities for advancement.

This chapter begins with an examination of some law enforcement positions including state trooper, municipal police officer, deputy sheriff, and constable. The general responsibilities, selection process, and training for each position are discussed.

The court component of the criminal justice system is discussed next. While there are other supportive positions within the court system, judges are the focus of this section. The responsibilities, selection, and training of magisterial district and court of common pleas judges will be addressed.

Finally, several positions within the corrections component are examined. The section begins with an examination of a correctional officer in the State prison system. Next, the county correctional officer is discussed. The section concludes with a review of probation/parole officers, including the increasingly sought out position of juvenile probation officer.

The chapter concludes with a discussion on the differences between education and training. The combined value of each is discussed. Also included in this section is an overview of a typical criminal justice degree program.

Police

Law enforcement employment remains a popular choice for those seeking employment within the criminal justice system. Working as a police officer is attractive to many job seekers for the following reasons:

- the opportunity to help others in many different situations;
- outdoor work;
- the ability to work independently;
- job security;
- the potential to save lives;
- the uncertainty of the potential of what each shift may pose; and
- salary and benefits.

While employment as a police officer won't make someone rich, the salary and benefits are attractive to many applicants. Applicants can generally expect to earn a decent "middle-class" wage, and have a health care plan, retirement, and other fringe benefits. However, due to rising personnel costs and cash-strapped government budgets, the amount, type, and continuation of certain types of compensation remains unclear. For example, many agencies typically have provided employer-paid health insurance for their criminal justice employees. It is now typical to find the employer attempting to have the employee share in the cost of health care premiums.

The application process for a law enforcement position may take a year for the applicant to complete. The process for many police-related positions often includes the following procedures:

- initial application;
- written exam;
- physical agility test;
- polygraph exam;
- background investigation;
- oral interview/oral board;
- psychological exam; and
- medical exam.

Law enforcement agencies may vary the order of the stages in the application process. For example, some agencies may administer the physical agility test to all applicants who meet the minimum qualification from the initial application. Those who pass the physical agility exam will be invited back to complete the written exam.

Pennsylvania State Police Trooper

For many police employment seekers, the Pennsylvania State Police (PSP) remains a popular career choice. The PSP's core purpose is "to seek justice, preserve peace, and improve the quality of life for all" (Pennsylvania State Police, 2013). Formed in 1905 as the first uniformed State Police agency in the United States, the Pennsylvania State Police are regarded by many as a premier law enforcement agency. The State Police have statewide jurisdiction and spend much of their time in a supportive role to local law enforcement, including assisting in criminal investigation. They are also known for traffic enforcement along Commonwealth Interstates and the Pennsylvania Turnpike (Pennsylvania State Police, 2013).

The patrol-related duties of a State Trooper are often very similar to those of a local police officer. Troopers respond to service calls, investigate auto accidents, and handle other routine patrol matters. However, due to the size of the agency, opportunities for specialization are more readily available. For example, some Troopers may be assigned to criminal investigation, narcotics, community relations, fingerprint identification, polygraph examination, or the training bureau. For many, this may be a key factor when considering employment. Considering that some local police departments may be composed of one full-time officer, State Police employment clearly offers unique advantages for specialization and promotion.

Upon the completion of a selection process, similar to the procedure outlined above, appointment as a State Police Cadet is offered to the applicant. The State Police Academy in Hershey is a residential training program of approximately 27 weeks. According to the Pennsylvania State Police (2013) website, the training program "is purposely designed to eliminate any Cadet who does not possess the necessary intelligence, emotional stability, or physical stamina to meet the requirements."

A physically rigorous and academically challenging paramilitary training program is offered by the State Police. The Cadet's day often begins at 5:30 a.m. and may run until 11 p.m. In addition, the cadet may be assigned to special duty assignments such as care of departmental horses. Some specific areas of instruction at the State Police Academy include:

- First Aid/CPR;
- Emergency water safety;
- Police operations;
- Pursuit driving;
- Instruction in departmental weapons, including exposure to pepper spray;
- Calisthenics;
- Boxing, fighting techniques and defensive tactics;
- Cross-country running; and
- Criminal law and procedure (Pennsylvania State Police, 2013).

Weekend leave is considered a privilege for cadets and may be restricted for failing to meet training standards. Upon successful completion of the Academy, the cadet is promoted to the rank of Trooper and is assigned to a State Police installation. This assignment may be anywhere within the Commonwealth. There is an 18-month probationary period (Pennsylvania State Police, 2013). State police employment offers several advantages:

- Increased opportunities for advancement over those of a small department;
- Specialization opportunities such as community relations, accident reconstruction, forensic unit, fingerprint identification, aviation, and K-9; and
- Enhanced training availability.

Municipal Police Officer

Municipal police officers provide patrol services, investigate crime, maintain order, and strive to keep the peace within their respective jurisdictions. Contrary to State Police, municipal police officers are employed by a political subdivision such as a city, borough, or township. The primary jurisdiction of the municipal police officer is within that political subdivision.

The training and certification of municipal police officers in Pennsylvania is regulated by Act 120. The Municipal Police Officers' Education & Training Commission (MPOETC) was established in 1974 to set certification and training standards for police officers employed in the Commonwealth of Pennsylvania by municipalities (MPOETC, 2013). Since then, MPOETC has established a comprehensive, innovative curriculum of basic and in-service training.

The basic training program is 754 hours. Students or newly hired police officers can take this program at any of the approximately 25 MPOETC-approved sites. The training facilities are usually college campuses, large police department academies (Allentown, Reading, Philadelphia and Pittsburgh), and Pennsylvania State Police training facilities. Instructors in these programs are often active or retired police officers.

The MPOETC Basic Curriculum is divided in 18 modules:

- Introduction to Academy Training;
- Introduction to Law Enforcement in Pennsylvania;
- Physical and Emotional Readiness;
- Laws and Procedures;
- Defensive Tactics;
- Motor Vehicle Law Enforcement;
- Motor Vehicle Collision Investigation;
- Patrol Procedures and Operations;
- Principles of Criminal Investigation;
- Human Relations;
- Crisis Management;
- Families in Crisis;
- Basic Firearms;
- Operation of Patrol Vehicles;
- Report Writing;
- Case Presentation;
- First Aid and CPR; and
- Handling Arrested Persons.

In addition to the basic training curriculum, MPOETC develops mandatory in-service training that municipal police officers must complete on a yearly basis. The courses are developed by course committees composed of MPOETC instructional staff, officers from various law enforcement agencies and other experts. In 2013, the mandatory in-service offerings were:

- Legal Updates;
- Threat Assessment and Management;
- Managing Public Events; and
- Emergency Vehicle Operations (Lackawanna College, 2013).

Since the mandatory in-service update training began, MPOETC has offered a variety of timely and innovative topics for police officers such as cultural diversity awareness, police stress management, and off-duty decision making. The course offerings vary yearly, although legal updates and officer safety themes are usually present. Recently, MPOETC and the Pennsylvania Chiefs of Police Association began offering update training via online instruction. Officers may complete the yearly required 12 hours of training at their convenience either at home or work. Additionally, officers must maintain First Aid/ CPR certification and weapon qualification.

Deputy Sheriff

In Pennsylvania, sheriffs are elected law enforcement officers who serve as the enforcement component of county courts. Sheriffs will hire deputy sheriffs to assist with these duties. Sheriffs and their deputies transport prisoners, provide court security (bailiff), and serve warrants for defendants who have not appeared in court. In addition, they have civil-law responsibilities such as serving lawsuits, Protection from Abuse (PFA) service, and enforcing court orders. Unlike sheriffs in the southern and western United States who may serve as county police, Pennsylvania Sheriffs primarily serve as court officers. Generally, Pennsylvania sheriffs do not "patrol" or respond to calls for service as a police officer or state trooper would.

The Pennsylvania Commission on Crime and Delinquency, through the Deputy Sheriffs' Education and Training Program, provides certification and re-certification training to all active deputy sheriffs in the Commonwealth (Pennsylvania Commission on Crime and Delinquency, 2013). A new sheriff's deputy is required to complete the 760-hour training program within one year of his or her hire date. The training program includes the following subject areas:

- Introduction to the Sheriff's Academy;
- The Pennsylvania Court System;
- Victim's Rights and Services;
- Civil Law and Procedure;
- Crimes and Offenses;
- Criminal Procedure;
- Motor Vehicle Code Enforcement;
- Use of Force;
- Oral and written communication;
- Ethics;
- Cultural Diversity;
- Physical Conditioning and Defensive Tactics;
- Firearms Training;
- Court Security and Prisoner Transportation;
- DUI Enforcement; and
- First Aid and CPR (Pennsylvania Commission on Crime and Delinquency, 2013).

A waiver of the mandated basic training is available if the applicant has completed Act 120 (Municipal Police Officer Training) or was a Pennsylvania State Police Officer. In addition, deputy sheriffs must complete an 80-hour basic training waiver course, obtain first aid/CPR certification, and qualify with their firearm.

Constable

Constables are elected law enforcement officers who serve as the enforcement arm of a Magisterial District Judge, similar to the functions of a sheriff on the Court of Common Pleas level. A typical function of a constable would be to serve summary offense warrants. For example, if someone receives a traffic citation in Pennsylvania and fails to respond to the charge, a district judge would issue a warrant. A constable will then serve this warrant on the violator. Constables also assist with landlord-tenant matters and evictions, and enforce civil judgments of the district court.

In order for an elected or appointed constable to perform his or her duties, they must complete an 80-hour basic training course. Exams are administered during the training and a 70% passing grade is required. The following topics are covered in basic constable training:

- Role of the Constable in the Justice System;
- Professional Development;

- Civil Law and Process;
- Criminal Law and Process;
- Use of Force;
- Mechanics of Arrest;
- Defensive Tactics;
- Prisoner Transport and Custody;
- Court Security;
- Crisis Intervention;
- Expandable Baton; and
- OC (oleoresin capsicum) Training (Indiana University, Pennsylvania, 2013).

In order to be successfully recertified, constables must complete a 20-hour in-service training program. The topics for 2013 were:

- Civil Law Review: Enforcement of Judgments;
- Criminal Law Review: Warrant Service;
- Surviving a Constable-Involved Shooting; and
- Defensive Tactics (Pennsylvania Commission on Crime and Delinquency, 2013).

Courts

Pennsylvania's court system is composed of 4 levels. Judges in Pennsylvania are elected. The first court component is the Magisterial District Judge who serves a six-year term. This is the only judicial office in the Commonwealth that does not require the judge to be a lawyer. District judges conduct summary offense trials, preliminary arraignments, and preliminary hearings, and preside over certain civil court matters. Upon completion of their six-year term, the district judge must run for re-election. New district judges who are not members of the bar are required to complete a 4-week course administered by the Minor Judiciary Education Board and complete a final course examination. Lawyers who will serve as a District Judge are exempt from this basic training program. In-service magisterial district judges receive yearly update training.

The initial certification educational program is composed of the following subject areas:

- Overview of judicial responsibilities;
- Judicial ethics;
- Criminal Rules of Procedure;
- Evidence;
- Pennsylvania Crimes Code;

- Search and Seizure law;
- The Controlled Substance Act;
- Pennsylvania Vehicle Code;
- Civil Rules and Procedure;
- Assumpsit (contracts and concepts of negligence);
- Trespass; and
- Landlord-Tenant (Minor Judiciary Education Board, 2013).

Conversely, Common Pleas Court judges are required to be attorneys. The Court of Common Pleas serves as Pennsylvania's trial court of general jurisdiction. Civil and criminal trials would be conducted at this level. Judges are elected to 10-year terms. Upon completion of a term, the judge is then subject to a retention election to keep his or her seat. Upon election to the bench, the new judge must complete a 7-day training session mandated by the Pennsylvania Supreme Court. The new judge will be educated at the Pennsylvania Judicial Center, located in Harrisburg, in key areas such as legal updates, communication skills, decision-making, and avoiding bias to ensure fairness.

Common Pleas judges attend the Pennsylvania Conference of State Trial Judges to receive in-service training twice yearly. In July 2013, hundreds of state judges made their way to this 4-day conference. Topics for discussion included medical malpractice cases, updates on new sex offender laws, a review of appellate court practices, the use of interpreters in court, and handling child witnesses (Delazio, 2013).

Judges in the higher-level courts (Superior, Commonwealth, and Supreme) in Pennsylvania are not statutorily required to complete additional training, however, training is made available.

Corrections

Correctional Officer

Within the Commonwealth, correctional institutions generally operate on the county, state, and federal level. Employment opportunities, salary, benefits, and opportunities for advancement may vary from one institution to the next.

The Corrections Officer Trainee is an entry-level position within the State Department of Corrections. Upon completion of the one-year training program, the trainee is promoted to Corrections Officer 1. Classroom and on-the-job training is offered during this first year of employment. The training focuses on developing the necessary skills and techniques in the care, custody, and control of inmates. A month-long training program is offered at the Department of Corrections Training Academy in Elizabethtown, Pennsylvania. Like many criminal justice agencies, the Department offers employment preference to qualified veterans.

In order to obtain employment with the Department of Corrections, the applicant must be a Pennsylvania resident, be at least 21 years of age, and pass a 120 question written test. The subject areas of the exam include:

- Judgment and Problem Solving;
- Observation;
- Following Oral Instructions;
- Understanding Rules and Regulations;
- Following Written Instructions; and
- Clarity of Expression (Corrections Officer Trainee Test Announcement, 2013).

The test is administered at various sites throughout the Commonwealth. Applicants may submit a new application and re-take the exam one year from their prior exam date. Applicants are then placed on an eligibility list.

On the county corrections level, for an example, the Luzerne County Correctional Facility offers a very comprehensive month-long (160 hour) training program for new correctional officers. Within one year of employment, the new officer must also complete a training program offered by the Pennsylvania Department of Corrections at the academy in Elizabethtown. The County Correctional Facility training division program consists of the following subject areas:

- Use of force;
- Booking procedures;
- O.C. spray;
- Professionalism;
- Positional asphyxia;
- EBID (Electric Body Immobilizer Device);
- First Aid/CPR;
- Cell extraction;
- Restraints;
- Suicide prevention;
- Testifying in court;
- Air pack usage;
- Fire suppression;
- Female cell block operations;
- Special duty (yard, tower, control room, transport, key control, visitor, hospital);
- Correctional officer survival;

- Inmate behavior;
- Correctional officer code of ethics;
- Inmate dress codes;
- County employment policies;
- Observation skills;
- Report writing;
- Firearm training; and
- Cell searches.

Any correctional officer may be required to work various shifts, holidays, and weekends as correctional facilities are staffed 24 hours a day, 7 days a week. In effect, they are also "locked in" the facility. They may be required to use physical force, respond to emergencies, and face physical danger.

Probation/Parole Officers

Probation and parole officers are also popular paths for those seeking employment in the corrections component of criminal justice. Officers supervise those on probation/parole, enforce terms and conditions imposed by the court, and assist with individual services such as employment, housing and treatment needs. Probation and parole officers have an interesting position in that they serve an enforcement function ensuring that court conditions are abided with, while also taking on a supportive role to ensure the probationer/parolee is successful in their correctional plan.

Probation officers are found at the county, state and federal level. Parole officers are more likely to be state employees. Since the Sentencing Reform Act of 1984 abolished parole, the federal court imposes supervised release during sentencing in addition to the sentence of imprisonment. Unlike parole, supervised release does not replace a portion of the sentence of imprisonment but is in addition to the time spent in prison. United States probation officers supervise persons on supervised release (United States Courts, 2013).

Working both in field offices and in correctional institutions, the probation or parole agent manages caseloads of probationers and parolees under State supervision. In order to obtain a position as a parole agent 1 (entry level position with the Pennsylvania Board of Probation and Parole) an applicant must meet the following requirements:

- Complete a written exam;
- Pass a background investigation;
- Be willing to travel;

- Complete a training program that include firearms, defensive tactics, and personal safety techniques;
- Be willing to work independently;
- Be able to interact with various types of offenders; and
- Be free of any felony convictions (Parole Agent 1 Test Announcement, 2013).

Generally, in Pennsylvania, county and state probation officers (including juvenile probation officers) are required to have a bachelor's degree.

While the functions of adult and juvenile probation officers are quite similar, the main difference is the age group of the persons under court supervision. In addition, juvenile probation officers are often involved in the criminal justice process at a much earlier time than are adult probation officers. In the adult system, the offender often does not have contact with the probation department until after sentencing. In the juvenile system, the offender may have first contact with the probation department soon after arrest. Juvenile probation officers often make decisions on detention, informal adjustment, and intake prior to the juvenile ever coming before a juvenile court judge. If a criminal justice job-seeker enjoys working with young people in combination with a law enforcement component, a juvenile probation officer may be the perfect job for them.

Pennsylvania probation/and parole agents are required to complete a basic training academy and on-the job training during the first six months of employment. In addition, agents are required to complete a minimum of 40 hours of annual training (Parole Agent 1 Test Announcement, 2013).

In addition, there are other minimum requirements including that the applicant have at least 2 years of experience as a parole investigator or institutional parole assistant and at least an associate's degree. The Department will also consider equivalent combinations of experience and training (Parole Agent 1 Test Announcement, 2013). Acceptable degrees areas are criminal justice, law enforcement, sociology, social work, legal studies, psychology or other related fields.

Juvenile probation officers undergo similar training to that of adult probation officers. The new juvenile probation officer will complete a 57-hour training program spanning 2 weeks. The topic areas in this training program include:

- Balanced and Restorative Justice;
- Evidence-Based Probation Practices;
- The Impact of Crime upon Victims;
- Detention Practices and Procedures;
- Officer Safety;
- Engaging the Community;

- Cultural Competency;
- Communication Skills;
- Working with Families; and
- Ethics (Center for Juvenile Justice Training and Research, 2013).

Similarly, juvenile probation officers must complete a minimum of 40 hours of training annually. There are many options available for this staff development training including the following:

- Mental Health Training for Juvenile Justice;
- Crime Victim Rights;
- Male Issues and Violence;
- The Trajectory of Gangs in the 21st Century;
- Post-Traumatic Stress Disorder;
- Addiction and Motivational Interviewing;
- Sexual Identity, Sexual Orientation and Gender Role Issues of Adolescence;
- Motivational Interviewing; and
- Criminal Minds, Criminal Behavior (Center for Juvenile Justice Training and Research, 2013).

Criminal Justice Education and Training

To many, the terms *education* and *training* have the same meaning. However, they are distinctly different, particularly as they pertain to the criminal justice profession. Education is essentially imparting the body of knowledge within a discipline. It focuses upon knowledge and understanding (Bennett & Hess, 2007, p. 190). Education most often occurs on college and university campuses. Training is often "skill-focused" or more "hands-on." Essentially, education may try to explain "Why do we do it this way?" Training will demonstrate "How do we actually do it in the field?"

For example, a criminal justice education program will focus on the 4th amendment of the United States Constitution, which impacts so many areas in criminal justice. Many "technicalities" in criminal cases often center on search and seizure issues. Education would explain the background and history of the 4th amendment and the sometimes complex application of the law today. What is an "unreasonable search"? What is probable cause? What are the essential parts of a warrant? Educational programs would strive to answer these questions.

Training programs might focus on the steps to take during a traffic stop. How to stop the vehicle, approach the violator, and write a citation might be addressed in the context of a traffic stop, which is regulated by the 4th amendment. Officers are trained on how to search a home or person and how to detect contraband. In effect, training puts the "theory" of education into practice.

In a practical application of the value of combining education *and* training, consider a runaway child scenario. Criminal justice education programs would discuss background information on adolescent behavior, family dynamics, and perhaps child psychology. Training programs, on the other hand, would focus more upon how to investigate a missing child case with the desired outcome being returning the child safely to his or her home. As educational programs might suggest, cases of runaway children might be the result of domestic violence in the home or child abuse. When an adolescent does not know what to do, he or she may run away from the situation. This information would be very valuable in combination with the training related to the investigation of the case. Certainly, a police officer would not want to find a missing child, only to unknowingly return the child to an abusive home.

Throughout the chapter, we have focused upon training. Let us consider educational programs. In the opinion of the chapter author, it is suggested that students pursue a bachelor's degree prior to seeking employment in the criminal justice field. Criminal justice remains one of the most popular programs on campus. Additionally, job seekers often flood agencies with applications when positions become available within those organizations. The competition for employment may be fierce. While employment in the field may be possible after completing a training program or associate's degree, having the bachelor's degree often improves employment potential and the opportunity for advancement. The additional education may also assist new applicants with the testing and application process by improving reading comprehension, as well as written and oral communication skills. Considering the reality that promotion within the criminal justice field may require the completion of additional written testing and other assessments, the value of education in improving the marketability of the individual is clear.

Students may begin their criminal justice studies at a two-year institution such as a community college and then transfer to the four-year school. Careful coordination by the student is needed to ensure the courses will appropriately transfer to avoid unnecessary duplication or to avoid missing requirements. Deciding what four-year college or university a student will eventually transfer to should be decided at the earliest possible point. Fortunately, many two-year and four-year schools have articulation agreements which help to streamline this process.

Whether students begin their academic careers at a community college or complete the entire bachelor's degree at a four-year institution, during their four-year course of study, criminal justice students should expect that approximately half of their credits will relate to their major and the other half of credits will be general education courses. The typical requirement for a bachelor's degree is approximately 120 credits. In any criminal justice program, students can usually expect to take courses in the following areas:

- Introduction to the Criminal Justice System;
- Criminal Investigation;
- Juvenile Justice;
- Police Community Relations;
- Criminology;
- Police Operations;
- Management and Supervision;
- Drugs;
- Specialized courses such as Terrorism, Gangs, Organized Crime, Child Abuse and Cyber Crime;
- Corrections;
- Probation and Parole;
- Court Administration;
- English Composition and Literature;
- Speech;
- Science;
- History;
- Political Science;
- Algebra;
- Sociology;
- Psychology; and
- Free electives.

Degree requirements often have "free elective" choices that students may take as they earn credits towards their degrees. Students are often advised to choose these electives in such a way as to enhance their résumés. For example, students might consider taking 1 or more semesters of Spanish, unless the student is already fluent in the language. A basic accounting and computer science course might also prove valuable considering the sometimes technical investigation of white collar crime. Abnormal psychology and ethics would also be great choices.

Conclusion

Educational and training requirements for employment in Pennsylvania's criminal justice system clearly vary based upon the individual position. By having a better understanding of these requirements, students will be better pre-pared to enter employment within the system. While working in the criminal justice system may not be financially lucrative, the non-tangible rewards such as the ability to help others, serve the community, and help keep people safe remain prime motivators for job seekers. Criminal justice employment also offers job stability in times of economic uncertainty. By combining the bene-fits of educational and training programs, the efficiency and effectiveness of the Commonwealth's criminal justice system can only be improved.

Key Terms

Act 120: A state statute that regulates Municipal Police training requirements.

Minor Judiciary Education Board: A Commonwealth agency charged with ed-ucating new magisterial district judges and providing continuing education for in-service judges.

Municipal Police Officers' Education & Training Commission (MPOETC): A Commonwealth agency charged with enforcing the provisions of Act 120 and establishing basic and in-service training programs.

Pennsylvania Commission on Crime and Delinquency: A Commonwealth agency with improvement of the criminal justice system as a primary objective. The agency also regulates constable and sheriff training. Crime and delin-quency prevention support is also provided to local agencies.

Websites

Criminal Justice Schools in Pennsylvania: www.criminaljusticeprograms.com.
National Council on Crime and Delinquency: www.nccdglobal.org.
Pennsylvania Department of Corrections: www.cor.state.pa.us.
Pennsylvania State Civil Service Commission: www.scsc.state.pa.us.
Pennsylvania State Police: www.psp.state.pa.us.

Review Questions

1. Identify the differences between "training" and "education."
2. List the reasons why people may seek police employment.
3. Describe the advantages of being employed by larger agencies, such as the Pennsylvania State Police.

4. Compare and contrast the different duties of a police officer, constable, and deputy sheriff.
5. Explain the benefits that a college degree would offer to a probation officer.

Critical Thinking Questions

1. Explore the Pennsylvania State Civil Service Commission website. Research various positions under the "Law Enforcement, Investigation and Safety" section. Discuss requirements for 3 positions that may be of interest to you.
2. To serve as a district judge, one need not be an attorney. Discuss the pros and cons of having someone without a legal degree serving in this position.
3. Analyze the training areas for the positions presented in the chapter. Do you see any topic areas that seem irrelevant to the position? Can you identify any topic area that should be added to the training?

References

Allentown Police Academy. (2013). Retrieved from: http://www.allentown.gov/.
Bennett, W., & Hess, K. (2007). *Management and Supervision in Law Enforcement* (5th ed.). Belmont, CA: Wadsworth-Thomson Learning.
Center for Juvenile Justice Training and Research. Pennsylvania Juvenile Court Judges Commission. Retrieved from: www.jcjcjems.state.pa.us.
Corrections Office Trainee Test Announcement (2013). Retrieved from: www.scsc.state.pa.us.
Delazio, S. (2013, July 25). County judges attending conference in Hershey. *Times Leader,* p. 5A.
Lackawanna College (2013). Retrieved from: www.lackawanna.edu.
Indiana University of Pennsylvania. Basic Constable Training Program. (2013). Retrieved from: http://www.iup.edu.
Minor Judiciary Education Board (2013). Retrieved from: http://www.mjeb.org/Certification.htm.
Municipal Police Officers' Education and Training Commission (2013). Retrieved from: www.mpoetc.state.pa.us/.
Parole Agent 1 Test Announcement (2013). Retrieved from: www.scsc.state.pa.us.
Pennsylvania Commission on Crime and Delinquency (2013). Retrieved from: www.pccd.state.pa.us.
Pennsylvania State Police (2013). Retrieved from: www.psp.state.pa.us/.
United States Courts (2013). Retrieved from: www.uscourts.gov.

Index

Page numbers in italics indicate figures; those in boldface, tables.